WORLD PEACE

VOLUME TEN

WOMAN AND PEACE

Suresh Chandra Mallick
Pritam Mallick

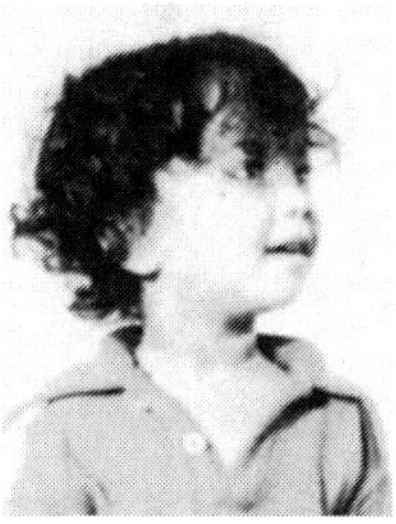

WOMAN AND PEACE

Institute of Development Studies and Policy research, Pritam Bhawan, 93- Dharma Vihar, Khandagiri, Bhubaneswar 751030 (Orissa), INDIA

ISBN: 978-81-924851-9-5

First Edition

2013

E-Publication Price: US $ 4

Dedicated to

Ms. Aung San Suu Kyi

Political Leader and Nobel Laureate in Peace (1991)

PROLOGUE

The manuscript on WORLD PEACE - VOLUME TEN highlights on 'Woman and Peace'. The study is intended to ascertain whether there is any possibility of empowerment of women in all countries. The women are tortured and are devoid of human rights in many countries, religions and societies.

Women are more intelligent, laborious, well behaved and religious as compared to men. They are more ambitious. They desire that well-being of all family members and expect them to achieve laurels in life. Women extend helping hands to the poor, needy and hungry. They live in a world dominated by men. All male writers and poets have offered high regards to the women world except Bernard Shaw, who had criticized the womenfolk as a mistake by the Almighty God.

In the first chapter, "Quotes by Women" has been reported to mobilize the whole world that women are advanced in knowledge, experience and inner thoughts for the welfare of the people and the world. Chapter II explains the sufferings and sacrifices of women in USA, India and Iran and Arab. Chapter III includes 'government support to women' in Siera Leone, Liberia, and India. It also includes suggestions of Inter - Parliament Union, and the United Nations. Chapter IV highlights healthcare support to women and children in USA, India, Ethiopia, Pakistan, Mali and Morocco. Chapter V discusses that the women have proved as successful ambassadors of peace. Chapter VI explains on the achievements of Women in politics.

Chapter VII includes interesting facts on International Marriage, History's most famous Weddings, When Marriage Dream fails, Division of Property after Separation, Salary of Wives of misogyny and Indian politics, Money and Marriage, Marriages in Different Religion, Unsuccessful marriages in India, The shrinking Universe: How convenient is your Marriage? Beautiful Woman, Women and war: Acclimated to Violence, Women fighting and dying in War, Despite Combat Exclusion Policy, Poetry and the War-II, and conclusion. Chapter VIII includes speeches of noble women in the world. Their experiences and observations would assist in law making for the benefits of women and the world. Chapter IX highlights that there is possibility to ensure World Peace through women empowerment.

We are grateful to Wikipedia, Google in search and a number of Newspapers for collection of facts on corruption. Journals and Internet enriched this manuscript. We acknowledge the contribution of authors, who have written articles, research papers, reports, resolutions, and reports on peace. They have contributed tremendously to solve the political problems of the entire world and suggested measures for improvement. We will appreciate for constructive criticism aiming at improvement of the subsequent editions of the book.

We will be happy, even if a small step towards world peace is contemplated through this endeavour.

January 15, 2013 Suresh Chandra Mallick

CONTENTS

INTRODUCTION

In the Aryan literature, women in ancient times were taking the same share as men; this is found in no other literature of the world. Our *Vedas* are the oldest literature the world possesses. Their oldest portion, *Rig Veda*, is composed of hymns, and these hymns are to the Gods whom the Aryans worshipped. I may be pardoned for using the word Gods; the literal translation is "the bright ones". These hymns are dedicated to Fire, to the Sun, to Varuna and other deities. The titles run: "Such-and-such a sage composed this verse, dedicated to such-and-such a deity".

In the tenth chapter comes a peculiar hymn — for the sage is a woman — and it is dedicated to the one God who is at the background of all these gods. All the previous hymns are spoken in the third person, as if someone were addressing the deities. But this hymn takes a departure: God (as the Devi) is speaking for herself. The pronoun used is "I". "I am the Empress of the Universe, the Fulfiller of all prayers." This is the first glimpse of women's work in the *Vedas*. As we go on, we find them taking a greater share — even officiating as priests. There is not one passage in the *Vedas* that can be construed even indirectly as signifying that woman could never be a priest.

Then we come to the last portion of these *Vedas*. There, too, we find women pre-eminent. Large portions of these books are words, which have proceeded from the mouths of women. It is there — recorded with their names and teachings.

There is that beautiful story of the great sage Yajnavalkya, the one who visited the kingdom of the great king Janaka. There in that assembly of the learned, people came to ask him questions. One man asked him, "How am I to perform this sacrifice?" Another asked him, "How am I to perform the other sacrifice?" And after he had answered them, there arose a woman who said, "These are childish questions. I take these two arrows, my two questions. Answer them if you can, and we will then call you a sage.

The first is: **What is the soul?**
The second is: **What is God?"**

Thus arose in India the great questions about the soul and God, and these came from the mouth of a woman. The sage had to pass an examination before her, and he passed well.

The oldest Sanskrit poem in existence, the *Ramayana*, has embodied the loftiest Hindu ideal of a woman in the character of Sita. We have no time to go through her life of infinite patience and goodness. We worship her as God incarnate, and she is named before her husband, Rama. We do not say "Mr. and Mrs.", but "Mrs. and Mr." and so on, with all the gods and goddesses, naming the woman first.

There is another peculiar conception of the Hindu. Those who have been studying with me are aware that the central conception of Hindu philosophy is of the absolute that is the background of the universe. This 'absolute being' has its powers spoken of as She — that is, the real personal God in India is She. This

Shakti of the *Brahman* is always in the feminine gender.

Rama is considered the type of the absolute, and Sita that of power. I will quote a passage from her life that is very much suited to the ladies of this country. The picture opens when she was in the forest with her husband, whether they were banished. There was a female sage whom they both went to see. Her fasts and devotions had emaciated her body.

Sita approached this sage and bowed down before her. The sage placed her hand on the head of Sita and said:

"It is a great blessing to possess a beautiful body; you have that. It is a greater blessing to have a noble husband; you have that. It is the greatest blessing to be perfectly obedient to such a husband; you are that. You must be happy". Sita replied, "Mother, I am glad that God has given me a beautiful body and that I have so devoted a husband. But as to the third blessing, I do not know whether I obey him or he obeys me. One thing alone I remember, that when he took me by the hand before the sacrificial fire — whether it was a reflection of the fire or whether God himself made it appear to me — I found that I was his and he was mine. And since then, I have found that I am the complement of his life and he of mine".

We come now to Manu, the great lawgiver. Now, there is an elaborate description of how a child should be educated. We must remember that it was compulsory with the Aryans that a child be educated, irrespective of his caste. After describing how a child should be educated, Manu adds: **Along the same lines, the daughters are to be educated — exactly as the boys.**

I have often heard that there are other passages where women are condemned. I admit that in our sacred books there are many passages, which condemn women as offering temptation. But there are also passages that glorify women as the power of God.

And there are other passages, which state that in that house where one drop of a woman's tear falls, the gods are never pleased and the house goes to ruin.

Drinking wine, killing a woman and killing a Brahmin are the highest crimes in Hinduism. [1]

But in the twenty-first century, we find that there has been progress in education, scientific achievements, income and knowledge of most of the people, but we are loosing the family bond, love, affection, friendship and attachment in the family itself. We earn more; spend more and achieve more, but we are feeling suffocated because the family relationship is distancing each day. We are searching for peace, but we are worried for self. Perhaps, the state of advancement has made the humanbeings self-centered and greedy. Each day, the newspapers are covered with bad incidents in all the countries.

In this manuscript, we have analyzed that every family could be secured and live in peace provided both husband and wife live peacefully; make adjustments in views and pay regards to the partner.

The world could assure peace everywhere, when women are regarded as partners of progress and peace in each family, caste, sect, religion or society. When women are awarded justice everywhere, WORLD PEACE would be possible. For this great achievement, we have to train our mind for peace.

---

[1] Excerpts from The Complete Works of Swami Vivekananda, Volume 9, quoted from the Pioneer, July 30, 2011

Chapter I

QUOTES BY WOMEN

A woman is a symbol of peace, prosperity and pain. All greatmen in the world are influenced by their mothers through persuation, divinal inspiration and sacrifices. But the womenfolk are neglected. They have the capacity to award peace to all people in the world and they should be the leaders of Peace Movement in all countries, states and settlements.

All great religions in the world have sacred scriptures. These scriptures prescribe advices to acquire good habits to prosper and progress. These religions have a great historical significance; not only have these religions influenced the lives of billions of people in the past; they continue to do so in today's society. These words of truth form the core beliefs of religion and thus have shaped civilization as we see it today.

Similarly, both women and men scholars of different religions and faiths have suggested advices for the benefits of all people without any boundaries of religion, colour, sex or country. It is universal sermons for all.

These distinguished women have contributed their advices for the wellbeing of humanity, which could change peoples' activities and character for achievements and prosperity. If these 'quotes' are practiced, a peaceful world would be possible. The **'one world family'** concept would prioritize good governance and would strengthen peace movement and a prosperous world devoid of conflicts and wars.

In the Twenty-first century, women have advanced so much that they are at par with men in all most all activities. They have shown more efficiency in politics, cinema, dances and singing.

The famous quotes of Madam Marie Curie, Helene Keller, Benazir Bhutto, Mother Teresa, Florence Nightingale, Susan B. Antony, Anna Eleanor Roosevelt, Mary Kay Ash, Audray Helpburon, Maya Angelou, Fashion Goddess Coco Chanel and Martha Graham are included to widen the scope of women world for peace. These are as follows:

Marie Curie
(1867 - 1934)

With her husband, Pierre, Marie Curie was the pioneer in researching radioactivity. When he died suddenly, she refused a government pension and instead took his place as a professor at the University of Paris. She was awarded a Nobel Prize in Physics in 1903 for her work, and then became the first person to win a second Nobel Prize in Chemistry in 1911, and she is the only Nobel Prize winner who is also the mother of another Nobel Prize winner – daughter of Marie Curie and Pierre Curie, Irène Joliot-Curie.

Selected Quotations:

I never see what has been done; I only see what remains to be done.

Nothing in life is to be feared. It is only to be understood.

We must not forget that when radium was discovered no one knew that it would prove useful in hospitals. The work was one of pure science. And this is a proof that scientific work must not be considered from the point of view of the direct usefulness of it. It must be done for itself, for the beauty of science, and then there is always the chance that a scientific discovery may become like the radium a benefit for humanity.

I am among those who think that science has great beauty.

I am one of those who think like Nobel, that humanity will draw more good than evil from new discoveries.

A scientist in his laboratory is not only a technician: he is also a child placed before natural phenomena, which impress him, like a fairy tale.

You cannot hope to build a better world without improving the individuals. To that end each of us must work for own improvement and at the same time-share a general responsibility for all humanity, our particular duty being to aid those to whom we think we can be most useful.

Humanity needs practical men, who get the most out of their work, and, without forgetting the general good, safeguard their own interests. But humanity also needs dreamers, for whom the disinterested development of an enterprise is so captivating that it becomes impossible for them to devote their care to their own material profit. Without doubt, these dreamers do not deserve wealth, because they do not desire it. Even so, a well-organized society should assure to such workers the efficient means of accomplishing their task, in a life freed from material care and freely consecrated to research.

Especially women have frequently questioned me, of how I could reconcile family life with a scientific career: Well, it has not been easy.

We must believe that we are gifted for something, and that this thing, at whatever cost, must be attained.

I was taught that the way of progress is neither swift nor easy.

Be less curious about people and more curious about ideas.

There are sadistic scientists who hurry to hunt down errors instead of establishing the truth.

When one studies strongly radioactive substances special precautions must be taken. Dust, the air of the room, and one's clothes, all become radioactive.

After all, science is essentially international, and it is only through lack of the historical sense that national qualities have been attributed to it.

One never notices what has been done; one can only see what remains to be done.

I have no dress except the one I wear every day. If you are going to be kind enough to give me one, please let it be practical and dark so that I can put it on afterwards to go to the laboratory. *About a wedding dress*

Quotes about Marie Curie:

Marie Curie is, of all celebrated beings, the only one whom fame has not corrupted. – ***Albert Einstein***

That one must do some work seriously and must be independent and not merely amuse oneself in life –

our mother has told us always, but never that science was the only career worth following.

– ***Irene Joliet-Curie***

Helen Keller
(1880 - 1968)

Famous for her many achievements in life despite being both deaf and blind, She has been a role model of achievement in the face of adversity.

Life is either a daring adventure or nothing at all. Security is mostly a superstition. It does not exist in nature.

One cannot consent to creep when one has an impulse to soar.

The best and most beautiful things in the world cannot be seen or touched ... but are felt in the heart.

When indeed shall we learn that we are all related one to the other, that we are all members of one body?

Keep your face to the sunshine and you cannot see the shadow.

I long to accomplish a great and noble task, but it is my chief duty to accomplish small tasks as if they were great and noble.

I seldom think of my limitations, and they never make me sad. Perhaps there is just a touch of yearning at times; but it is vague, like a breeze among flowers.

What we have once enjoyed we can never lose. All that we love deeply becomes a part of us.

When we do the best that we can, we never know what miracle is wrought in our life, or in the life of another.

Everything has its wonders, even darkness and silence, and I learn whatever state I may be in, therein to be content.

Be of good cheer. Do not think of today's failures, but of the success that may come tomorrow. You have set yourself a difficult task, but you will succeed if you persevere; and you will find a joy in overcoming obstacles.

Although the world is full of suffering, it is also full of the overcoming of it.

Optimism is the faith that leads to achievement. Nothing can be done without hope or confidence.

Avoiding danger is no safer in the long run than outright exposure. The fearful are caught as often as the bold.

Faith is the strength by which a shattered world shall emerge into the light.

Life is an exciting business, and most exciting when it is lived for others.

It is wonderful how much time good people spend fighting the devil. If they would only expend the same amount of energy loving their fellow men, the devil would die in his tracks of ennui.

Science may have found a cure for most evils; but it has found no remedy for the worst of them all – the apathy of human beings.

It is hard to interest those who have everything in those who have nothing. Until the great mass of the people shall be filled with the sense of responsibility for each other's welfare, social justice can never be attained.

A child must feel the flush of victory and the heart sinking of disappointment before he takes with a will to the tasks distasteful to him and resolves to dance his way through a dull routine of textbooks.

Smell is a potent wizard that transports you across thousands of miles and all the years you have lived.
It is a terrible thing to see and have no vision.

I have often been asked, "Do not people bore you?" I do not understand quite what that means. I suppose the calls of the stupid and curious, especially of newspaper reporters, are always inopportune. I also dislike people who try to talk down to my understanding. They are like people who when walking with you try to shorten their steps to suit yours; the hypocrisy in both cases is equally exasperating.

It gives me a deep comforting sense that "things seen are temporal and things unseen are eternal."

I sometimes wonder if the hand is not more sensitive to the beauties of sculpture than the eye. I should think the wonderful rhythmical flow of lines and curves could be more subtly felt than seen. Be this as it may, I know that I can feel the heartthrobs of the ancient Greeks in their marble gods and goddesses.

The problems of deafness are deeper and more complex, if not more important, than those of blindness. Deafness is a much worse misfortune. For it means the loss of the most vital stimulus–the sound of the voice that brings language, sets thoughts astir and keeps us in the intellectual company of man.

Have you ever been at sea in a dense fog, when it seemed as if a tangible white darkness shut you in and the great ship, tense and anxious, groped her way toward the shore with plummet and sounding line, and you waited with beating heart for something to happen? I was like that ship before my education began, only I was without compass or sounding line, and no way of knowing how near the harbor was. "Light give me light!" was the wordless cry of my soul, and the light of love shone on me in that very hour.

College isn't the place to go for ideas.

Literature is my Utopia. Here I am not disenfranchised. No barrier of the senses shuts me out from the sweet, gracious discourses of my book friends. They talk to me without embarrassment or awkwardness.

The highest result of education is tolerance.

We could never learn to be brave and patient, if there were only joys in the world.

Many persons have a wrong idea of what constitutes true happiness. It is not attained through self-gratification but through fidelity to a worthy purpose.

I do not want the peace that passes understanding. I want the understanding, which brings peace.

It is not possible for civilization to flow backward while there is youth in the world. Youth may be headstrong, but it will advance its allotted length.

What a blind person needs is not a teacher but another self.

It is for us to pray not for tasks equal to our powers, but for powers equal to our tasks, to go forward with a great desire forever beating at the door of our hearts as we travel toward our distant goal.

Character cannot be developed in ease and quiet. Only through experience of trial and suffering can the soul is strengthened, ambition inspired, and success achieved.

Walking with a friend in the dark is better than walking alone in the light.

As the arrow winged with his own feather killed the eagle, so the hand of the world is wounded by its own skill.

Toleration is the greatest gift of mind; it requires the same effort of the brain that it takes to balance oneself on a bicycle.

My share of the work may be limited, but the fact is, it is work that makes it precious.

The world is moved along, not only by the mighty shoves of its heroes, but also by the aggregate of tiny pushes of each honest worker.

The heresy of one age becomes the orthodoxy of the next.

Unless we form the habit of going to the Bible in bright moments as well as in trouble, we cannot fully respond to its consolations because we lack equilibrium between light and darkness.

There is much in the Bible against which every instinct of my being rebels, so much that I regret the necessity, which has compelled me to read it through from beginning to end. I do not think that the knowledge, which I have gained of its history and sources, compensates me for the unpleasant details it has forced upon my attention.[2]

Death is no more than passing from one room into another. But there's a difference for me, you know because in that other room I shall be able to see.

Benazir Bhutto
Former Prime Minister of Pakistan

Benazir Bhutto, fondly called "the Daughter of the East," became a victim of terror attacks. She joins the rank of leaders who have been felled by those who are against democracy. Twice elected the Prime Minister of Pakistan, Benazir faced many challenges. But she refused to be cowed down. Benazir Bhutto quotes inspire us to rally against mindless dominance and injustice.

Statements on Death Threats:

Despite threats of death, I will not acquiesce to tyranny, but rather lead the fight against it.

We are prepared to risk our lives. We're prepared to risk our liberty. But we're not prepared to surrender this great nation to militants. The attack was on what I represent. The attack was on democracy and very unity and integrity of Pakistan.

Just before the attacks happened, I was very happy. The procession was one enormous party, the atmosphere was joyful, people were dancing in the street; it was magnificent. For me, that was the real Pakistan.

We have to modify our campaign to some extent because of the suicide bombings. We will continue to meet the public. We will not be deterred.

---

[2]Jone Johnson Lewis, About.com Guide

Don't worry; I'm going to be safe, and God willing I'm going to be safe.

Benazir Bhutto's Political Views:

Pakistan is at crossroads. We citizens are faced with a decisive choice this January 8th (2008) election day. We can turn our backs on the years of dictatorship, fundamentalism, and economic decline.

Democracy needs support and the best support for democracy comes from other democracies. Democratic nations should come together in an association designed to help each other and promote what is a universal value - democracy.

All our problems, all our disputes, all our disagreements can be resolved quickly to mutual satisfaction if we address the question.

I think it's very unfortunate for Pakistan that yet another government, a democratically-elected government elected by the people has been dismissed. I think it says something about the fact that our democratic institutions haven't worked.

Democracy is necessary to peace and to undermining the forces of terrorism.

You can imprison a man, but not an idea. You can exile a man, but not an idea. You can kill a man, but not an idea.

It pains me that they are using the judicial authorities here to score certain political points back home in Pakistan.

The government I led gave ordinary people peace, security, dignity, and opportunity to progress.

Given the right to a free ballot, the people would support my return.

Now, when people are dying, you don't really look at who's offering the help. You take it. The first issue should be to help the people.

The military wants a system that protects its policies and privileges.

The political parties have unanimously rejected the one-man constitutional changes. [3]

Mother Teresa

When Mother Teresa speaks on issues like family, children, or God, her words overwhelm the reader by their profoundness. Mother Teresa was not just another protagonist for the weak. Her acts of selfless service to humankind touched people of all strata. She was a darling of the masses; a messiah in the garb of a nun. Let us gain from these Mother Teresa quotes.

Be faithful in small things because it is in them that your strength lies.

Everybody today seems to be in such a terrible rush, anxious for greater developments and greater riches and so on, so that children have very little time for their parents. Parents have very little time for each other. And in the home, begins the disruption of peace of the world.

I am not sure exactly what Heaven will be like. But I don't know that when we die and if comes the time for God to judge us, He will not ask, "How many good

[3] These quotes are collected from: Simran Khurana, about. Com Guide

things have you done in your life?" Rather He will ask, "How much love did you put into what you did?"

In light of heaven, the worst suffering on earth, a life full of the most atrocious tortures on earth, will be seen to be no more serious than one night in an inconvenient hotel.

It is easy to love the people far away. It is not always easy to love those close to us. It is easier to give a cup of rice to relieve hunger than to relieve the loneliness and pain of someone unloved in our own home. Bring love into your home for this is where our love for each other must start.

Kind words can be short and easy to speak, but their echoes are truly endless.

Love cannot remain by itself... it has no meaning. Love has to be put into action, and that action of service.

Our life of poverty is as necessary as the work itself.

Only in heaven will we see how much we owe to the poor for helping us to love God better because of them.

Sweetest Lord, make me appreciative of the dignity of my high vocation, and its many responsibilities. Never permit me to disgrace it by giving way to coldness, unkindness, or impatience.

Florence Nightingale

The name Florence Nightingale is synonymous with selfless service. The 'lady with the lamp,' as she was fondly referred to, saved many wounded patients with her compassion. Though Nightingale was born in the lap of luxury, with all the creature comforts that one could hope for in those days, she chose to follow her calling. She believed that God had sent her to Earth to take care of the sick. She eventually became the founder of modern nursing, and espoused the values of sanitation and nutrition in healthcare facilities. Her books set the foundation for modern nursing.

These texts such as:

(a) Notes on Nursing
(b) Notes on Hospitals
(c) Notes on Matters Affecting the Health and
(d) Efficiency and Hospital Administration of the British Army

These are also widely used in the nursing curriculum. Here are some memorable Florence Nightingale quotes. Use these quotes as a source of inspiration and power.

There were many nurses before Florence Nightingale. It was only after Nightingale entered the profession that nursing earned such a respectable name. With her steely resolve to change the living conditions of sick patients, she showed the world that love heals the deepest wounds. Here are some memorable Florence Nightingale quotes. Use these quotes as a source of inspiration and power.

Rather, ten times, die in the surf, heralding the way to a new world, than stand idly on the shore.

So never lose an opportunity of urging a practical beginning, however small, for it is wonderful how often in such matters the mustard-seed germinates and roots itself.

No man, not even a doctor, ever gives any other definition of what a nurse should be than this – 'devoted and obedient'. This definition would do just as well for a porter. It might even do for a horse. It would not do for a policeman.

Women should have the true nurse calling, the good of the sick first the second only the consideration of what is their 'place' to do – and that women who want for a housemaid to do this or the charwomen to do that, when the patient is suffering, have not the making of a nurse in them.

The amount of relief and comfort experienced by the sick after the skin has been carefully washed and dried is one of the commonest observations made at a sick bed.

The only English patients I have ever known refuse tea, have been typhus cases; and the first sign of their getting better was their craving again for tea.

The very first requirement in a hospital is that it should do the sick no harm.

The craving for 'the return of the day', which the sick so constantly evince, is generally nothing but the desire for light.

The martyr sacrifices themselves entirely in vain. Or rather not in vain; for they make the selfish more selfish, the lazy more lazy, the narrow narrower.
There is no part of my life, upon which I can look back without pain.

To understand God's thoughts one must study statistics... the measure of his purpose.

So never lose an opportunity of urging a practical beginning, however small, for it is wonderful how often in such matters the mustard-seed germinates and roots itself.

Were there none who were discontented with what they have, the world would never reach anything better.

What the horrors of war are, no one can imagine. They are not wounds and blood and fever, spotted and low, or dysentery, chronic and acute, cold and heat and famine. They are intoxication, drunken brutality, demoralization and disorder on the part of the inferior... jealousies, meanness, indifference, and selfish brutality on the part of the superior.

Susan B. Anthony

Susan B Anthony (1820 - 1906) was an American social reformer and suffragist. Some of her quotes can affect you at the core. Here is a collection of the most popular Susan B Anthony quotes.

I always distrust people who know so much about what God wants them to do to their fellows...

It was we, the people; not we, the white male citizens; nor yet we, the male citizens; but we, the whole people, who formed the Union...

Join the union, girls, and together say Equal Pay for Equal Work...

If all the rich and all of the church people should send their children to the public schools they would feel bound to concentrate their money on improving these schools until they met the highest ideals...

Cautious, careful people, always casting about to preserve their reputation and social standing, never can bring about a reform. Those who are really in earnest must be willing to be anything or nothing in the world's estimation, and publicly and privately, in season and out, a vow their sympathy with despised and persecuted ideas and their advocates, and bear the consequences...

I tell them I have worked 40 years to make the W.S. platform broad enough for Atheists and Agnostics to stand upon, and now if need be I will fight the next 40 to keep it Catholic enough to permit the straightest Orthodox religionist to speak or pray and count her beads upon.

Men, their rights, and nothing more; women, their rights, and nothing less...

Independence is happiness...

Sooner or later we all discover that the important moments in life are not the advertised ones,, not the birthdays, the graduations, the weddings, not the great goals achieved. The real milestones are less prepossessing. They come to the door of memory unannounced, stray dogs that amble in, sniff around a bit and simply never leave. Our lives are measured by these.

Failure is impossible.

Resolved, that the women of this nation in 1876, have greater cause for discontent, rebellion and revolution than the men of 1776.

Suffrage is the pivotal right.

Bicycling has done more to emancipate women than any one thing in the world. It gives her a feeling of self-reliance and independence the moment she takes her seat; and away she goes the picture of untrammeled womanhood.

I can see that "reap" and "deep," "prayers" and "bears," . . . do rhyme, and so I suppose it is a splendid effort, but if you had written it in plain prose, I could have understood it a great deal better and read it a great deal more easily.

I can't say that the college-bred woman is the most contented woman. The broader her mind the more she understands the unequal conditions between men and women, the more she safes under a government that tolerates it.

Many abolitionists have yet to learn the ABC of woman's rights.

Modern invention has banished the spinning wheel, and the same law of progress makes the woman of today a different woman from her grandmother.

Oh, yes. I'd do it all again; the spirit is willing yet; I feel the same desire to do the work but the flesh is weak. It's too bad that out bodies wear out while our interests are just as strong as ever.

Sooner or later we all discover that the important moments in life are not the advertised ones, not the birthdays, the graduations, the weddings, and not the great goals achieved. The real milestones are less prepossessing. They come to the door of memory.

The older I get the greater power I seem to have to help the world; I am like a snowball – the further I am rolled the more I gain.

There never will be complete equality until women themselves help to make laws and elect lawmakers.

Woman must not depend upon the protection of man, but must be taught to protect herself.

What you should say to outsiders that a Christian has neither more nor less rights in our Association than an atheist. When our platform becomes too narrow for people of all creeds and of no creeds, I myself shall not stand upon it

To no form of religion is woman indebted for one impulse of freedom...

The religious persecution of the ages has been done under what was claimed to be the command of God.

There is not the woman born who desires to eat the bread if dependence, no matter whether it be from the hand of father, husband, or brother; for any one who does so eat her bread places herself in the power of the person from whom she takes it.

I think the girl who is able to earn her own living and pay her own way should be as happy as anybody on earth. The sense of independence and security is very sweet.

Anna Eleanor Roosevelt

Anna Eleanor Roosevelt was a woman with great sensitivity for the underprivileged. She did not limit herself to the role of "wife of President Franklin Roosevelt." She created her own identity by being an active protagonist for the poor. Here are some quotes of Eleanor Roosevelt.

Friendship with oneself is all-important because without it one cannot be friends with anyone else in the world.

He, who loses money, loses much; He, who loses a friend, loses much more; He, who loses faith, loses all.

If we want a free and peaceful world, if we want to make the deserts bloom and man grow to greater dignity as a human being – we can do it.

It is not fair to ask of others what you are not willing to do yourself.

Life was meant to be lived, and curiosity must be kept alive. One must never, for whatever reason, turn his back on life.

Since you get more joy out of giving joy to others, you should put a good deal of thought into the happiness that you are able to give.

The future belongs to those who believe in the beauty of their dreams.

No one can make you feel inferior without your permission.

Mary Kay Ash

At a time when women struggled to break out of stereotypes, Mary Kay Ash proved her mark in business. As a founder of Mary Kay Cosmetics, Mary Kay Ash showed the world that women can excel in business too. She faced many challenges with fortitude. Here are inspiring words from Mary Kay Ash that will bring light into the lives of aspiring businesswomen.

A mediocre idea that generates enthusiasm will go further than a great idea that inspires no one.

Aerodynamically, the bumble bee shouldn't be able to fly, but the bumble bee doesn't know it so it goes on flying anyway.

An average person with average talents and ambition and average education, can outstrip the most brilliant genius in our society, if that person has clear, focused goals.

Dare to risk public criticism.

Don't limit yourself. Many people limit themselves to what they think they can do. You can go as far as you mind lets you. What you believe, you can achieve.

Achievements: Everyone has an invisible sign hanging from their neck saying, "Make me feel important. Never forget this message when working with people.

Everyone wants to be appreciated, so if you appreciate someone, don't keep it a secret.

For every failure, there's an alternative course of action. You just have to find it. When you come to a roadblock, take a detour.

Give yourself something to work toward constantly.

Honesty is the cornerstone of all success, without which confidence and ability to perform shall cease to exist.

If you think you can, you can. And if you think you can't, you're right.

Mediocre idea that generates enthusiasm will go further than a great idea that inspires no one.

Most people live and die with their music still not played. They never dare to try.

No matter how busy you are, you must take time to make the other person feel important.

Pretend that every single person you meet has a sign around his or her neck that says, Make Me Feel Important. Not only will you succeed in sales, you will succeed in life.

Perseverance, Persistence: When you come to a roadblock, take a detour.

Audrey Hepburn

Famous Hollywood actress Audrey Hepburn was an iconic beauty of the sixties. She won the Academy Award for her role in **Roman holiday**. She led a troubled childhood as her country grappled with the Nazis. After immense success in Hollywood, Audrey Hepburn shifted her focus to humanitarian activities. As the UNICEF Goodwill Ambassador, she often visited third world nations. In 1992, President George Bush presented her with the Presidential Medal of Freedom. The Academy of Motion Picture Arts and Sciences awarded her The Jean Hersholt Humanitarian Award.

Your heart just breaks, that's all. But you can't judge, or point fingers. You just have to be lucky enough to find someone who appreciates you.

I was born with an enormous need for affection, and a terrible need to give it.

Remember, if you ever need a helping hand, it's at the end of your arm, as you get older, remember you have another hand: The first is to help yourself, the second is to help others.

People, even more than things, have to be restored, renewed, revived, reclaimed, and redeemed; never throw out anyone.

Success is like reaching an important birthday and finding you're exactly the same.

I never think of myself as an icon. What is in other people's minds is not in my mind.

I just do my thing. I probably hold the distinction of being one movie star who, by all laws of logic, should never have made it. At each stage of my career, I lacked the experience.

Pick the day. Enjoy it – to the hilt. The day as it comes – People as they come... The past, I think, has helped me appreciate the present – and I don't want to spoil any of it by fretting about the future.

Living is like tearing through a museum. Not until later do you really start absorbing what you saw, thinking about it, looking it up in a book, and remembering – because you can't take it all in at once.

For attractive lips; speak words of kindness.

For lovely eyes; seek out the good in people.

For a slim figure; share your food with the hungry.

For beautiful hair; Let a child run his/her fingers through it once a day.

For poise,
Walk with the knowledge that you never walk alone.

People, even more than things,
Have to be restored, renewed, revived, reclaimed,
And redeemed; never throw out anyone.

Remember, if you ever need a helping hand,
You will find one at the end of each of your arms.

As you grow older, you will discover that you have two hands one for helping yourself, and the other for helping other.

Maya Angelou

Poet, philosopher, civil rights activist, dancer, playwright, author, actor, black activist, woman, and mother – that is Maya Angelou for you. It is interesting to note that though most of us barely manage to play two or three roles in our life, Angelou could balance so many balls in the air with finesse.

Maya Angelou has been a shining light of inspiration for people around the world. With a smile on her lips and a generous heart, she conquered the world with her words of inspiration and wisdom. She taught people to rediscover themselves and understand the true meaning of life. Through these Maya Angelou quotes, her legacy will live on. Her pearls of wisdom will guide many generations, and will be the eternal lamppost for despairing souls.

A bird doesn't sing because it has an answer, it sings because it has a song.

Bitterness is like cancer. It eats upon the host. But anger is like fire. It burns it all clean.

Determine to live life with flair and laughter.

I've learned that you can tell a lot about a person by the way (s)he handles these three things: a rainy day, lost luggage, and tangled Christmas tree lights.

We allow our ignorance to prevail upon us and make us think we can survive alone, alone in patches, alone in groups, alone in races, even alone in genders.

There is no greater agony than bearing an untold story inside you.

If you have only one smile in you, give it to the people you love. Don't be surly at home, then go out in the street and start grinning 'Good morning' at total strangers.

For Africa to me... is more than a glamorous fact. It is a historical truth. No man can know where he is going unless he knows exactly where he has been and exactly how he arrived at his present place.

History, despite its wrenching pain, cannot be unlived, however, if faced with courage, need not be lived again.

Hoping for the best, be prepared for the worst and unsurprised by anything in between.

I can be changed by what happens to me. But I refuse to be reduced by it.

I do not trust people who don't love themselves and yet tell me, 'I love you.' There is an African saying which is: Be careful when a naked person offers you a shirt.

If you find it in your heart to care for somebody else, you will have succeeded.

You alone are enough. You have nothing to prove to anybody.

There's a world of difference between truth and facts. Facts can obscure truth.

I've learned that making a 'living' is not the same thing as 'making a life'.

Life is not measured by the number of breaths we take, but by the moments that take our breath away.

Most people don't grow up. Most people age. They find parking spaces, honor their credit cards, get married, have children, and call that maturity. What that is, is aging?

Nature has no mercy at all. Nature says I'm going to snow.

If you have on a bikini and no snowshoes, that's tough. I am going to snow anyway.

The need for change bulldozed road down the center of my mind.

There is a very fine line between loving life and being greedy for it.

We delight in the beauty of the butterfly, but rarely admit the changes it has gone through to achieve that beauty.

Coco Chanel

Fashion Goddess

Millions of women have Coco Chanel to thank for their favorite LBD (little black dress). The smart and sassy priestess of haute couture learnt the ropes of high fashion on her own. Her life was peppered with many hurdles, but she did not let that keep her away from her dreams. From the dungeons of poverty, Coco Chanel clawed her way to the top. Many call her an opportunist and traitor, but she did not care too much for the whining world. She was not the one to bow down, or let fate dictate how her life should turn out.

Coco Chanel exerted a modernizing influence on European fashion. She outlawed the rigid and overbearing skirts of those times, and made casual dressing trendy. She also introduced men's blazers and shirts into women's wardrobes; thereby changing the dynamics of feminism. Her dresses could be worn without tight corsets, and were made out of men's jerseys.

Daredevilry was in her veins, and probably helped her catapult to fame. Coco Chanel lives even today, through her brands.

Chanel No. 5, the first perfume launched by Coco Chanel, is one of the most popular perfumes sold in France, the Mecca of fashion. Coco Channel's life has inspired many filmmakers to produce movies on the enigmatic couturier. These Coco Chanel quotes reveal the raw passion of a woman who had the world wrapped around her manicured fingers.

A girl should be two things: classy and fabulous.

Elegance does not consist in putting on a new dress.
A woman has the age she deserves.

Fashion fades, only style remains the same.

Success is often achieved by those who don't know that failure is inevitable.

The best color in the whole world is the one that looks good, on you!

The most courageous act is still to think for you aloud.

A woman who doesn't wear perfume has no future.

Dress shabbily and they remember the dress; dress impeccably and they remember the woman.

As long as you know men are like children, you know everything!

Coquetry, it's a triumph of the spirit over the senses.

Don't spend time beating on a wall, hoping to transform it into a door.

Elegance is not the prerogative of those who have just escaped from adolescence, but of those who have already taken possession of their future.

Nature gives you the face you have at twenty; it is up to you to merit the face you have at fifty.

Fashion has become a joke. The designers have forgotten that there are women inside the dresses.

Most women dress for men and want to be admired. But they must also be able to move, to get into a car without bursting their seams! Clothes must have a natural shape.

Simplicity is the keynote of all true elegance.

An elegant woman should be able to do her marketing without making housewives laugh. Those who laugh are always right.

I don't do fashion, I am fashion.

How many cares one loses when one decides not to be something but to be someone.

In order to be irreplaceable one must always be different.

Luxury must be comfortable otherwise, it is not luxury.

My life didn't please me, so I created my life.

Fashion is not something that exists in dresses only.

Fashion is in the sky, in the street; fashion has to do with ideas, the way we live, what is happening.

One can get used to ugliness, but never to negligence.

Great loves too must be endured.

Nothing goes out of fashion sooner than a long dress with a very low neck.

Since everything is in our heads, we had better not lose them.

Some people think luxury is the opposite of poverty. It is not. It is the opposite of vulgarity.

Fashion is architecture: it is a matter of proportions. Fashion is made to become unfashionable.

There are people who have money and people who are rich.

There is no fashion for the old.

I don't understand how a woman can leave the house without fixing herself up a little – if only out of politeness. And then, you never know, maybe that's the day she has a date with destiny. And it's best to be as pretty as possible for destiny.

If you were born without wings, do nothing to prevent their growing.

I wanted to give a woman comfortable clothes that would flow with her body. A woman is closest to being naked when she is well dressed.

Youth is something very new: twenty years ago, no one mentioned it.

If a man talks bad about all women, it usually means he was burned by one woman.

There is no time for cut-and-dried monotony. There is time for work. And time for love. That leaves no other time.

Martha Graham
Famous American dancer

She danced as if nobody was watching. Martha Graham danced to evoke strong emotion in her audience. She danced into the hearts of millions of fans around the world. She taught the world to communicate using body movements. Martha

Graham, famous American dancer, changed the definition of modern dancing. Her dance style was unique with a blend of spasmodic motions and pronounced expressions. She brought about a dance renaissance with powerful visuals and dramatic movements. Her dance was a medium to bring about social change, by moving the audience from its apathetic stupor.

Martha Graham was in the profession of dancing for over seventy years. She devoted her entire life to fine-tuning her art. She won accolades and prestigious awards, including the Presidential Medal of Freedom.

Martha Graham remained true to her profession throughout her life. She danced, choreographed, and taught many aspiring dancers. These Martha Graham quotes give us an insight into her life.

Looking at the past is like lolling in a rocking chair. It is so relaxing and you can rock back and forth on the porch, and never go forward.

In a dancer, there is a reverence for such forgotten things as the miracle of the small beautiful bones and their delicate strength.

It is difficult to see the great dance effects as they happen, to see them accurately, catch them fast in memory. It is even more difficult to verbalize them for critical discussion. The particular essence of a performance, its human sweep of articulate rhythm in space and in time has no specific terminology to describe it by.

It takes ten years, usually, to make a dancer. It takes ten years of handling the instrument, handling the material with which you are dealing, for you to know it completely.

My dancing is not an attempt to interpret life in the literary sense. It is an affirmation of life through movement.

A building – if it's beautiful – is the love of one man; he's made it out of his love for space, materials, and things like that.

First, we have to believe, and then we believe.

Great dancers are not great because of their technique; they are great because of their passion.

Dance is the hidden language of the soul of the body. A dancer must listen to his body and pay homage to it. Behind the movement lies this terrible, driving passion, this necessity. I won't settle for anything less.

Age is the acceptance of a term of years. But maturity is the glory of years.

Censorship is the height of vanity.

Every dance is a kind of fever chart, a graph of the heart.

No artist is pleased. There is no satisfaction whatever at any time. There is only a queer, divine dissatisfaction, a blessed unrest that keeps us marching and makes us more alive than the others.

Nobody cares if you can't dance well.

Just get up and dance. Great dancers are great because of their passion.

The only sin is mediocrity. Dance is communication, and so the great challenge is to speak clearly, beautifully, and with inevitability.

Fire is the test of gold... adversity, of strong men. Dancers today can do anything; the technique is phenomenal. The passion and the meaning to their movement can be another thing. Dancing is just discovery, discovery, and discovery. Theater is a verb before it is a noun, an act before it is a place.

There is a fatigue so great that the body cries, even in its sleep. There are times of complete frustration; there are daily small deaths.

There is vitality, a life force, energy, a quickening that is translated through you into action, and because there is only one of you in all time, this expression is unique. And if you block it, it will never exist through any other medium and will be lost.

Nothing is more revealing than movement.

People have asked me why I chose to be a dancer. I did not choose. I was chosen to be a dancer, and with that, you live all your life.

Practice means to perform, over and over again in the face of all obstacles, some act of vision, of faith, of desire. Practice is a means of inviting the perfection desired.

Some men have thousands of reasons why they cannot do what they want to, when all they need is one reason why they can.

You can be Eastern or Burmese or what have you, but the function of the body and the awareness of the body results in dance and you become a dancer, not just a human being.

You see, when weaving a blanket, an Indian woman leaves a flaw in the weaving of that blanket to let the soul out.

The next time you look into the mirror, just look at the way the ears rest next to the head; look at the way the hairline grows; think of all the little bones in your wrist. It is a miracle. And the dance is a celebration of that miracle.

No artist is ahead of his time. He is his time; it is just that others are behind the times.

The body is your instrument in dance, but your art is outside that creature, the body.

Some men have thousands of reasons why they cannot do what they want to, when all they need is one reason why they can. The body is shaped, disciplined, honored, and in time, trusted. The body is a sacred garment. The body says what words cannot.

I did not want to be a tree, a flower or a wave. In a dancer's body, we as audience must see ourselves, not the imitated behavior of everyday actions, not the phenomenon of nature, not exotic creatures from another planet, but something of the miracle that is a human being.

Think of the magic of the foot, comparatively small, upon which your whole weight rests.

It's a miracle and the dance is a celebration of that miracle. The center of the stage is where I am.

+++++

Chapter II

LIFE OF WOMAN

Life is not easy for any of us. But what is of that life? We must have perseverance and above all confidence in ourselves. We must believe that we are gifted for something and that this thing must be attained. ---- Marie Curie

A society is civilized when it shows respect to its women. In every society, human rights and social imperatives will collide: security and liberty, equality and justice. To adjudicate between such competing claims, people need reliable methods of investigation, evidence and impartiality. But miscarriage of justice happens in most of the countries. Lack of clear legal provisions also encourages crime. The eruption of public anger over a heinous action to a girl in Delhi has called for the protest against the government and police system in India in December 2012. Crime against women is increasing in Somalia, India and other countries. People feel that democracy has created goons, law-breakers and cheats.

Each democracy needs suitable economic policies, humane maintenance of peace and law and order.

In all arranged marriages, brides are forced to bring dowry to the mother-in-laws houses. It is because of poverty and social dogma. All the countries have enacted 'Dowry Prevention Act' to check dowry tortured deaths; yet it is continuing.

In this chapter, sufferings and sacrifices of women in different countries are discussed. In the Twenty – first century heinous activities like forced marriages, diverse and rape continue all over the world more or less.

U S A: **Free Women**

With hindsight, we may find that the 2016 U.S. presidential race began last week, when Hillary Rodham Clinton made a politically electrifying point. "Why extremists always focus on women remains a mystery to me," she said at the Women in the World conference in New York. "But they all seem to. It doesn't matter what country they're in or what religion they claim. They want to control women."

At a time when birth control has re-emerged as a political issue in the United States, 94 years after the first legal ruling to permit it, Clinton's comments were an inspiring rallying cry for worried American women. But what about the mystery she identified? Why, as the secretary of state asserted, do extremists, from the Taliban to conservative Christians, want to control women?

An intriguing new study by two professors at the Rotman School of Management at the University of Toronto suggests a possible answer. (Disclosure: I am on the school's dean's advisory board.) Soo Min Toh and Geoffrey Leonardelli didn't set out to discover why extremists want to control women.

Their question was more familiar: Why aren't there more female leaders?

Toh and Leonardelli argue that women are held back by "tight" cultures and can emerge more easily as leaders in "loose" cultures. "Tight" cultures are ones that have clear, rigid rules about how people should behave and impose tough sanctions on those who color outside the lines. Socially conformist, homogeneous societies like Japan, Malaysia, Norway and Pakistan are tight cultures.

Tight cultures, Toh and Leonardelli believe, hold women back because "cultural tightness provokes a resistance to changing the traditional and widespread view that leadership is masculine."

Loose cultures, by contrast, do not have clear norms and are more tolerant of deviation from the rules. Heterogeneous societies and countries in the midst of social and political transition, like Australia, Israel, the Netherlands and Ukraine are loose cultures.

These are cultures in which "societal members tend to be more open to change, and this openness may become manifest in changing expectations and attitudes about the masculinity of leadership."

Here is where Clinton's mystery comes in. Tight cultures are not necessary sexist ones - witness the inclusion of Norway in the list. But extremist subcultures are certainly tight cultures, and they are built on historical assumptions of male dominance. The perspective of Toh and Leonardelli helps to explain why these rigid ideologies are so fixated on keeping women down.

But what about the places like Norway: tight cultures where women do extremely well? Toh's and Leonardelli's answer to that apparent paradox is that, where there has been a top-down decision to support female leaders, tight cultures are very good at executing that directive. That is because these societies are effective at acting on the collective will. If the decision is made to elevate women, tight societies will implement it.

"Although a culturally tight country, Norway ranks high in terms of gender egalitarianism," the study's authors point out. In Norway, egalitarianism is not a rebellion against prevailing cultural norms. It is, instead, what Norway's new top-down consensus requires: "Norway has among the most ambitious equal opportunity legislation in the world that legally requires firms to reach a 40 percent women board representation by 2017."

The study's framework also helps to explain one peculiarity of women in the workplace. Tight societies that choose egalitarianism, like Norway, have been good at pushing women into the corporate establishment. Loose societies that are open to change have been good at empowering women more broadly, encouraging them to join the workforce and to start their own small businesses.

But the one thing women around the world have failed to do is create paradigm - shifting companies. None of the great technology start-ups - for example, Google, Apple and Face book - were founded by a woman. Nor were any of the leading hedge funds, the innovators in the world of money, established by a woman. Women are not just under-represented in this space of transformative entrepreneurs - they are entirely absent.

At first blush, this gap seems to contradict the analysis by Toh and Leonardelli. After all, start-ups embody a profoundly loose culture. It does not matter whether you are a misfit or an ultra-conformist, so long as you have a brilliant idea and are able to implement it.

But the authors point out that leadership is not just about how others view you, it is also about how you view yourself.

Centuries of sexism, they argue, mean that "even when possessing and demonstrating leadership behavior that is superior to others in the group, women leaders may sometimes prefer to cede the formal leadership role to men in the group because they, too, believe that being male or masculine is more leaders like."

Loose cultures can counteract those self-imposed stereotypes to some degree. But the final frontier for women, even in societies that allow them to lead established institutions, is to be ruthless and to take big risks, essential qualities in world-changing entrepreneurs. Instead, as the authors found of female entrepreneurs in Malaysia, women often have to "lead as if they were mothers or teachers."[4]

U S A:

House Vote Sets Up Battle on Domestic Violence Bill

After a fierce fight, full of gender politics, the House passed a Republican bill on Wednesday to combat violence against women, over objections from President Obama and other Democrats, who said it would reduce protections for many battered women, including lesbians, American Indians and illegal immigrants.

The 222-to-205 vote clears the way for negotiations with the Senate, which passed a more expansive version last month by a vote of 68 to 31.

---

[4] Chrystia Freeland (2012), " Free women", NEW YORK, Www Reuters Com, March 15, 2012

Some version of the legislation is likely to become law before elections this fall. But first, Democrats said, they want to force the likely Republican presidential nominee, Mitt Romney, to choose between the House bill and the Senate measure, which was approved with support from 15 Republicans.

Mr. Obama threatened to veto the House bill. But it passed, with support from 216 Republicans and 6 Democrats. Twenty-three Republicans joined 182 Democrats in voting against the bill.

The bill would reauthorize programs operated under the 'Violence against Women Act of 1994', which has provided lifesaving assistance to hundreds of thousands of women. In the past, it was renewed with bipartisan support.

Representatives Sandy Adams, Republican of Florida, and Gwen Moore, Democrat of Wisconsin, both said they had experienced domestic violence, but they took radically different positions. Mrs. Adams, a former deputy sheriff in Orange County, is the chief sponsor of the House bill, while Ms. Moore was one of the most outspoken critics.

Mrs. Adams said that "Democrats had created a phony war on women to score political points. Turning this re-authorization into a political issue is not only wrong. It is dangerous. We can't allow domestic violence to become a campaign issue."

Ms. Moore said that under the bill "abusers' rights prevail over the rights of the victim," and she assailed the measure as "a direct assault on women's lives."

Representative Lamar Smith, Republican of Texas and chairman of the House Judiciary Committee, said Democrats were exploiting the legislation for political gain, "instead of working with Republicans to protect women from domestic violence, rape and stalking."

But Democrats said major provisions were opposed by groups representing women, law enforcement officers and churches. The American Bar Association also opposed the House bill, calling it "a retreat from the battle against domestic and sexual violence."

Democrats said they were dismayed by the House bill, but delighted at the prospect that Republicans would alienate female voters by pushing the legislation in this election year — after battles over contraception and other issues of concern to women.

The House bill omits three provisions of the Senate measure. One would allow Indian tribal courts to try certain non-Indians accused of committing crimes of domestic violence on reservations. Another would expand the number of temporary visas for illegal immigrant victims of domestic violence. The last would extend protections to lesbian, gay, bisexual and transgender victims of domestic violence.

Representative Zoe Lofgren, Democrat of California, said: "The House bill rolls back protections for battered spouses and victims of serious crimes such as rape and sexual assault. It does so by weakening or repealing provisions that have had near-unanimous support of Democrats and Republicans in years past."

Representative Rubén Hinojosa, Democrat of Texas, said the bill "shifts power into the hands of abusers."

But Representative Virginia Foxx, Republican of North Carolina, said "it really pains me" to hear Democrats assert that Republicans do not care about domestic violence.

"We are strengthening the 'Violence against Women Act', not weakening it," Ms. Foxx said. "We want to see women served better and money spent better. Our goal is to ensure that more money is spent on direct services and less on administrative bureaucracy."

Representative Lynn Jenkins, Republican of Kansas, said, "Any attempt to exploit this bill as a partisan political issue is contemptible."

Representative John Conyers Jr. of Michigan, the senior Democrat on the Judiciary Committee, said that the bill — even with last-minute changes by House Republican leaders — was "worse than current law." It would, he said, make it more difficult for immigrants to obtain visas so they could help law enforcement officials investigate and prosecute domestic violence and similar crimes.

Leaders of 31 religious groups, including the United States Conference of Catholic Bishops, the National Association of Evangelicals and the Episcopal Church, opposed immigration provisions of the House bill.

These provisions "would actually roll back protections in current law for battered noncitizens, making them more vulnerable and, in some cases, endangering their lives," the groups said in a letter to House leaders.

Democrats tried unsuccessfully to expand protections for gays and lesbians.

"Studies show that lesbian, gay, bisexual and transgender victims experience domestic violence at roughly the same rate as the general population," but they are less likely to receive help, said Representative Jared Polis, Democrat of Colorado.[5]

---

[5] Robert Pear (2012), "House Vote Sets Up Battle on Domestic Violence Bill", The New York Times, Washington, May 10, 2012

The United Nations

It lashes out at Taliban for violence against Women

A United Nations human rights investigator Sunday called for the dismantling of the ruling Taliban's religious police because of systematic discrimination against women in Afghanistan. "We found official, widespread, systematic violations of the human rights of women in the Taliban areas of Afghanistan," Radhika Coomaraswamy, UN Special Rapporteur for violence against women, said on return from Afghanistan. She said women's rights to education, health and employment and freedom of movement and association were restricted in Afghanistan.

The militia, which controls some 80 percent of the war-torn country, has enforced its ultra-puritanical interpretation of Sharia. Coomaraswamy told a news conference here that the Taliban's ministry for propagation of virtue and suppression of vice, known as the religious police had enforced its edicts, which were "quite unacceptable." "If you compare these edicts with any of the international standards, they are in complete violation," she said. Women are beaten publicly and public lashings of women are held on Fridays, mainly for the violation of the ministry's edicts, she added.

The Afghan government has an "official policy" of discrimination against women, she observed, adding in many rape cases women were punished publicly for adultery. "I think the dismantling of this ministry is something the international community should call for." The UN rapporteur said she was told that because of war and poverty and loss of jobs, the level of begging by women was "extremely high." She said she received reports prostitution did exist in Kabul and many people told her about trafficking of Afghan women abroad.

However, the UN was yet to confirm these reports, she added. Coomaraswamy, a Sri Lankan and lawyer by training, said the freedom of movement of women was restricted and women were not allowed to go out without a "Mehram," a closely related male companion. The UN rapporteur, who held talks with the Taliban, said she was not optimistic about an improvement in the situation in the near future. She said she asked the authorities in Kabul if they were committed to the development of women and their education, but received no reply. However, they reiterated their commitment to all international agreements signed by Afghanistan.

The UN investigator said despite dire poverty, the state of women's rights was "much better" in northern Afghanistan, which is controlled by the anti-Taliban alliance. But she added there were "grave" human rights violations and violence against women during the rule of former president Burhanuddin Rabbani who was ousted by the Taliban. Coomaraswamy, who will shortly submit her report to the UN Human Rights Commission, suggested humanitarian aid to non-governmental organizations in Afghanistan should not be stopped.[6]

The Ministry of vice and virtue is the most misogynist department in the whole world.

The UN Special Rapporteur for Violence against Women Radhika Coomaraswami Sunday lashed out at the ruling Taliban for systematic violation of the human rights of women. She said, "We found widespread systematic violation of the human rights of women in the Taliban areas of Afghanistan," Coomaraswami told a news conference on return from a 4-day visit to Afghanistan.

---

[6] AFP, Islamabad - September 13, 1999

She said public beating of women, by a leather cricket bat continues in Afghanistan, which is mainly for the violations of edicts by the department of virtue and vice. The UN rapporteur urged the Taliban authorities to respect international conventions on human rights and dismantle Ministry for Promotion of Virtue and Prevention of Vice.

"We found violations in the areas of physical security, the right to education the right to health the right to employment of movement freedom of association, protection of the rights of women, protection of the family and trafficking and prostitution. Public lashing of women on Fridays for violations of the Hadood Ordinance also continue. She said because of war and poverty many of the women cannot work, level of begging by women is extremely high and "we did find that prostitution does exist in Kabul and that many people told us that it was on the increase".

She said the freedom of movement of women is extremely restricted. "There are allegedly no passports for women in Afghanistan. But we still have not confirmed it. There seems to be a fact that women cannot go out without a Mahram".

The Taliban's ministry of vice and virtue has authored edicts that ban women from working, going to school, forces them to wear the all-economy-passing burqa, ordered people to paint their first floor windows black so passers by could not see women inside.

She said the ministry issued edicts saying women should travel outside their home only when accompanied by a close male relative. She said violators are publicly beaten, sometimes with a car antennae ripped off the nearest vehicle.

The ministry of vice and virtue is the most misogynist department in the whole world their edicts are quite unacceptable. She interviewed scores of Afghan women, both in Afghanistan and - - neighboring Pakistan, where tens of thousands live as refugees. She said discrimination against women exists throughout the world but in Afghanistan it is the official policy of the Taliban. The ruling militia has imposed their interpretation of Islamic laws. She said also visited the areas controlled by the opposition United Front led by Burhanuddin Rabbani adding she was shown girls school and was told of the opposition's support for women.

However, she said "for the record" Rabbani's government ruled Afghanistan from 1992 until 1996 when bitter factional fighting destroyed 70 percent of the city and "some of the worst violence against women in a war" was committed.

She said women's begging is on the increase in capital Kabul adding that depression among women is rampant. There were reports of trafficking in women, forced marriages and prostitution. She said women were separated from their husbands and relocated to camps from the Shomali Plains. There also were reports of sexual assaults, which should be investigated.

She said that she has never seen the people's suffering as much as in Afghanistan. "The situation looks very bleak in terms of poverty, in terms of war, in terms of the rights of women." [7]

No country for young women

Whatever else one might think of the anti-corruption movements, they give the lie to the conventional notion that the middle class is politically apathetic. Likewise, unprecedented public protests that have broken out in Delhi against the horrific gang rape of a

[7] News Network International, September 13, 1999, Islamabad

young woman in a moving bus — leading to baton charges, use of water cannon, lockdown of central Delhi and closure of Metro stations — open a crack in the narrative that the reason such horrific crimes against women happen is because society doesn't care.

This is not to say that the reasons for such violence aren't social. Sexual crimes are committed across the world, but elsewhere they tend to be individual crimes committed in private circumstances. It's only in India that gang rapes are uploaded as MMS clips, or carried out in moving vehicles in metropolitan cities, suggesting collective impunity for the perpetrators. While indicative of a social pathology that's specific to us, it's clearly also being resisted by significant segments of society. There's a social and sexual churning that's afoot, with which India's archaic administrative and political systems are failing to cope.

To proceed by way of an analogy, look at Delhi's own development. It is an imperial city, and that character has sustained post-independence. The British built New Delhi to reflect the pomp and glory of the imperial state (prior to that Old Delhi was the seat of the Mughal empire and the Delhi Sultanate). Thus the imperial hauteur of home minister Sushil Shinde's statement, that if he were to go out and meet student protestors today, next he would be expected to meet Maoists just because they turn up at India Gate.

Yet precisely because Delhi is home to the sarkar, resources have been lavished on building its infrastructure. That, along with the migration of talent from all over the country, makes it a dynamic commercial city as well, contributing to its Janus-faced character. Delhi's collisions occur because commercial and citizen activity must peep out from within the interstices of a disdainful government mindset.

This reflects in the nature of policing as well, with large numbers of policemen being corralled for VIP duty. A cop told me that while his compatriots assigned to VIP security in Delhi serve only 6-8 hours a day, the rest could be expected to put in as many as 22 hours. That was because, as he pointed out, authorities are well aware that excessive hours impact badly on the alertness of policemen.

Not only are the facilities they are provided with poor and degrading, sometimes they are even expected to pay for fuel for their motorbikes to travel to the crime spot, out of their own meagre salaries! If a cop in such circumstances doesn't turn out corrupt, brutal, negligent or sexist, that in itself is a small miracle. Citizens' safety is not seen as worth investing in, and women's safety comes last on the priority list. A policeman's death at the hands of some protesters in Delhi can only be expected to further this cycle of de-humanization.

If Gujarat and Tamil Nadu are industrial powerhouses, Delhi and the national capital region perform the same function for services — with strengths in IT and IT-enabled services, fashion, healthcare, entertainment, finance, education, media, professional services, hotels and tourism. This post-industrial landscape gives rise to a large middle class and places Delhi at the cusp of modernity. It leads to a great social churning as young people earn far more than their fathers, women earn as much as men. With social hierarchies unsettled, the scene is set for a traditional and patriarchal backlash.

Women are supposed to be the standard bearers of tradition. But note that with liberalisation and the launch of market forces, the market is also a feminised space (hence the association of women with shopping). Both in the aristocratic and socialist imagination the market, fashion and post-industrialist consumer culture are spaces of frivolity, and the woman as consumer becomes a threat. It means they are no longer looked at but also looking, no longer passive objects of exchange but actively exercising choice and autonomy, which could also include sexual autonomy.

It's no wonder that the assault on Delhi's gang rape victim started out with taunts directed at her boyfriend. It's no wonder that women sitting in a bar or pub become an affront, whether to Sri Ram Sene goons in Mangalore or to self-righteous cops in Mumbai. And it's no wonder that "love marriages" become an issue, leading to lynch mobs being set on lovelorn couples. The prospect of women exercising autonomy and the consequent challenge to the way things were must be met by subjecting them to sadistic violence (or harassing them with the full force of the law, if you happen to be a lawman).[8]

The Indian constitution, however, gives equal rights to women. And citizens have the right to security. Instead of keeping up our ambivalence about modernity — evident in suggestions that women themselves are partially responsible for violence against them — we need to see security as an essential element of infrastructure and development planning. It's as critical to building thriving cities and decent lives for Indians as roads, electricity or breathable air.

Women's Support for Fundamentalist Islam

Why do some women in Muslim countries adopt fundamentalist Islamic value systems that promote gender-based inequalities while others do not? This

---

[8] Swagato Ganguly (2012), "No country for young women", The Times of India, December 26, 2012

article considers the economic determinants of fundamentalist beliefs in the Muslim world, as women look either to marriage or employment to achieve financial security. Using cross-national public opinion data from eighteen countries with significant Muslim populations, we apply a latent class model to characterize respondents according to their views on gender norms, political Islam, and personal religiosity. Among women, lack of economic opportunity is a stronger predictor of fundamentalist belief systems than socioeconomic class. Cross-nationally, fundamentalism among women is most prevalent in poor countries and those with a large male-female wage gap. These findings have important implications for the promotion of women's rights, the rise of political Islam, and the development of democracy in the Muslim world.

This study provides empirical evidence for a mechanism linking a lack of economic opportunity to support for fundamentalist belief systems among Muslim women worldwide. We do not claim that economic considerations are the only relevant factors. Rather, we demonstrate that among the many forces that may impel Muslim women to adopt a fundamentalist value system, one significant one is the quest for financial security.

Women with unfavorable economic prospects have more to gain on the marriage market by adopting fundamentalist beliefs than they do on the employment market by adopting secular or even just non-traditionalist beliefs. In particular, women without jobs or with lower levels of formal education have a greater tendency to view the world from a traditionalist or fundamentalist perspective. And countries that are poorer and provide fewer economic opportunities for independent women contain more women (on a percentage basis) that hold fundamentalist beliefs.

An important goal of this article has been to consider some of the economic motivations of Muslim women in a strategic context. This approach is in stark contrast to the usual treatment of the Islamic world, which some seem to believe is dominated by immutable cultural, historical, and religious forces. Our intent has not been to target Islam as a religion with particular gender practices, but instead to try to explain the variation in attitudes that we observe across the Muslim world. We are interested in determining when Western norms regarding gender are adopted and by whom.

What are the implications of these findings? Consider three broad areas.

First, if we care about women's rights in family protection, employment, and education in and of themselves then these findings suggest that increasing economic opportunities for women in the Muslim world will lead to a decrease in fundamentalism.

Second, Natchwey and Tessler (1999) have argued that support for political Islam tends to be associated with cultural factors, like personal religiosity and attitudes toward gender equality. While Islamists in government are still a relatively rare phenomenon, the recent victory of Hamas in Palestine and the electoral successes of the Muslim Brothers in Egypt and the Islamic parties in Turkey suggest that political Islam is increasingly an important political phenomenon.

Third, Fish (2002) posits that the inferior status of women in Muslim countries accounts for at least part of the link between Islam and authoritarianism. From a normative perspective, if gender attitudes are a determinant of democratic capacity, then these findings shed light on the possibility for the development of more democratic government in the Islamic world.

Finally, this study has shown that there exists tremendous variation in ideological beliefs both within the Islamic world and among individual Muslims. This suggests that interpretations of Islam are mutable. While fundamentalist attitudes toward women are widespread, being Muslim does not mean that one need adopt particular beliefs with regard to the sexes.

Binder (1988) has argued that there exists the potential for Islamic liberalism and this article has suggested one way that this liberal tradition may be activated. The strategic basis for male support for fundamentalism is just beginning to be explored and provides another potentially fruitful research area.[9]

Islam and the sufferings of women

There are many things that go on in Islam regarding women that are barbaric. Untold suffering has been heaped upon women due to these practices. There seems to be no one in the world of Islam that is willing to speak out and bring an end to these practices. Imams are silent, the women's movements of the world are silent, particularly women's studies in the universities, and reform seems impossible given the secondary position of women in the Qur'an and the hadiths. There are many practices that demean women and subject them to barbaric and evil conditions.

1. Female Genital Mutilations

Consider the following news story:

---

[9] Lisa blaydes and Drew A. Linzer (1997), "The Political Economy of Women's Support for Fundamentalist Islam", Annual Meetings of the American Political Science Association, 2006

(a) Iraq - Sheelan Anwar Omer, a shy 7-year-old Kurdish girl, bounded into her neighbor's house with an ear-to-ear smile, looking for the party her mother had promised.

There was no celebration. Instead, a local woman quickly locked a rusty red door behind Sheelan, who looked bewildered when her mother ordered the girl to remove her underpants. Sheelan began to whimper, and then tremble, while the women pushed apart her legs and a midwife raised a stainless-steel razor blade in the air. "I do this in the name of Allah!" she intoned.

As the midwife sliced off part of Sheelan's genitals, the girl let out a high-pitched wail heard throughout the neighborhood. As she carried the sobbing child back home, Sheelan's mother smiled with pride.

"This is the practice of the Kurdish people for as long as anyone can remember," said the mother, Aisha Hameed, 30, a housewife in this ethnically mixed town about 100 miles north of Baghdad. "We don't know why we do it, but we will never stop because Islam and our elders require it."

More than 60 percent of women in Kurdish areas of northern Iraq have been circumcised, according to a study conducted this year. In at least one Kurdish territory, 95 percent of women have undergone the practice, which human rights groups call female genital mutilation.[10]

(b) Ayaan Hirsi Ali, in her book, INFIDEL, describes her experience as a young female.

"In Somalia, like many countries across Africa and the Middle East, little girls are made "pure" by having

---

[10] "For Kurdish Girls, a Painful Ancient Ritual," by Amit R. Paley for the Washington Post, December 29, 2008

their genitals cut out. There is no other way to describe this procedure, which typically occurs around the age of five. After the child's clitoris and labia are carved out, scraped off, or, in more compassionate areas, merely cut or pricked, the whole area is often sewn up, so that a thick band of tissue forms a chastity belt made of the girl's own scarred flesh. A small hole is carefully situated to permit a thin flow of pee. Only great force can tear the scar tissue wider, for sex.

"Female genital mutilation predates Islam. Not all Muslims do this, and a few of the peoples who do are not Islamic. But in Somalia, where virtually every girl is excised, the practice is always justified in the name of Islam. Uncircumcised girls may be possessed by devils, fall into vice and perdition, and becomes whores. Imams never discourage the practice: it keeps girls pure.

"Many girls die during or after their excision, from infections, other complications cause enormous, and more or less lifelong pain." (New York: Free Press, 2007, p. 31)

There are testimonies of Muslim girls who are frightened to death of their wedding night when they are forced to have sex under these conditions. Not only is sex a problem, but also delivering is a child abnormal. One would think that Muslim men would rise up and condemn the practice for there are men who married women and could not enter the woman on their wedding night. This reflects poorly on a man's image of himself.

I consulted a friend who is an ob-gyn doctor and asked his views on the implication of this mutilation. He wrote:

"I looked up Frank Netter's drawings of the procedure (Netter is a well honored MD/medical artist who is famous for his drawings of anatomical and surgical subjects). Netter shows various degrees of mutilation involved with female "circumcision". It may involve "only" a partial removal of the anterior labia minora and clitoral hood, to the total removal of the labia minora, partial removal of the labia majora and extirpation of the total clitoris. This is the same as we do for cancer of the vulva (called a simple vulvectomy). In both cases with "circumcision", the labia are the sutured TOGETHER! (With vulvectomy we attempt to resuture residual anatomy to appropriate residual anatomy). The net results leave a nearly impenetrable vulva...or what I would think an actually impenetrable vulva.

The following are some possible/probable side effects:

1) Physical obstruction of the introituses may lead to a condition of hematocolpos and hematometria...the accumulation of menstrual blood in the vagina and endometrial cavity of the uterus which would cause (likely) sterility as well as endometriosis (a condition of small implants of endometrium in the lower abdominal cavity that causes pockets of blood in the abdomen and severe pain in the abdomen...and even potential death should the enlarging blood cysts rupture).

2) A misdirection of the urinary streams--the labia minora fundamentally direct or point the flow of urine. This side effect is worse than it sounds...it may cause the smell of urine on the person so affected.

3) Severe scarring of the vulva, which would lead to a predisposition to severe tearing during childbirth. This (tearing) could lead to severe hemorrhage and the formation of huge hem Tomas of the vulva...I've seen them the size of a football and require several units of blood transfusion. As a corollary of this, scarring

could cause dystocia (an increased disability, or even inability, to deliver.)

4) Infection at the time of the procedure or shortly thereafter...infection with attempted intercourse or any trauma that might lacerate the scar tissue.

5) Massive dyspareunia (pain with intercourse) due to the scar tissue. This would probably be a lifetime problem unless obviated by surgery. Normal sexual function would likely be impossible.

6) The psychological effects would be massive. It seems to certainly have the grotesque psychological side effects as childhood rape has, which often leads to a number of problems, such as drug and alcohol addiction (high correlation), antisocial behavioral disorders (moderate correlation) and remarkably promiscuous behavior, including prostitution (high correlation)

7) It has been my observation that many women who are self-described lesbians have had traumatic incidents analogous to this that are associated, in the victim's opinion, with men."

The questions are:

(a) One has to ask about this practice in the minds of people. Did the Creator make a mistake in making females the way they are?
(b) Do Muslims feel the need to improve on what He did?
(c) Is this not an insult to the Creator?
(d) What does this do for the female in terms of sexual pleasure?
(e) It is not commanded in the Qur'an, so why not reject the practice?
(f) Why do imams not condemn the practice?

The story of Genesis 1-2 is that God created man and woman. No improvements were necessary. No barbaric operations were ordered. In fact the Hebrew was forbidden to cut the body. "You are the sons of the LORD your God. You shall not cut yourselves or make any baldness on your foreheads for the dead. (Dt. 14:1) In the New Testament we read: "And the God of peace himself sanctify you wholly; and may your spirit and soul and body be preserved entire, without blame at the coming of our Lord Jesus Christ. " (I Thess. 5:23 ASV) The body, both male and female, is to be kept in its created state.

The lone exception is male circumcision, which was the sign of Yahweh's Covenant with Abraham. As such the foreskin was cut, but the organ was not mutilated. Nor does it impose a hardship on the man. This was commanded for the Jewish people only. The Qur'an does not command female cutting. If one attempted to justify the practice from the hadiths it must be remembered they are not "revelation."

Moreover, there are so many fraudulent hadiths that one cannot be sure about using them to justify an evil practice on women.

It is a horrible sin to mutilate little girls in the name of custom, Allah, religion, or tradition.

2. Wearing the burqa

This is the most extreme form of covering for females. One of the most barbaric examples of this was in March 2002 in Mecca when fifteen girls were killed in a fire at their school. The Saudi Religious police would not allow the girls out of the building without the proper dress.

They battled the police and the firemen who were trying to open the school's doors. Is this not an evil practice that required the girls to die rather than being seen without the burqa? What kind of value system is this?

Can you imagine as a man wearing a tent to cover your whole body and not exposing any part of your body to be viewed by others? Not only is it demeaning to women, it is also unhealthy.

"Muslim women who wear the burqa in Ireland are at increased risk of pelvic fractures during childbirth because of vitamin D deficiency due to a lack of sunlight, a consultant warns.

Babies born to women with vitamin D deficiency are also more prone to seizures in their first week of life, according to Dr Miriam Casey, of the Osteoporosis Unit in St James's hospital in Dublin.

Casey said she was aware of cases involving pelvic fractures, and warned that these could become more frequent as Ireland's Muslim population increased. "Ireland's temperate climate doesn't have the intense sunlight that keeps burqa-clad women from becoming vitamin D-deficient in their own countries," she said.

Vitamin D helps the body to absorb calcium and is crucial for making bones strong. The greatest source is sunlight.

Casey said the fractures occur at sites of particular weakness, which develop in under-mineralized pelvic bones. In these women's babies, low calcium can cause "serious complications such as seizures, growth retardation, muscle weakness and fractures".

"As a toddler, carrying the weight of the torso can force the development of a bow-legged appearance and a waddling gait," she said. "Later, there can be rickets, which is caused by vitamin D deficiency, with swollen wrists and bones that fail to fuse in adolescence."

Darker skins can produce as little as 1 percent of the vitamin D that fair skins produce. Moreover, studies have found that the rate of many diseases rises the further north one moves, leading researchers to suspect that vitamin D may play a greater role in health than previously thought. [11]

It seems that the Creator made us to be exposed to the sun for our health's sake, but many Muslim cultures require a female to be covered and that is more important to Islam than health. It is irrational to think that viewing women will excite only men. Why do not the men cover themselves as required of the women? Women are not without passion. How would a man feel wearing a black tent that covers his entire body and his face covered so no one would recognize him?

3. Honor killings

No one knows the number of "honor killings" that occur each year. The estimates run into the thousands. Frequently the police do not investigate and bring charges against the murderer in Muslim cultures.

Honor killings are primarily related to the females who may be suspected of having sex before marriage, flirting with someone, talking to a stranger, failing to serve a meal on time, rape by a relative, cousin, uncle, or brother. There is no limit to the reasons given for honor killings. One of the more notorious honor killings occurred in the Dallas, Texas area where their father killed two sisters because

---

[11] "Ireland too grey for the burqa," by Colin Gleeson for the Times Online, December 28, 2008

they were being too influenced by western culture and music.

Ayaan Hirsi Ali has reported that family members killed 11 Muslim girls between October 2004 and May 2005 in just two regions. There are 25 such regions in Holland.

Shawbo Ali Rauf was a 19-year-old Iraqi girl who was murdered by her own in-laws. Her crime was to have an unknown number on her mobile phone. Her "honour killing" is just one in a grotesque series emerging from Iraq, where activists speak of a "genocide" against women in the name of religion.

A 17-year-old girl, Rand Abdel - Qader, was stabbed to death by her father for becoming infatuated with a British soldier serving in southern Iraq. In Basra alone, police acknowledge that 15 women a month are murdered for breaching Islamic dress codes.

Campaigners insist it is a conservative figure. Violence against women is rampant, rising every day with the power of the militias. Beheadings, rapes, beatings, suicides through self-immolation, genital mutilation, and trafficking and child abuse masquerading as marriage of girls as young as nine are all on the increase.

A sixteen-year-old Palestinian girl became pregnant after being raped by her younger brother. Once her condition became known, her family encouraged her older brother to kill her to remove the blemish from their honor. Her brothers, the rapist and the murderer, were exonerated. The girl was blamed. "She made a mistake," said one of her male cousins. "She had to pay for it.

European police report that Islamic honor killings are on the rise. In 2005, for instance, a review by British police of 22 domestic homicides led to 18 of the cases being reclassified as "murder in the name of so-called 'honor.'

Polls routinely find that a disturbingly large percentage of Muslims – one in 10 according to a 2006 BBC poll – would condone the murder of someone seen to have disrespected their families' honor.

The claim is that the female has brought shame to the family. The greater shame is that they have no shame for what they do to the women.

The Christian response to the issue of shame is that my identity is in Christ, not in my family.

Jesus said, "God will bless you when others hate you and won't have anything to do with you. God will bless you when people insult you and say cruel things about you, all because you are a follower of the Son of Man." (Luke 6:22 CEV) Revenge is not something a follower of Christ can allow. Christians are told: "Dear friends, don't try to get even. Let God take revenge. In the Scriptures the Lord says, "I am the one to take revenge and pay them back." (Rom. 12:19) Moreover, "Don't let evil defeat you, but defeat evil with good." (Rom. 12:21)

The Apostle Peter wrote to the Christians concerning Jesus, "Although he was abused, he never tried to get even. And when he suffered, he made no threats. Instead, he had faith in God, who judges fairly. Christ carried the burden of our sins. He was nailed to the cross, so that we would stop sinning and start living right. His cuts and bruises heal you. You had wandered away like sheep. Now you have returned to the one who is your shepherd and protector. (1 Peter 2:23-25)

As long as the "shame culture" exists there will be lots of innocent victims put to death. Medical examinations have revealed that innocent girls accused of immorality were still virgins and the real evil was in the minds of the fathers, or brothers, or relatives. The principle of "innocent until proven guilty" doesn't seem to operate in the minds of these people.

4. Wife beating

The practice of beating a wife is not new in many societies. It may come about because of jealousy, laziness, indifference, or distrust. There are lots of irrational excuses for this in many cultures. Even among Christians there are those who beat their wives.

There are no religious verses commanding a Christian to beat his wife. Most non-Muslims who beat their wives do not have any religious justification for it. There are Muslim men who do not beat their wives; however, the Muslim context is different. There is a religious directive for it. The Qur'an says, "Men are the protectors and maintainers of women, because God has given the one more (strength) than the other, and because they support them from their means. Therefore the righteous women are devoutly obedient, and guard in (the husband's) absence what God would have them guard. As to those women on whose part ye fear disloyalty and ill-conduct, admonish them (first), (Next), refuse to share their beds, (And last) beat them (lightly); but if they return to obedience, seek not against them Means (of annoyance): For God is Most High, great (above you all)." (Surah 4:34 Yusuf Ali's Trans)

Pickthall uses the word "scourge them." Six other translations of the Qur'an use the word "beat them."

Obviously this is a command that gets a lot of attention both in and out of Islam. Inside are the defenders saying that it is such a mild beating as with a "toothbrush." Those outside of Islam have seen the results of the beating of neighbors who have been bruised, battered, thrown against the walls of their apartments. Often nothing happens when the police arrive because the wives will not file charges. So it goes on and on.

Statistics are hard to come by for obvious reasons. "The Pakistan Institute of Medical Sciences has determined that over ninety percent of Pakistani wives have been struck, beaten, or abused sexually — for offenses on the order of cooking an unsatisfactory meal. Others were punished for failing to give birth to a male child. In Spring 2005, when the East African nation of Chad tried to institute a new family law that would outlaw wife beating, Muslim clerics led resistance to the measure as un-Islamic."

Muslim leaders do affirm the view of the Qur'an and teach the idea of beating a disobedient wife.

On October 5, 2004, France expelled Algerian-born Imam Abdel Qader Bouziane for telling a French magazine that Muslim husbands may beat their wives. This follows the sentencing on January 14 of the Egyptian-born Sheik Muhammad Kamal Mustafa, the imam of the mosque of the Spanish city of Fuengirola, Costa del Sol, for publishing a book that explains that wife beating is in accordance with Shariah law.

Sheik Yousuf Qaradhawi, one of the most influential clerics in Sunni Islam and head of the European Council for Fatwa and Research and the International Council of Muslim Clerics, has also advocated wife-beating on multiple occasions in his 1984 book "The Lawful and the Prohibited in Islam," and on his weekly Al Jazeera program, which is popular among the surging number of European Muslims who increasingly look to religious leaders from the Middle

East for religious guidance. This is particularly true with the growth of viewers watching Arab TV stations, available on satellite TV in Europe, which frequently airs shows dedicated to teaching a husband how to beat his wife. The following examples on this subject can be viewed at www.memritv.org (MEMRI | Friday, November 05, 2004)

For an extensive treatment on the issue of wife beating go here.

There are probably many explanations why men do beat their wives. One may be that many marriages are arranged and neither person knows the other. If the marriage has a large age gap as in a 10-year-old girl and a 40-year-old man the marriage is doomed to have lots of problems. A recent story from Saudi Arabic tells of a girl who was 5 who appeared to be tested for marriage. The doctor denied the test and she could not get married. What companionship is there between two such spans of ages? What is the basis of love in an arranged marriage?

The lack of education for females is also a source of problems. The Taliban has been burning down schools, threatening people who send their girls to schools, and the end result is an enforced ignorance of the females. Can there be any preparation for marriage in ignorance?

There will be no change in this situation since the word from Allah and Mohammed is to beat the disobedient wives.

5. Rape

In a number of western countries, Sweden, Norway, Denmark, Australia, there have been a large increase in the rape of non-Muslim women some as young as a 13 year old Swedish girl gang raped by 5 Kurds. The victims in Australia were called "sluts" or "Aussie pigs."

A Lebanese Sheik Faiz Mohammed blamed the women themselves for wearing skimpy clothing, which invites men to rape them. In Copenhagen, Islamic mufti Shahid Mehdi declared that women who did not wear a headscarf were asking to be raped.

What is the psychology behind all these rapes? (Someone has written that most of the men who rape had the name of Mohammed.) The answer lies in the example of Mohammed. Rape was permitted and encouraged by Mohammed. Rape is a part of jihad. It is a part of war. The women captured in battle were raped and the husbands humiliated.

Mohammed participated in this horror. After the battle of Khaybar the spoils were given out. One warrior, Dihya bin Khalifa requested of Mohammed that he be given a slave girl from the captives. He chose a woman name Safiyya bint Huyayy. Her husband had been captured, tortured and killed by the Muslims. Later when Mohammed saw her he told Dihya to take another girl from the captives.

Mohammed freed her and married her upon her agreement to convert to Islam. That night she was dressed in a wedding dress and Mohammed consummated the marriage. What was it like to see your husband tortured, killed, and then forced into a marriage on the same day?

One of the problems discussing rape is that Muslims do not consider raping a non-Muslim as a sin or a problem. It is justified because Mohammed did it.

Rape is not only bad in the western countries where there can be punishment for the offenders when caught and tried, but in Muslim countries there is a different problem. If a woman makes charges at the police station that she has been raped, she must produce 4 male witnesses to justify her accusations.

If she cannot produce these four witnesses, she is often charged with adultery or fornication and may be imprisoned herself. In Pakistan 75 percent or more of the women in prison are victims of rape. To report a rape may mean nothing more than a confession of guilt. Little is done to investigate the charges. Can you imagine the chagrin of women who reports a rape at a police station to seek justice and to her dismay finds that she is put in jail for committing fornication or adultery?

For more information on the issue of rape in Islam, go here and here and here.

These are a few problems for women in the Muslim culture. Unfortunately, there will be little change for improvement of the lives of half a billion women. Conditions vary from country to country, some worse than others, but none with real freedom and position.

When women cannot be allowed a real education there will be problems borne of ignorance whether in growing up, marriage, raising a family, being a wife, being a real companion, or whatever. Ignorance is not bliss. Women can make a phenomenal contribution to the rising of culture if they are allowed this freedom. Only when one can escape the influence of a seventh century culture does this happen.

Jesus told the people who had faith in him, "If you keep on obeying what I have said, you truly are my disciples. You will know the truth, and the truth will set you free." (John 8:31-32)

"Christ has set us free! This means we are really free. Now hold on to your freedom and don't ever become slaves of the Law again." (Gal. 5:1) One could very well say, don't ever become slaves of sharia again.

This is easy to say to a person who becomes a believer in Jesus who lives in a Muslim culture whose life may be threatened by his confession. There will not be any great relief until the culture is changed and becomes Christian where there is freedom to be transformed by the Holy Spirit. For this reason among others there are people praying that great changes will take place in the Muslim culture that people will be free to believe in Jesus as Lord and Savior. Join in that prayer for the Glory of God.[12]

Alfred Nobel's Legacy to Women

Ellen Johnson Sirleaf, the President of Liberia and Nobel Peace Laureate 2011, has explained her experiences and thoughts on women of the world. She narrates as follows:

On Saturday I was in Oslo with two of my sisters from Africa, Leymah Gbowee and Tawakkol Karman, to receive the Nobel Peace Prize in recognition of — according to the Nobel Prize committee members — our "non-violent struggle for the safety of women and for women's rights to full participation in peace-building work."

On Tuesday, I will be in Paris to talk more generally about the role of women in shaping Africa's future and also to pay my respects to the man who created the prize I am taking with me back to Liberia: Alfred Nobel.

It was in Paris in November 1895 that this Swedish inventor, who made a fortune with the invention of dynamite, wrote his last will and testament leaving

---

[12] Answering Islam 1999 – 2011 – A Christian – Muslim dialog

much of his estate to establishing the prizes that bear his name.

Nobel is said to have been motivated to this act by a misunderstanding: In 1888, a French newspaper published an article stating that he had died. The headline was "The Merchant of Death is De4ad," and it said that "Dr. Alfred Nobel, who became rich by finding ways to kill more people faster than ever before, died yesterday."

The newspaper was doubly mistaken. First, Alfred Nobel had not died — it was his brother. Second, and much more consequential, Alfred Nobel's dynamite did not kill people. People kill people, whether it is with a knife or a machete, with a handgun or a rifle or a machine gun or an explosive device packed with Mr. Nobel's potent tincture.

The murder of 77 innocent people by a man with explosives and weapons in Norway last summer underscored this point with tragic clarity. It may have been a rare moment in the history of that prosperous and mostly peaceful Scandinavian country, as I observed in Oslo last Saturday, but it has often occurred with appalling frequency in other parts of the world, especially on my continent. I need only mention the Democratic Republic of Congo, Rwanda, Sierra Leone, Sudan, Somalia and my own Liberia.

And we must not forget that some of the most heinous crimes in war have been committed without explosives, indeed, without the need for any particular weapon at all. Too often simple brute force has sufficed. Rape remains one of the tested and most enduring weapons of war. I said this at the Nobel Peace Prize ceremony, and I would like to repeat here verbatim what I said three days ago in Oslo:

"Although international tribunals have correctly declared that rape, used as a weapon of war, is a crime against humanity, rapes in times of lawlessness continue unabated. The number of our sisters and daughters of all ages brutally defiled over the past two decades staggers the imagination, and the number of lives devastated by such evil defies comprehension."

"Through the mutilation of our bodies and the destruction of our ambitions, women and girls have disproportionately paid the price of domestic and international armed conflict. We have paid in the currencies of blood, of tears, and of dignity."

But wherever there have been men willing to commit this double transgression against the human body and spirit, there have always been other men, and perhaps even more women, who have committed themselves to the cause of peace. These were the people Alfred Nobel wanted to identify for celebration and, even more important, emulation.

In his testament establishing the foundation to fund his prizes, Nobel stipulated that each year a prize be given to a person who "shall have done the most or the best work for fraternity between the nations and the abolition or reduction of standing armies and the formation and spreading of peace congresses."

Unlike war, which has remained almost exclusively the domain of men, the project of peace and healing has belonged to men and women alike. The awarding of Nobel's peace prize has generously given recognition to this fact almost from its inception with 15 women to date.

In 1905, Baroness Bertha Felicie Sophie von Suttner was honored for her efforts in promoting the Hague Peace Conference of 1899. Since then, there have been 11 additional women, the most recent of whom was the late Wangari Maathai, who received Nobel's honor in 2004 "for her contribution to sustainable development, democracy and peace."

This courageous professor from Kenya, who died much too young, was the first woman from Africa to be honored by the Nobel committee, and this past weekend she was doubly honored as the trailblazer for her three African sisters who have now followed in her footsteps.

It is not just the memory of Professor Maathai that we must honor, but also the countless women across Africa, around the world, who work relentlessly, and selflessly to prevent or overcome the ravages of war.

As I said in Oslo, the award that Leymah Gbowee, Tawakkol Karman and I received belongs in fact to all those whose efforts we have the privilege to represent and whose rights we have the obligation to defend. We are but their reflection.

And let me repeat another observation I made at the podium in Oslo:

With such a distinction comes great responsibility. History will judge us not by what we say in this moment in time, but by what we do next to lift the lives of our countrymen and women. It will judge us by the legacy we leave behind for generations to come.

Just like the man whose legacy, I intend to honor on Tuesday in Paris.[13]

[13] Ellen Johnson Sirleaf (2011), " Alfred Nobel's legacy to women", The New York Times, The Opinion Page, December 12, 2011

Ellen Johnson Sirleaf, the president of Liberia, was awarded the 2011 Nobel Peace Prize with Leymah Gbowee of Liberia and Tawakkol Karman of Yemen.

Arab Spring

(A)Women and the Arab Spring

It is matter of universal human rights. No country can realize its potential if half its population cannot reach theirs.

Women in Tunisia, Egypt, and Libya played a frontline role in bringing down entrenched dictatorships. And now they are eager to reap the rewards of full political participation in their respective countries. "However," said Melanne Verveer, U.S. Ambassador-at-large for Global Women's Issues, "there are actors in these societies who clearly intend, and even often vocally express their desire, to push women back. Some claim the West is trying to impose its values on the Arab people by promoting women's rights, but this is neither a Western issue, nor an Arab issue, nor a religious issue. It is matter of universal human rights."

In Tunisia, women won around twenty-five percent of the seats of the new Constituent Assembly. Tunisia has a history of women's rights, said Ambassador Verveer. It was the first Arab state to abolish polygamy; the first to grant women professional rights; and it was at the forefront in establishing progressive family laws. Women took an active role in administering the October election. All parties who won significant seats responded to Human Rights Watch's pre-election survey indicating their support for the principles of gender equality.

In Egypt, there are concerns that the previous gains made by Egyptian women will be reversed and that they will be increasingly excluded from the process. The role of women in Egypt's transitional government has been very limited. No women were included on the committee that drafted Egypt's transitional constitutional declaration. Nevertheless, women will take part in the upcoming elections as voters, candidates, and political party members, and the U.S. government is supporting such efforts.

Women in Libya played a critical role in the country's liberation. There are small but very active groups of women across the country who expects to take their place in the leadership of the new Libya. U.S. Secretary of State Hillary Clinton laid out the United States' clear expectation for the full participation of women in the transition.

In an effort to empower women in Tunisia, Egypt, and Libya, the United States is supporting leadership skills training for women. These skills are critical if women are to take their rightful place in these transitioning societies.

As President Barrack Obama noted: **No country can realize it's potential if half of its population cannot reach theirs**.[14]

(B) Women and the Arab Spring

As change sweeps through the Arab world and dictatorships are toppled, will women's rights be forgotten as it happened in Iran?

As the Arab Spring moves through the Arab Autumn towards winter, there is hope but also anxiety and apprehension about the future. The elections in Tunisia — with a record 90 per cent turnout — have triggered the hope that countries like Egypt and Yemen and now Libya, will also witness a peaceful transition to a democracy they have never known. But the grounds for apprehension are abundant.

---

[14] Editorial, Voice of America, November 12, 2011

As the world watches, a key question that is being raised is that of women's rights in the new political arrangements emerging in these countries. Arab women have spoken out, emphasizing that a guarantee of their human rights is a prerequisite to a just society. But in the noise of the celebrations as dictators get toppled, these voices are sometimes being drowned out.

Arab voices

I was privileged to attend a fascinating discussion on the future of women in the Arab world at a recent conference in France. The Women's Forum for Society and the Economy 2011 drew together over a thousand women from around the world. But what turned out to be the most riveting session was the one where women from Egypt, Tunisia and Yemen and the renowned human rights activist and 2003 Nobel Peace Award winner Shirin Ebadi from Iran discussed how the future of Arab women would emerge following the Arab Spring. It threw up a relevant discourse on religion, secularism and law.

If women's rights are also human rights, then should societies fighting for the reassertion of human rights also first guarantee women their rights? Is it possible to allow religion to dictate law if the interpretation of that religion is left to men? Are rights that women have won, even in a dictatorship, still valid even after the overthrow of the dictator? Is it possible to have a 'secular' constitution and still respect religion and religious laws?

These were some of the questions that wove their way through the remarks made by the participants. Moushira Mahmoud Khattab, an impressive woman from Egypt who has been a diplomat and a Minister for Family and Population and is now a human rights activist, pointed out that even under Hosni Mubarak, women had won many rights. In fact, she was one of those central to bringing in laws to criminalize female genital mutilation (FGM) that is widespread in Egypt and other north African countries, raise the minimum age of marriage to 18, give women the right to initiate divorce, give women the right to custody of their children after divorce and allow children born outside wedlock to be registered. But now, after the January 25 uprising that led to the overthrow of Mubarak, she says there are voices that have been raised against these rights calling them "Suzanne's laws". Suzanne was Mubarak's wife and all these changes were initiated in her name. But, asked Ms. Khattab, why should rights that women had won after a struggle be negated just because they had been initiated during a hated dictatorship? The role of women in the January 25 revolution was crucial, she said. Women challenged tradition when they went out and protested and even spent nights out in Tahrir square. Yet, today in Egypt, women's rights are being questioned.

Nadwa Al Dawsari is a young activist from Yemen. She has spent many days in Freedom Square in the Yemeni capital of Sana'a with this year's Nobel Peace Prize winner Tawakkul Karman, who lives in a tent in the square. Ms. Dawsari said there was an assumption that in tribal societies, like the one in Yemen, women had no rights. Yet, over 30 per cent of the protestors in Freedom Square were women. The young people of Yemen wanted a civil state, not an Islamic state, she said. She insisted that what was important now was to get the dictator to leave Yemen and for free elections to be held. Other issues could be tackled later, even if the election brought the Islamists to power.

Tunisian women, however, are not as confident as Ms. Dawsari about the Islamists coming to power. In fact, many have gone on record to say they fear for the future if the Islamist party, al Nahda, wins the elections. But what primarily concerned Amira

Yahyaoui, a young blogger and militant human rights activist from Tunisia, was that women's rights in Tunisia ought not to be compared to other Arab countries but to those where women are better off. "We want women and men to have real equality. Women need to be considered not as women but as human beings. What we have at present is not enough," she said. Currently, although Tunisian women have more rights than their counterparts in some other Arab countries, they do not have equal rights of inheritance. They also cannot marry non-Muslims.

Ms. Yahyaoui was also not confident that women would have enough of a say in the process of constitution-making in Tunisia. Under the list system of proportional representation, women did not stand a chance of winning in substantial numbers as political parties tended to push male candidates to the top of their lists.

After listening to the young women from Tunisia and Yemen, Shirin Ebadi spoke. "Look at Iran", she told them, "Do not repeat our mistakes." When she saw images of the protestors in Syria, Yemen, Tunisia, she saw them demanding democracy. "Did anyone say we are against polygamy? That we want divorce rights? That we are human beings and need equal rights? You are making the same mistake Iranian women made. We thought we could demand women's rights after the revolution", she said.

Ms. Ebadi said that the Iranian women, who participated in the 1979 revolution that overthrew the Shah of Iran, knew what they did not want. They wanted an end to dictatorship. What they did not demand and insist upon were the rights that they did want. They did not go on the streets and demand an end to polygamy, or the right to divorce. It was taken for granted that these rights could be negotiated later.

Biased interpretation:

"I am a practicing Muslim woman", said Ms. Ebadi, "but when a government is based on Sharia law, it can be interpreted in different ways." She said that she did not believe that Sharia law was against human rights and democracy. But when it is left to men within a patriarchal system to interpret that law, inevitably the suppression of women's rights is justified.

The best way to prevent that, she advised her Arab sisters, was to push for women's rights during the struggle. "Don't wait for the victory. Choose your allies. Dictate these conditions before the alliance", she said.

She reminded the Tunisian about a recent incident where a TV channel was attacked for telecasting the film "Persepolis", an animated feature film about women's rights in Iran. The director of the channel had to give a public apology. "These are not good signs", she said. Ms. Ebadi said that although Iranian women had succeeded, even under a fundamentalist regime, in wresting many rights, these were not enough. "We are expecting a bigger victory. Aim for complete equality between the rights of women and men", she said.

As the Arab world goes through a political churning, the voices of these women need to be heard, and heeded.[15]

Chronic Hunger and the Status of Women in India

The persistence of hunger and abject poverty in India and other parts of the world is due in large measure

---

[15] Kalpana Sharma (2011), " Women and the Arab Spring", The Hindu, Sunday October 30, 2011

to the subjugation, marginalization and disempowerment of women. Women suffer from hunger and poverty in greater numbers and to a great degree then men. At the same time, it is women who bear the primary responsibility for actions needed to end hunger: education, nutrition, health and family income.

Looking through the lens of hunger and poverty, there are seven major areas of discrimination against women in India:

Malnutrition: India has exceptionally high rates of child malnutrition, because tradition in India requires that women eat last and least throughout their lives, even when pregnant and lactating. Malnourished women give birth to malnourished children, perpetuating the cycle.

Poor Health: Females receive less health care than males. Many women die in childbirth of easily prevented complications. Working conditions and environmental pollution further impairs women's health.

Lack of education: Families are far less likely to educate girls than boys, and far more likely to pull them out of school, either to help out at home or from fear of violence.

Overwork: Women work longer hours and their work is more arduous than men's, yet their work is unrecognized. Men report that "women, like children, eat and do nothing." Technological progress in agriculture has had a negative impact on women.

Unskilled: In women's primary employment sector - agriculture - extension services overlook women.

Mistreatment: In recent years, there has been an alarming rise in atrocities against women in India, in terms of rapes, assaults and dowry-related murders. Fear of violence suppresses the aspirations of all women. Female infanticide and sex-selective abortions are additional forms of violence that reflect the devaluing of females in Indian society.

Powerlessness: While women are guaranteed equality under the constitution, legal protection has little effect in the face of prevailing patriarchal traditions. Women lack power to decide who they will marry, and are often married off as children. Legal loopholes are used to deny women inheritance rights.

India has a long history of activism for women's welfare and rights, which has increasingly focused on women's economic rights. A range of government programs have been launched to increase economic opportunity for women, although there appear to be no existing programs to address the cultural and traditional discrimination against women that leads to her abject conditions.

The Inextricable Link: The greatest tragedy facing humanity today is the persistence of chronic hunger - an intolerable phenomenon that takes the lives of 24,000 of us every day. For fully one-fifth of humanity, life is a daily struggle to survive in conditions of relentless poverty. Day after day, the lives of one billion individuals are cut short or terribly diminished by chronic, persistent hunger. Day after day, one billion people are denied the opportunities they need to lead healthy and productive lives.

People living with chronic hunger exist in conditions of severe poverty. What they lack is the chance to change their situation, to develop their own self-sufficiency. The most potent confirmation of this fact can be seen in the lives of women. They, along with their children, are the main victims of hunger, and they are also most lacking in opportunities to end their own and their families' hunger.

The Hunger Project has come to the recognition that the persistence of hunger in India - and elsewhere in the world where hunger is still an overriding social issue - is, to a large degree, due to the subjugation, marginalization and disempowerment of women. Furthermore, women's suppression is rooted in the very fabric of Indian society - in traditions, in religious doctrine and practices, within the educational and legal systems, and within families. Ironically, much of the essential work of ending hunger rests in women's hands.

Traditionally, women bear primary responsibility for the well-being of their families. Yet they are systematically denied access to the resources they need to fulfill their responsibility, which includes education, health care services, job training, and access and freedom to use family planning services.

In order to gain a shared understanding of the condition of the status of women in India and its impact on the persistence of hunger, this document surveys papers done by leading scholars in Indian development issues. It is organized in a framework of seven issues that characterize the plight of resource-poor women, with a focus on rural women, in India: malnutrition, poor health, and lack of education, overwork, lack of skills, mistreatment and powerlessness.[16]

The link between these issues and the persistence of hunger in India was underscored in a 1996 study: The Asian Enigma, by Vulimiri Ramalingaswami.

In short, the poor care that is afforded to girls and women by their husbands and by elders is the first

---

[16] Carol S Coonard (1998), " Chronic Hunger and the status of Women In India", Empowering Women and Men to end their own hunger, The Hunger Project, Union Square West, New York, NY 10003

major reason for levels of child malnutrition that are markedly higher in South Asia than anywhere else in the world.

Killing of Women

ASSAM is not a safe place for women. Every second day for the past several years the media has been reporting stories of elderly women who are labelled "witches" being brutally killed. The latest incident (12 February 2012) occurred in Tezpur in Sonitpur district where Lakshmi Gaur was murdered and buried. The day before, another 45-year-old tribal woman, a mother of five children, was burnt alive, also for "allegedly" practising witchcraft. This was in Sonari in Sibsagar district. Although the phenomenon is common among the Bodos, the social malady is fast spreading across the state.

Till date, not a single article has appeared in the newspapers of Assam to challenge this shocking, inhuman behaviour. Yet the state claims to be a culturally evolved habitat of highbrows. Assam has a rich literary culture but perhaps there are too few women columnists. The galaxy of male writers is unlikely to take up an issue concerning women. They are more comfortable writing about politics and the more eclectic issues of statecraft.

Women who are branded witches are usually elderly widows or spinsters and the reason for killing them is to usurp their property. That such brutality can be allowed to happen with such impunity in the 21st century shows the complete failure of the state. Can kangaroo courts made up of mindless mobs be the judge and jury and give the call to "kill" someone because she is "allegedly" a witch? Where is the scientific evidence? How can anyone possess super-human powers to cause harm to another human being? Can the state simply sit back and watch while this pernicious witch-hunt against women of a certain age continues?

As a woman I am saddened that women with four and five children should be murdered through the active connivance of their own children. I am sure that all other women in the villages of Assam, with grown up children and who are no longer in a position to perform hard manual labour or to earn and invest in the family kitty, will be feeling very insecure. They, too, might wonder when they will be branded witches and done to death. The killings are so brutal that one wonders which age Assam is living in? Is this 21st century Assam whose metros are dotted with swanky malls and palatial homes? That barely 200 km away there are acts of savagery the state in unable to prevent?

I want to ask the government of Assam and the two women parliamentarians — Bijoya Chakraborty and Rani Narah — what they have done to contain this menace of witch-hunting of their own kind? Are they aware about the ritual of first accusing women of practising witchcraft and then lynching them to death? Is this not the single biggest threat to all women widows of Assam across society? Have these two women leaders called public meetings to awaken society to this atrocious gender discrimination? Why are only women accused of having the powers to practice witchcraft? And why are widows the targets? I want to ask the district administration of Sonitpur whether the body of Lakshmi Gaur has been exhumed and cases drawn up against her killers.

How many past cases of witch-burning and witch-killing have there been in that district? What is the fate of the accused? Are they out on bail? Have they been acquitted? We need to know this and we need to know it fast.

No popular government can stand by and allow these archaic practices to continue in the age of rocket science. Some women activists I spoke to said they rushed to these places when they heard of such witch-hunts but were unable to do much since the communities were wildly averse to any outside interference. Apparently the district administration also prefers to look the other way. Is the state not supposed to defend the weak? But in the case of poor, widowed women, there are obviously very few people to take up their cause.

Last year, on a visit to Bongaigaon for a meeting largely attended by Bodo people, one heard this issue of witch-hunting being discussed. The majority of people at the meeting were men but they seemed to feel the agony of helpless women meeting a cruel end after they had performed their maternal duties. One learnt, as one had done in the past too, that the prime reason behind the killing of elderly women was to get hold of their property, which had probably come to them after the death of their husbands.

The sons are impatient to wait for their mothers to die natural deaths so they connive to kill them, albeit with an excuse that they are witches, so they escape arrest. This has to be the grossest violation of human rights in Assam today.

Assam is also known for its academic and intellectual grasp. But the scholars have skirted this issue. Is it because the subject is not as explosive as insurgency? Truly, the hypocrisy rankles. And what about women's studies centres and women's organisations across the state? Why are they allowing a mob to rule the fates of women?

This is a time when we need the likes of a Raja Ram Mohan Roy to lead the campaign. In his time, Ram Mohan Roy fought the evils of sati and child marriage. Today, someone with courage must emerge to challenge the witch-hunting of elderly women.

Sadly, the media too has paid scant attention to witch-hunting. The story of the two women who were killed within a day of each other after being accused of practising witchcraft received scant reportage. No comments were taken from the district administration as to why it could not prevent the killings. No coverage was given about the reactions of the people around that village. Did they all believe that Lakshmi Gaur was a witch? If so, how did they arrive at that conclusion? Is there anything suspicious behind her killing?

I know such investigations are the work of the police, but aren't we journalists also supposed to do our own spooking so we can arrive at the truth? This could trigger some concerned citizens to start a campaign against this systematic, ruthless extermination of elderly women.

There is no bigger curse for a woman as when her own son or daughter is unable to protect her life or becomes a conspirator in her death.

It's time for women's organisations across the country to intervene. This outrage against women has to stop.[17]

Innocence interrupted

They should be the most protected, yet they are the ones at greatest risk. In Delhi alone almost 9000 kids went missing till September this year. Unspeakable crimes continue to be committed in India against those who are least able to defend themselves.

All this and more happened in just this month. Unspeakable crimes continue to be committed in India against those that are the most vulnerable, the most defenseless, the most innocent — kids being battered, beaten, and raped. And the perpetrators could be anyone — parents, relatives, hostel

[17] Patricia Mukhim (2012), " Assam's Moment od Shame", The Statesman , February 20, 2012

wardens, strangers. The bad news is that, as the National Crime Records Bureau (NCRB) figures show, matters are only getting worse.

While kidnapping and abduction of children accounted for 46.2 percent of the cases, rapes were 21.5 percent and other crimes 25.8 percent. In Delhi alone, 8,956 kids have gone missing till September this year. The 2007 National Study on Child Abuse which surveyed 12,447 children from 5-12 years came up with shocking statistics. It found two in every three children suffered physical abuse. Two-year-old Falak, admitted to AIIMS this year with severe head injuries, broken arms and bite marks, was probably the worst of the victimized lot. In 88.6 percent of the cases, parents were the perpetrators. Sexual abuse was faced by 53.22 percent children, mostly on the street, at work and in institutional care. What was most frightening was that every second child reported emotional abuse.

The deviant behaviour meted out to them is numbing. One NGO got a call from a woman who said that a CD left at her doorstep showed her powerful father-in-law in Pune abusing a boy employed as a help by pushing sticks up his anus. But despite two NGOs filing FIRs, the man was given a clean chit. In another case, a 15-year-old girl from Maharashtra reported that her father, an alcoholic and drug addict, repeatedly raped her in front of family members. "He would threaten to throttle her if she spoke up," says Nishit Kumar of Childline India Foundation.

And increasingly, technology is being used to threaten and stalk children, blighting them forever. On August 14, a 16-year-old girl from Delhi was abducted and raped by two men who filmed the act and leaked it to others. Many school-based abuses have teachers using mobiles, says Vidya Reddy of Tulir, a Chennai-based centre dealing with child sexual abuse. But what's heartening is that children are also using mobiles, internet and Facebook to report crimes, says Rajat Mitra of Swanchetan Society for Mental Health.

In Lucknow and Allahabad, an alarming trend is the use of bombs to target kids. Ankush, a teenager, died on April 29 after four miscreants hurled a bomb at him in Saraisheikh village in Chinhat. There's also been a rise in juvenile offenders. In Maharashtra, they've gone up from 4,315 in 2010 to 4,775 in 2011. On September 23, five-year-old Shubh Rawal was abducted and murdered in Pune by two students for a ransom of one hundred thousands of Indian rupees.

While some quietly tolerate the abuse, many reach out for help — these days increasingly so. Childline, which runs a helpline, gets close to four million calls annually. Of these, 40% are directly by children, says Kumar. "There are SOS calls from street children as young as six years. The maximum calls are from 11-15 year-olds who just want someone to talk to. A new trend is that many middle class children too are calling up."

Just as well, as the police often doesn't show enough alacrity or interest in solving cases. On May 19, 2009, the body of Yogita Thakre, 7, was found inside a car in the then BJP state president Nitin Gadkari's residence. Postmortem report indicated blood stains and abrasions in various parts of the body. It was referred to the CID but a year later it sent a report to the court stating the case be closed. In Patna, despite the gang rape of a school girl at a residence in Shastri Nagar, no action was initiated till the state's women commission took the matter up with the DGP. The main accused is still at large. The lackadaisical probe into the Nithari case in Noida where many children were abducted, abused and killed by a psychopath, shows that young lives, especially from weaker sections, aren't valued enough.

Arvind Verma, a former IPS officer who is now in the Department of Criminal Justice at Indiana University, Bloomington, says, "For years, there has been non-registration and minimization of crimes by the police. And yet, there's been no systematic effort to even compare data from different states." Also, official crime figures don't tell the real picture. "Does anybody know how many cases of sodomy (which attracts Section 377) have been filed where the victim is a child? These are clubbed with Other Crimes," says Reddy. But change is slowly seeping in.

For the first time in India, a special court for child victims was recently inaugurated in Karkardooma in Delhi. The room for children was painted cheerfully and had toys; there's no intimidating contact with the accused either. In Kerala, there are school protection groups, says Kochi range Inspector General K Padmakumar. "Complaints submitted by children are immediately registered and an investigation conducted." Parents of victims too are ready to file complaints, whereas earlier they would hush up matters, says A Sheela, a Child Welfare Committee member.[18]

Indian baggage

Sex determination tests and abortions happen not only in India but also in those parts of the West with sizable population of Indians

In mid-April, a reproductive clinic's ad appeared in a newspaper for the Indo-Canadian community in British Columbia, inviting readers to "create the family you want, boy or girl, for family balancing" with the help of pre-conception sex selection. The two children in the ad wore ethnic Indian clothes.

---

[18] Shobha John (2012), " Innocence, interpreted", Times of India, September 30, 2012

The newspaper withdrew the ad following public outrage, while the clinic was accused of targeting cultural attitudes that perpetuate discrimination against girls. But the writing was on the wall. For long, sex selection and female foeticide have been issues identified with countries like India and China where the usual rationales given include dowry, patriliny (descent or inheritance by the male line), one-child policy or dependence on kids' support in old age. But now, studies in Canada, Norway, US and UK show the persistence of this cultural attitude within the diaspora too.

Dr Shiv Pande, a Liverpool-based general practitioner and a former treasurer of the General Medical Council in Britain, says: "As they say, Indians, wherever they go, carry their curry, customs and cultural baggage. Sex selection of the foetus is quite common among British Indians, though not known widely."

In 2007, two Oxford academics, Sylvie Dubuc and David Coleman, carried out a study of the sex ratio, using the annual birth registrations in England and Wales between 1969 and 2005, and found that there was "indirect quantitative evidence of prenatal sex selection against females performed by a small minority of India-born women in England and Wales" . Interestingly, the study found no such evidence regarding Pakistan-born and Bangladesh-born women living in England and Wales.

Says Sylvie says that based on numbers from my previous work, I estimated the number of missing baby girls for the period 1990-2005 to be about 1500. Note that these figures relate to immigrant (i.e. India-born) women only (and not UK-born women of Indian origin)."

In February 2012, an investigation by the UK's Daily Telegraph newspaper discovered that some clinics were prepared to carry out such abortions with few, if any, questions asked. Likewise, the British Columbia newspaper ad came just days after a study published in the Canadian Medical Association Journal (CMAG) analyzed 766,688 births in Ontario and found mothers born in South Korea and India were more likely to have boys for their second child. When it came to having a third child, the male-to-female ratio grew even more skewed for India-born mothers, who had 136 boys for every 100 girls (the world average ratio is 105:100).

Lead researcher of the study and scientist at St Michael's hospital in Toronto, Joel G Ray, says, "Women from India and South Korea who had previous children were significantly more likely to give birth to males. For India-born women with more than one prior child, the male-female ratios were even more pronounced." Ray, however, cautions that "we (or anyone else) do not have direct evidence this is due to foetal sex selection." But Mahvish Parvez of the Indo-Canadian Women's Association in Edmonton, says, "There is a strong suggestion that the skewed ratio is due to sex-selective abortion. We know that son preference strongly persists in immigrant communities."

Many western nations have banned sex selection for non-medical purposes - the US is a notable exception. It is a profitable business there, with gender determination technologies easily available, both online and offline, and clients flying in from the UK, Australia and probably India too. In 2006, two professors from Columbia University, Douglas Almond and Lena Edlund, examined the year 2000 US Census data and found that while more boys than girls are born by a ratio of 1.05 to 1 among families of Chinese, Korean and Indian descent, the ratio increased if the first child was a girl. If the first two children are girls, the ratio was 50 percent greater in favour of boys.

It's no surprise to community activists. Maneesha Kelkar, women's rights activist and former executive director of Manavi, a New Jersey-based organization, remembers taking a call from a woman who said she was sitting on the operating table in an abortion clinic and was being forced to have an abortion. "She didn't tell me if the foetus was a girl, or why she was being told to have the abortion. When I asked what was preventing her from walking out, she said, 'my in-laws are in the waiting room'."[19]

Death by gender

A battered, bitten and burnt baby battled for her life in Bengaluru. Sounds like a crass tongue-twister but was a real life horror story which unfolded layer by layer over the past week. As I write, news has just come in: the battle is over. Three-month-old Afreen, who was struggling for survival in the intensive care unit of a Bengaluru hospital, died of cardiac arrest Wednesday morning.

Tuesday night, as I was watching the news on television, the macabreness hit me: even as Afreen was struggling for survival, the city's corporators were spewing rage. The object of their fury was not Afreen's father who had severely injured his daughter, and wanted her dead, nor the social system which allows such savagery towards little girls. They were outraged at being denied free passes to the Indian Premier League cricket matches. Last heard, the miffed corporation was refusing to clear garbage from the stadium.

Baby Afreen had been burnt with cigarette butts, bitten and banged against a wall, allegedly by her 25-year-old father Umar Farooq. In Farooq's eyes, she deserved to die because she was born a girl. He

---

[19] Saira Kurup (2012), " Indian Baggage", The Times of India, Sunday, June 03, 2012

wanted a son, according to Reshma Banu, Afreen's 19-year-old mother who finally mustered up courage to speak out, after putting up with abuse and harassment for dowry. The father had also tried to murder the child on earlier occasions.

Now Afreen is dead. Even if she had lived, the chances of the little girl leading a normal life would have been slim. The cycle carries on, according to Dr Preeti Galagali, a Bangalore-based paediatrician and coordinator (south) for the Indian Child Abuse and Neglect and Child Labour Group. Afreen's father has been arrested and furious soul searching is underway in the media. Earlier this year, another battered baby girl, Falak, had grabbed national headlines. Despite two months of the best medical care in Delhi's All-India Institute of Medical Sciences, the baby could not be saved. Like Afreen, she too succumbed to cardiac arrest.

India mourns these deaths. Or does it?

Few places in the world have seen the dramatic effects of globalisation as Bengaluru. And yet, as we wring our hands and grieve over Afreen, the bitter truth stares us in the face. All the trappings of progress notwithstanding, little girls continue to be unwelcome even in this "progressive and cosmopolitan" part of India. The grim stories of Falak and now Afreen are just the tip of the iceberg. On Tuesday, a father was arrested in Gwalior for killing his two-day-old daughter by feeding her nicotine. But there is another instance of desperation for a son.

The problem is neither specific to a people or a region. Despite the laws, the committees, and the rest of it, unwanted little girls are either exterminated inside the womb or crushed outside. India's already skewed infant sex ratio is getting worse. There were only 914 girls for every 1,000 boys under the age of six in India, according to the 2011 census, compared to 927 for every 1,000 boys in the 2001 census. Today's ratio marks the highest imbalance since the country won Independence in 1947. Economic growth, urbanisation and rising literacy have made little impact on the widespread revulsion towards girls.

So while it is absolutely essential to punish the baby-batterers, it is critical to look at the other vital part of the story — the mother — who is also subjected to abuse. There is very little being done in the country to support young women and mothers to opt out of abusive relationships which put their children and them at risk. Afreen was born a perfectly healthy baby as the images on television showed. She would have stayed that way had the mother felt emotionally and economically equipped to take on her abusive husband. That did not happen. She stuck to her husband despite the harassments for dowry, despite the abuse and despite the torture of her little girl. When she finally picked up courage to speak out, it was too late. The battered baby is dead. But what were her options?

"There is no quick response mechanism on the ground. There are no 'crisis shelters' which are readily accessible to poor, uneducated women like Afreen's mother," says Nina Nayak, chairperson of the Karnataka State Commission for the Protection of Child Rights.

The ministry for women and child development sanctioned nearly 1.50 billion to states and Union Territories under the Integrated Child Protection Scheme (ICPS) on March 26, 2012. ICPS was introduced in 2009-10 to improve the well-being of children in difficult circumstances, and to reduce vulnerabilities to situations and actions that lead to abuse, neglect, exploitation, abandonment and separation of children from their families. The money is meant to strengthen institutional services. But what is needed along with that is a campaign so that those in need know where these services are available and how they can be accessed.

Such services are necessary but not sufficient. Women without education and economic options often continue in a relationship, no matter how abusive it gets. To break this vicious cycle, many things have to be done. It means, as Ms Nayak points out, cracking down unequivocally on child marriages which are banned by law but continue in practice. Young girls do not only need to have basic minimum education and skills to find remunerative work which can sustain them, they also need to feel emotionally empowered to break out of an abusive relationship.

There is no magic pill that can empower women, but clearly the place to start is to drastically improve the education system, especially vocational education. Today, if a woman stays with her abusive husband, it is because of the stigma of separation and because she knows she cannot make an honest living by herself. She also knows that going back to already-burdened parents is not an option. From policymakers to police constables, almost everyone in authority says these are social and domestic issues about which they can do little. But that is not true. They can, for starters, honestly implement the many policies for women's education — especially vocational education — that exist on paper. There are plenty of examples of women standing up for their basic rights at home and outside, once they have the ability and the confidence to earn a living. It is not enough to decry gender discrimination and grieve for battered babies. The women who nurture them need real options so that they can protact themselves, and their babies.[20]

---

[20] Patralekha Chatterjee (2012), "Death by gender", the Asian Age, April 12, 2012

India: **No country for women**

Rashme Sehgal (2012) has analyzed the pathetic conditions of women in India. India's women have been brutalised down the ages. Nothing is new there. But the Guwahati incident earlier this month when a 17-year-old girl was molested by a mob signals a new and dangerous low. It confirmed that public, free-for-all, mob assaults are the order of the day.

For another, the mob wasn't afraid of doing their worst on camera, in fact, they seemed happy to show their faces. Which leads us to the conclusion: Sexual predators are by now confident that they need not fear the law enforcement agencies — the police and the courts, says Rashme Sehgal.

A17-year-old, High School girl student along with four other friends chose to celebrate a birthday party in a pub at nine o'clock at night. And as parties often go, this one ended in a tiff with this schoolgirl ending up in an argument with a male friend.

She left the pub in a huff. Her male friend tried hard to persuade her to sit on his motorbike so he could drop her home.

She declined and the rest is, unfortunately, history. Video footage on YouTube shows her being slapped, dragged, cursed at and finally stripped on a busy Guwahati street last week although the police station happened to be located just ten minutes away.

The police may have failed to come to her rescue but one news journalist spent the next thirty minutes filming this girl pleading with her assaulters to leave her alone till finally, an elderly man came to her rescue.

Guwahati-based Nandita Konwar, of Women Power Connect who has followed this assault case very closely is surprised at just how many counts the local cops played false. The local police chief, when asked why the police failed to rescue the teenager, said, "The police is not an ATM machine dispensing instant justice."

The police decision to finally initiate action against the inebriated thugs who had assaulted this teenager is of little consolation to her parents who are planning to leave the city fearful that some new vendetta may be planned against their daughter in the coming months. Women have little to celebrate in a country like India where surveys rank its treatment of women as being better only than Pakistan and Afghanistan.

The result is there for everyone to see. The National Crimes Record Bureau informs us that rape is the fastest growing crime in India and has seen an exponential 600 per cent explosion from 1971 followed by kidnapping (again, largely women victims) which has seen an over 350 per cent increase.

Brinda Karat, member of the CPI (M) Politburo admits that crimes against women are on the rise and one of the main reasons for this is 'the low rates of conviction'.

"People seem to believe they can get away with these crimes. The assertion of women in public life is something that our patriarchal India is finding it difficult to accept," she said.

Jyotsna Chatterjee heading Joint Women's Program puts the blame squarely on the lack of political will to take culprits to task.

"Take the case of the recent khap panchayat in Asara village in Baghpat which had issued a diktat that women must cover their heads when they leave home, they have imposed a complete ban on love marriages and no mobile phones for girls while only women above the age of 40 years should be allowed to venture out of house for work."

Chatterjee finds it strange that the entire political class has failed to condemn this diktat. Rather, the Samajwadi party leader and minority affairs minister Azam Khan issued a statement saying there was nothing wrong if a 'group of villagers come together to express their opinion'.

Meanwhile, in an obviously orchestrated show of solidarity, women from three UP villages in Muzaffarnagar district have vowed to 'burn their jeans and tops and to dress much more judiciously'.

Khap panchayats have joined hands at a crucial juncture. But Naresh Tikait, president of the Bharatiya Kisan Union and chief of the Baliyan khap panchayat insists their diktats are not anti-woman.

"We also oppose the dowry system and female foeticide but that is not being highlighted. Instead the decisions we take for orderliness in the society in accordance with our traditions are dubbed as 'taliban'."

Akhila Shivdas of the Centre for Advocacy and Research believes the rumblings in these khap panchayats have been triggered by the release of a recent study of the Population Council of India that found that rate of premarital sex as higher amongst girls than boys.

Girls, according to the study, are also willing to indulge in risky sex without using contraceptives. Police believe the attitude of the younger generation of girls has undergone a sea change.

The Noida police, following a case of a girl being gang raped in a car concluded their investigation with the comments: "The girl is a habitual vodka drinker following a vodka party (sic); she wanted Rs 6000 to have sex. When the money wasn't paid, she registered a case of rape."

Breakdown of law and-order (chain snatchings - seven within two hours one day in Mumbai apart from rape, molestation and its lesser version called eve-teasing on the roads, buses and suburban trains) has seen some writers come out in support of hockey stick wielding controversial assistant commissioner of police Vasant Dhoble in his efforts to control drugs and prostitution in Mumbai's parties and bars.

Women activist Sujata Madhok attributes the increasing lumpenisation in our cities to growing migration from the villages.

"There are no social restraints (in our cities) and the obsession with national security and VIP security has forced the police to move away from their traditional duties of looking after law-and-order."

India needs a separate law to deal with sexual harassment and assault. Introducing new laws alone is not the answer. The streets of our cities need to be patrolled with greater strictness in order to secure the safety of our women, today and in the future.

Reported Events in India:

A young woman holds up a placard during a protest, sparked by remarks by government authorities in various parts of India that women invite sexual assault by dressing "provocatively".

New Year's Eve, 2008: Two women coming out of a pub were molested by a mob of 70-80 men. The courts are yet to rule in the case.

24 Jan, 2009: A mob of Sri Ram Sene hooligans attacked a group of girls at a Mangalore pub, ostensibly to teach the girls 'Indian values'.

July 17, 2012: Jagatsinghpur, Odisha: Dalit woman dies of injuries after being assaulted by some villagers on June 14, when she objected to some men defecating on her fields. Police did not act promptly. SHRC directed district SP to submit case report. Husband has alleged some politicians and policemen are shielding the accused.

July 9, 2012: Guwahati: A 17-year-old girl is dragged, beaten, stripped and molested — on camera — on a busy street by a mob of some 50 men. Police, from a station 1 km away, arrive after 45 minutes. Action is taken only a video of the assault goes viral on YouTube and sparks national outrage.

June 29, 2012:, Karimganj, Assam: Congress MLA Rumi Nath is attacked in a hotel room by a hundred-strong mob, allegedly for marrying a Muslim man in a second marriage she undertook without divorcing her first husband.

July 17, 2012: Belgaum, Karnataka: 33-year-old Ujwala Jinappa sustains severe burns after miscreants attack her at home and throw acid on her face. She had been receiving threats of acid attack for over a year. She had complained to police in November 2011, but police did not act. The woman had to attend a special 'Janata Darshan' by the district SP to report the July 17 attack.

July 18, 2012: Mumbai: A rowdy attempts to molest a woman, but the woman escapes. Later, the rowdy and two others barge into her house in Shivajinagar and assault her brother and mother, while she escapes again.

July 20, 2012: Panaji, Goa: Constable Sarvesh Naik booked for assaulting woman home guard Sunita Gaonkar in Ponda police station.

July 20, 2012: Kochi, Kerala: Train pantry worker on Maveli Express arrested for sexually assaulting a woman passenger.

Numbers speak for India

- **(a) 2,61,000 cases of crimes against women, including sexual harassment, cruelty by husband/his relatives, kidnapping, human trafficking in 2011**
- **(b) 42,968 cases of molestation of women in 2011.**
- **(c) 873 percent rise in rape cases between 1953 and 2011.**
- **(d) A case of rape every 22 minutes**
- **(e) A case of bride burnt for dowry every 58 minutes[21]**

Curb Sex Crimes:

Broadening definition of rape is a good first step, but higher conviction rate is a must

The government's move to make rape a gender-neutral crime is a welcome step towards harmonising current anomalies in laws relating to sexual offence. The proposed changes are aimed at broadening the definition of rape, so far restricted to penile and vaginal penetration. The replacement of the word 'rape' with 'sexual assault', a gender-neutral distinction, will also bring male victims within the legal ambit. Endorsing the proposal the Law Commission has observed that "Not only women but young boys are being increasingly subjected to forced

---

[21] Rashme Sehgal (2012), "India: No country for women", Deccan Chronicle, July 22, 2012, NCRB

sexual assaults...[which] causes no less trauma and psychological damage to a boy than to a girl subjected to such offence." It's important to consider in this context that the Delhi High Court in 2009 decriminalised homosexuality as far as it pertained to consensual sexual acts of adults, thereby demarcating such acts from sodomy, the equivalent of rape.

The best among the government's proposals is the one that will bar cross-examiners from bringing into question the character and previous sexual experiences of the victim, very often used to dilute the victim's case and even discourage her from coming forward, allowing the perpetrator to go scot free. Given the patriarchal mindset of crucial institutions like the police, it's hardly surprising that the present legal lacuna has been used at will against women, heightening the victim's trauma.

It's time that laws related to sexual offence - from eve-teasing, molestation, rape to acid throwing and stalking - are made more sensitive and in sync with changing times. Rape, as activists have correctly pointed out, must be understood as an experience of brutal violation and degradation and not just the act of penetration. However, some activists believe that clubbing 'rape' with 'sexual assault' and other crimes might dilute the gravity of rape itself. To factor in this criticism the law should define various grades of sexual assault, with more grievous categories attracting correspondingly more stringent punishment. International best practices can be invoked in this regard.

Such legislative changes will, no doubt, have positive implications for female and male victims. And very stringent punishment must be decreed in case of custodial rape - in police stations, shelter homes and orphanages. It must be remembered, however, that legislative interventions and up-scaling of punishment alone won't act as deterrents. At the heart of the present problem lies the abysmal rate of conviction and a corresponding culture of impunity. It's equally important, therefore, to implement existing laws and increase the conviction rate. That alone will really deter sexual offenders.[22]

Stop the waffling

Crimes against women reflect a crisis of machismo - and administration

Recent attacks on women in two far-flung locations - Guwahati, Assam and Baghpat, Uttar Pradesh - are shocking. But not surprising. Both mirror each other with disturbing neatness. A teenage girl was attacked in Guwahati by a 30-strong mob of men. Exiting a pub, she was seized by the mob which beat and stripped her. Meanwhile, in Baghpat, a khap panchayat decreed local women be stripped of the right to even possess mobile phones as apparently women were choosing their own marriage partners and often eloping, phones helping them assert free will.

Both incidents reflect the violent tension surrounding women's access to modernity in India, bitterly resented by conservative groups, furiously ripped into by men in mobs. Examples include the right-wing Hindu group Sri Ram Sena assaulting girls in Bangalore pubs, a mob trying to strip two women outside a hotel in cosmopolitan Mumbai, Gurgaon's gangs raping women returning from multinationals and malls. As India moves towards post-modern enterprise, where women have an equal role to play, attitudes of the so-called guardians of our morality - ranging from apathetic policemen more sympathetic to perpetrators than victims, to political parties like UPA ally Rashtriya Lok Dal - stay sunk in prehistory.

---

[22] Editorial , The Times of India, July 20, 2012

A woman enjoying the fruits of modernity - free will, consumption, mobility - is often set upon by men seething with frustration, encouraged by a political and administrative vacuum in the country. Take Guwahati - the disgrace happened early last week but it took a media-led storm for the administration to wake from its siesta. By then, the accused had fled. Six days later, only six men involved in the video graphed episode have been arrested. Such sluggishness reflects how victims of such crimes receive zero support from the quarters meant to support them.

This must stop. Women have an equal right to free movement and choice. Local administrations must intensively police and prevent crimes against women. Expecting women to retire behind curtains or be assisted only by individuals like Keenan or Reuben, slain in Mumbai by a mob harassing a female friend, is ridiculous. That's the job of the police - we pay them for it and demand results. Further, political leaders must make a sharp example of those perpetrating violence against women. A good place to start - Baghpat, where it must be ensured women don't fear any bans. Ajit Singh needs to withdraw his party's support of the khap panchayat bullies. Women are not the wretched of the earth - they are half of it. All administrations must accord these citizens the equality and security they deserve.[23]

The right to our bodies:

Who would decide her gender identity?

In a case where the "facts" are both complex and yet also the question at hand let us start with one that should be undisputed: **PINKI Paramanik says she is a woman.** She has lived as one, competed as one, and identifies as one. She and no other person or

---

[23] Editorial, "Stop the waffling ", The Times of Ideas, The Times of India, July 16, 2012

institution - particularly the law or medical science - has the right to decide what her gender identity is regardless of her anatomy, her chromosomes or her hormones. As the investigations against her began, her claim to be a woman should have been accepted at face value regardless of whether narrow judgments of her appearance, manner, physicality or dress led some to believe otherwise.

The list of systematic violations of her rights by the police is a long one: being kept initially in a male prison; being handled and then sexually harassed by male police officers; the filming and then leaking of an alleged MMS of her in the hospital undergoing a gender test that, by many accounts, was forced on her as part of the conditions of her bail without an order from a magistrate. It is a welcome first step that the West Bengal Human Rights Commission, the Cyber Crimes Bureau and the Kolkata high court have demanded and initiated inquiries into these rights abuses.

Yet we must also stop and ask why these rights abuses occurred. PINKI"s case is a marker of a more fundamental struggle that we as a society have with the body. We, as a society, allow bodies thought to be different or of lesser value (at times marked by sexual or gender difference but equally with caste or religion) to be publicly stripped, examined, probed, debated, paraded, marked and judged. Examples abound: two finger tests to check the sexual character of a woman who has made a rape accusation; repeated cases of sexual assault of bi-sexual with impunity in police custody; Scheduled caste women and men who are stripped naked and publicly paraded as punishment in cities and villages across India; or the bodies of young Muslim men suspected of "terror" that are fair game for police torture. These bodies hold no real right to dignity, safety and privacy. The initial question that the country asked of PINKI was not who she is but "what" she is - a public spectacle that reduced her to an object to be classified as per the needs of law.

It is indeed between law and medical science that this case will precede. The question of "what she is" will supposedly be answered by a "gender test". In it, PINKI's entire life lived as a woman - her sense of her own gender - will be discounted and reduced to measures of chromosomal and hormonal behaviour that measure biological sex on the assumption that it can be neatly categorized into "male" and "female". Yet even recent scientific writing in the Journal of the American Medical Association describes gender tests as "difficult, expensive, and potentially inaccurate". Hormones and genital development, the study argues, vary significantly within "women" and "men". The science itself, it is important to remember, is far from certain.

Yet from laws to social norms and our own internalized fears, we go to a great deal of effort to police and protect the boundaries that separate "male" and "female" even though the realities of our lives repeatedly show us that biological sex cannot so easily be tabulated into XX and XY, hormones do not line up to be counted either in the pink or blue line, and biological men and women don't always choose to be either masculine or feminine as per "the rules". Many people are intersex, i.e. biologically both male and female. Even otherwise, our biology can change through sex reassignment just like our hearts can be transplanted or mechanically run. Our understandings of our own gender identities can, as they do with transgender people, be independent of our biological sex. The question we must ask then is this: What kind of answer is Pinki allowed to give to the question of who she is? What answer will we be willing to accept?

We have struggled to accept gender variance and fluidity in our society and it has left us with legal regimes and languages that often violently force all difference into categories we understand. The recent inclusion of "other" gender categories in many state documents is a small beginning that sees the state bend to actual complexities of gender.

We have much to learn from countries like Argentina where citizens can legally choose their gender identity regardless of their biological sex. What would our laws look like if we re-imagined them to reflect more fluid gender identities? PINKI's case reminds us of how far we must go and that, until we get there, it is those presumed "different" - and it is only a presumption since PINKI maintains that she is a woman and neither intersex nor transgendered - that are the most vulnerable.

PINKI faces serious accusations that must, let me say clearly be fully investigated. Yet what must be on trial are her acts and not her person. In the procedural violations that have already occurred and the trial that she has already been put through, the process of a fair trial for both PINKI and her accuser are delegitimized.

There are critical lessons to be learnt here about due process, the presence of gender variant citizens and their rights, and the role of privacy and dignity to all. As her bail hearing approaches, let us remember the basic question of justice: if PINKI has indeed committed acts of violence, let her be tried for them. Until that moment, however, her right to be judged as an equal with her own understanding of her gender identity must be protected by the state and by all of us.[24]

---

[24] Gautam Bhan (2012), "The right to our bodies", The Times of India, July 9, 2012,

Harassment of women

The steady growth in the graph of rape cases worldwide is about male hegemony smashing back with a vengeance.

Let's shed our ostrich-like mentality and take a reality check on the 40-year debate on women's rights and equality of the sexes.

Britain's youngest (and increasingly most articulate) feminist, Kat Banyard, has through her book, "The equality illusion" — the truth about women and men today (Faber & Faber, 2011), has broken the myth of so-called signs of "gender equality" that are all around us — female prime ministers, diplomats, CEOs. CFOs, constables, armed combatants, etc.

"Throughout the 90s and much of the naughtiness, we were sold a lie on an almighty scale. That equality had been won, that the battle was over, and now was the time to enjoy our rights. I think what really helped contribute to that was how institutions and corporations who rely on sexism, who rely on women's inequality, adapted and changed. And co-opted the language of feminism very, very cleverly," said the influential founder of UK Feminista, a grassroots movement which has become wildly popular.

"Feminists of previous generations really got these ideals of independence, equality and agency accepted as standards and values society holds dear. So this didn't escape the notice of people like Hugh Hefner, the sex industry, the beauty industry. They knew that to survive they had to adapt. So all of a sudden putting on makeup was a major route to empowerment; visiting or performing in a lap dancing club was evidence of your independence and how sexually liberated you were. The sex industry held itself up as the promised land of feminism. Everything that feminists had been fighting for — sexual liberation, economic independence, control over their own bodies and so forth. When in fact what they represented was the complete opposite of feminism."

Since India's forever embryonic feminist movement has no comparable spokesperson, it relies on dolled up news anchors to decode patterns of exploitation. Sadly, they are getting nowhere. The growing incidents of crimes against women — and I don't mean just the reported rapes but also the silent indignities - unleashed on Indian women day in and day out by India Inc. through its 'ideals' of feminity; the kickback of medievalism through khap panchayats; the disappearance of hard-won rights at the workplace, etc.

If an organization could take its eyes off ugly politicians and petty bureaucrats and focus on the new misogyny which is sweeping social and economic institutions, a Tahrir encore would be on the cards. The women of India, like their sisters all over the world, feel nothing for this serial exposure of loot. To them these are déjà vu in a man's world. The real problems which bind womenfolk in the second decade of the 21st century is humiliation — of a kind not experienced before.

The variables

We read that in the 1960s there was a sexual revolution, whose impact was felt in India before long. Sex was brought out of the closet and discussed/exploited in the public space. Women and men defied social norms and became more sexually liberated. Now, in the 2010s, has the wheel come full circle with men once again arbitrating over sexual freedom of the human race? Consider the trends —

1. Rapid legitimacy acquired by the western, free market model has led to the return of the female

body as a multipurpose vehicle for selling products. The sixties' sexual revolution happened in a world that celebrated socialistic ideals. Most western countries themselves had the welfare model of governance. Today, it's each man for him. The question to be asked is — are women losing out in this jungle raj? Are they surrendering their bodies once again for survival?

2. There are signs that they are. Look, for instance, the celebration of aspects of female sexuality which satisfy only male needs. For instance, why are young women edging out older women in every field? BBC and CNN have two sets of rules for male and female news anchors. The men symbolise experience and depth. But women of the same age are dismissed by being described as 'over the hill' and relegated to the backroom. Bimbettes have become the public face of news channels —this is a global phenomenon.

3. The queer thing is that women are not complaining. In the 1960s, female presence was rare in boardrooms/decision making centres. In the 2010s, women have broken the glass ceiling (read: become CEOs, PMs, etc). But it's as if they have become men in skirts, because they have to excel in the traditionally male domain - and this includes participating in the culture of commode-fying women for profits. In the 1960s through 80s, there used to be magazines like FEMINA (from The Times of India stable) which ran articles protesting against the use of scantily clad women to sell products. They even objected to the use of female models to sell unrelated products like heavy machinery, petrol lubricants, etc. But today, it's as if protecting the female form from exploitation has itself become taboo.

4. Rape is not only growing, but a layer of controversy has been cleverly added to its definition. All over the world, cities are becoming unsafe for women. Independent newspaper of London recently

reported that only one-third of rapes and female molestation are reported by the victims themselves because they know the police will not believe them. This is true of India too. A woman with a sexual history with more than one partner is not likely to be considered a rape victim; rather she stands the risk of being vilified as the enticer/seducer.

5. Women are encouraged to be more "open", which means even in formerly conservative societies like India, they are welcomed in drinking places, hookah bars, etc. But little do they know how they are being used. When an incident of rape or violence happens, the same women are described as sluts, loose women. This shows a pattern in male dominance. The males are in a win-win scenario. When the girls are "open", they exploit them. Then, when ugly situations arise, they don the conservative hat and recall the virtues of their mothers and grandmothers which are so missing in today's women. Everyone, from ministers to policemen to bank clerks undergo this transformation without so much as batting an eyelid.[25]

Conclusion

In 2006, the Supreme Court of India had mandated sweeping police reforms including a police complaint authority to pronounce binding recommendations in response to public complaints in every district. There has been little progress on this, mainly because control over police force is seen as a fundamental perk of political power.

There should be first-track courts to try crimes against women. The culprit should not be allowed to appeal higher courts. The case for heinous activities

---

[25] Swarn Kumar Anand (2012), "A lie on an almighty scale", the Pioneer, October 27, 2012

should be finalized within two months before it fades away from the public memory.

As part of zero-tolerance policing, it is essential to have a system of calibrated and proportionate system of punishing crimes against women, depending on the degree of the offence. The Singapore model of canning to the culprits within a week might be followed in other countries.

Man is a social animal. So, animal instinct in love and romance grows at the shortest possible time in failures. This leads to torture, and murder.

The Television, cinema and print media should not be permitted to publish erotic photos, slides or scenery by law. The media cannot repeat ugly and dangerous news or events continuously in length. It could show or publish the facts only for once in summary form in one or two paragraphs.

The girls and women should protect themselves by avoiding rush travel. They should restrict travel during evening and must be confined in their residences at nights to avoid unwanted attacks from mischiefs.

The Countries with Maximum Rape Records include the United States of America followed by South Africa, Sweden, England, France, India, Germany, Sri Lanka and Canada. Hence, economic development, education, society and culture have contributed more of offense than other countries. (Report 2014)

Women must be in groups or with family members during pleasure trips to distant locations, the governments should consider framing business time-table for cinema halls and business establishments for each day. These establishments should operate from 7 AM to 7 PM for the entire country or towns.

There should be separate news papers for cinema and separate news papers for sports. The media should not teach the technique of bank robbery, murder, ghost appearance or corruption that creates bad impression on young minds. They cannot report misdeeds of cheats daily to create anti-socials in the country.

Women should not take part in road marches for political reasons. They should fight for education, justice and female empowerment. All women hostels and girls' hostels must be protected from miscreants. All boarders must be provided facility for YOGA classes and medical facility in the hostel. The hostel superintendents must hold responsible for any unwanted happenings leading to death in disease.

The serious culprits should be awarded chemical castration or 5 years of imprisonment. And minor culprits would be punished by caning in open places.

+++++

Chapter III

WOMEN EMPOWERMENT

When one door of happiness closes, another opens; but often we look so long at the closed door that we do not see the one, which has been opened for us. ---Helen Keller

The great genius Kabir advised that "If India is to be free; women must be given their freedom. If you try and stop them, we will face the consequences." Honour killings persist in India because police and state agencies fail to take them seriously.

In every society, human rights and social imperatives will collide: security and liberty, equality and justice. To adjudicate between such competing claims, we need reliable methods of investigation, evidence and impartiality.

The state cannot delay overhauling the criminal justice delivery system, improving our poor population-linked ratio of policemen and judges besides establishing more fast-track courts and modernizing law enforcement and judicial infrastructure. It is because these institutions are over-burdened that crimes against women are often treated as low priority. Nor have we worked at sensitizing policing to encourage reporting of crimes, including by recruiting more women police. Lack of clear legal provisions also encourages crime. The U S states have criminalized stalking, recognizing its potential for seriously endangering victims. Hence, India and other countries should ensure effective crime prevention by strict implementation of law and expeditious justice delivery to save attacks to women. In an independent country people must be safeguarded by the state.

In the present chapter, Women gaining ground in politics, Egypt: Authorities Support women-empowerment efforts, Liberians in revolt: Male supremacy quakes and quivers, honoured woman at home, Women's education 'smartest global investment'. Top ten most powerful women in the World and 'No woman no peace' have been included and conclusion has been drawn for furthering their rights.

Sierra Leone

Women Gaining Ground in Politics

When Marie Jalloh first ran for office in 2007, resistance to women in politics in Sierra Leone was so strong she faced harassment and intimidation from local authorities. Now, not only is she a member of parliament; she and other women, along with local NGOs, have brought the country closer to a legal quota for women in decision-making posts.

Campaigners say more women in power would go a long way to improving people's living conditions and fostering development.

A draft bill to be voted on in October, ahead of the 2012 presidential and legislative elections, would require that women hold 14 seats in parliament and four places among the 12 paramount chiefs (traditional leaders), and make up 20 percent of candidates fielded by a political party.

In the 2007 elections female candidates won just 17 out of 112 elected seats, and were not awarded any of the seats allocated to paramount chiefs.

"Female politicians tend to be more development-oriented," said Barbara Bangura, the national coordinator of Women Solidarity Support Group and the women's NGO Grassroots Empowerment for Self Reliance. They tend to be more focused on nation-building - building the home, communities and country through (for example) availability of schools, health facilities, and safe drinking water.

Bangura added: "Failing to eliminate gender inequality in governance has and will continue to have long-term consequences on the development of the country. The exclusion of women from decision-making structures adds to the problems that many Sierra Leonean women face, such as extreme poverty, ill health, less education, sexual and gender-based violence."

Hopes for October Bill

Jalloh is a founding member of the All Political Parties Women's Association (APPWA) - a platform for women across different parties collaborating to boost women's participation in politics. She said she was confident the bill, drafted by NGOs, had the support needed to pass in October. "We (lobbied) men to support the enactment of this bill," she said, adding that men had formed a group to back the move. "We are beginning to see male politicians support women in key positions."

It is not just men who opposed women entering politics, but culture and tradition have meant many women did not see it as their place, said Nabeela Tunis, who has supported APPWA since 2008 through the UN Integrated Peace-building Mission in Sierra Leone. They had problems with confidence adding that APPWA has worked to help women see themselves as potential political candidates.

Inatorma Coomber, a women's rights project coordinator with Oxfam in Sierra Leone, pointed to President Ernest Bai Koroma's recent statement of support for the bill as cause for optimism. But she noted that support was not universal in Sierra Leone. There are still areas (where people) believe women should not take leadership (positions).

APPWA members are lobbying for the bill within their own parties and to make sure women who are strong candidates are put forward.

Less harassment

Whether or not a legal quota passes, change is already apparent.

Jalloh said: Women now face less harassment and intimidation adding she has not personally faced any since the events in 2007. Women in the past were victims of political violence but since the inception of APPWA this has changed.

Oxfam currently runs programmes in two districts (such as Koinadugu and Kailahun) supporting women representatives on the local council through training in delivering good government services. Getting women into political positions is a multi-faceted process.

Coomber said: You don't just get women into politics, you give them the tools, build up their capacity so they can deliver and serve as a good example. Oxfam also runs education sessions for prominent men - and sometimes women as well - on gender equality. We show them the benefits of empowering the opposite sex. If half your population are not empowered it is harder (for everyone).

The 2004 Truth and Reconciliation Commission report pointed to the need to boost the role of women in politics: The institutions and processes of peace, security and development, as well as societies at large, are made stronger and more effective by the full and equal participation of women.

The report recommended that 30 percent of candidates put forward for all public elections be women, and that the 2014 target should be a 50-50 gender balance in representative politics.[26]

Egypt

Authorities support women-empowerment efforts

Egyptian First Lady Suzanne Mubarak said that Egyptian political authorities have been a great support of women-empowerment efforts.

Suzanne Mubarak, head of the Egyptian National Council for Women, made the remarks in an interview broadcast Thursday by the Dubai-based satellite TV channel al-Arabiya news channel, underlining the political support Egyptian women are enjoying.

---

[26] IRIN News - Women Gaining Ground in Politics in Sierra Leone, Africa – the good news, the voice of Africa, AFRONLINE, Monday, 22 August 2011

Established in 2000 following a political resolution, the National Council for Women is in charge of reviewing all draft laws on the Egyptian woman and family and expressing its opinions among other jobs, she noted. So far, the council has backed all the laws that have to do with women and family issues, she added, indicating programs to mainly support rural women breadwinners with a small-loan project meant to help women improve their income. Moreover, she said that investments must be made to improve Egyptian women's capabilities and potentials so that they can take part in social development.

As for the achievements made by Egyptian women in the different fields, the Egyptian First Lady said that Egypt have succeeded to have a female judge after a 20-year-long struggle. She also noted that Egyptian women oppose setting a certain quota for women in the People's Assembly (the lower house the Egyptian parliament) and official institutions. It is high time for women to feel confident in their abilities and experience, she added, calling for equal chance for women to practice their rights with men.[27]

Lesbians in Revolt: **Male Supremacy Quakes and Quivers**

The development of Lesbian-feminist politics as the basis for the liberation of women is our top priority; this article outlines our present ideas. In our society which defines all people and institutions for the benefit of the rich, white male, the Lesbian is in revolt. In revolt because she defines herself in terms of women and rejects the male definitions of how she should feel, act, look, and live. To be a Lesbian is to love oneself, woman, in a culture that denigrates and despises women. The Lesbian rejects male sexual/political domination; she defies his world, his social organization, his ideology, and his definition of

[27] Xinhua, May 9, 2007

her as inferior. Lesbianism puts women first while the society declares the male supreme. Lesbianism threatens male supremacy at its core. When politically conscious and organized, it is central to destroying our sexist, racist, capitalist, imperialist system.

Lesbianism is a political choice:

Male society defines Lesbianism as a sexual act, which reflects men's limited view of women: they think of us only in terms of sex. They also say that Lesbians are not real women, so a real woman is one who gets fucked by men. We say that a Lesbian is a woman whose sense of self and energies, including sexual energies, center on women -- she is woman identified. The woman-identified woman commits herself to other women for political, emotional, physical, and economic support. Women are important to her. She is important to herself. Our society demands that commitment from women be reserved for men.

The Lesbian, woman-identified woman, commits herself to women not only as an alternative to oppressive male/female relationships but primarily because she loves women. The Lesbian has recognized that giving support and love to men over women perpetuates the system that oppresses her whether consciously or not, by her actions. If women do not make a commitment to each other, which includes sexual love, we deny ourselves the love and value traditionally given to men. We accept our second class status. When women do give primary energies to other women, then it is possible to concentrate fully on building a movement for our liberation.

Woman-identified Lesbianism is, then, more than a sexual preference, it is a political choice. It is political because relationships between men and women are essentially political, they involve power and dominance. Since the Lesbian actively rejects that relationship and chooses women, she defies the established political system.

Lesbianism by itself is not enough:

Of course, not all Lesbians are consciously woman-identified, nor are all committed to finding common solutions to the oppression they suffer as women and Lesbians. Being a lesbian is part of challenging male supremacy, but not the end. For the Lesbian or heterosexual woman, there is no individual solution to oppression.

The Lesbian may think that she is free since she escapes the personal oppression of the individual male/female relationship. But to the society she is still a woman, or worse, a visible Lesbian. On the street, at the job, in the schools, she is treated as an inferior and is at the mercy of men's power and whims. (I've never heard of a rapist who stopped because his victim was a Lesbian.) This society hates women, who love women, and so, the Lesbian, who escapes male dominance in her private home, receives it doubly at the hands of male society; she is harassed, outcast, and shuttled to the bottom. Lesbians must become feminists and fight against woman oppression, just as feminists must become Lesbians if they hope to end male supremacy.

U.S. society encourages individual solutions, apolitical attitudes, and reformism to keep us from political revolt and out of power. Men who rule, and male leftists who seek to rule, try to depoliticize sex and the relations between men and women in order to prevent us from acting to end our oppression and challenging their power. As the question of homosexuality has become public, reformists define it as a private question of who you sleep with in order to sidetrack our understanding of the politics of sex.

For the Lesbian-feminist, it is not private; it is a political matter of oppression, domination, and power. Reformists offer solutions which make no basic changes in the system that oppresses us, solutions which keep power in the hands of the oppressor. The only way oppressed people end their oppression is by seizing power: People whose rule depends on the subordination of others do not voluntarily stop oppressing others. Our subordination is the basis of male power.

Sexism is the root of all oppression:

The first division of labor, in pre-history, was based on sex: men hunted, women built the villages, took care of children, and farmed. Women collectively controlled the land, language, culture, and the communities. Men were able to conquer women with the weapons that they developed for hunting when it became clear that women were leading a more stable, peaceful, and desirable existence. We do not know exactly how this conquest took place, but it is clear that the original imperialism was male over female: the male claiming the female body and her services as his territory (or property).

Having secured the domination of women, men continued this pattern of suppressing people, now on the basis of tribe, race, and class. Although there have been numerous battles over class, race, and nation during the past 3000 years, none has brought the liberation of women. While these other forms of oppression must be ended, there is no reason to believe that our liberation will come with the smashing of capitalism, racism, or imperialism today. Women will be free only when we concentrate on fighting male supremacy.

Our war against male supremacy does, however, invovle attacking the later day dominations based on class, race, and nation. As Lesbians who are outcasts from every group, it would be suicidal to perpetuate these man-made divisions among ourselves. We have no heterosexual privileges, and when we publically assert our Lesbianism, those of us who had them lose many of our class and race privileges. Most of our privileges as women are granted to us by our relationships to men (fathers, husbands, boyfriends) whom we now reject. This does not mean that there is no racism or class chauvinism within us, but we must destroy these divisive remnants of privileged behavior among ourselves as the first step toward their destruction in the society. Race, class, and national oppressions come from men, serve ruling class elite men's interests, and have no place in a woman-identified revolution.

Lesbianism is the basic threat to male supremacy:

Lesbianism is a threat to the ideological, political, personal, and economic basis of male supremacy. The Lesbian threatens the ideology of male supremacy by destroying the lie about female inferiority, weakness, passivity, and by denying women's 'innate' need for men (even for pro-creation if the science of cloning is developed).

The Lesbian's independence and refusal to support one man undermines the personal power that men exercise over women. Our rejection of heterosexual sex challenges male domination in its most individual and common form. We offer all women something better than submission to personal oppression. We offer the beginning of the end of collective and individual male supremacy. Since men of all races and classes depend on female support and submission for practical tasks and feeling superior, our refusal to submit will force some to examine their sexist behavior, to break down their own destructive privileges over other humans, and to fight against those privileges in other men. They will have to build new selves that do not depend on oppressing women and learn to live in social structures that do not give them power over anyone.

Heterosexuality separates women from each other; it makes women define themselves through men; it forces women to compete against each other for men and the privilege which comes through men and their social standing. Heterosexual society offers women a few privileges as compensations if they give up their freedom: for example, mothers are respected and 'honored', wives or lovers are socially accepted and given some economic and emotional security, a woman gets physical protection on the street when she stays with her man, etc. The privileges give heterosexual women a personal and political stake in maintaining the status quo.

The Lesbian receives none of these heterosexual privileges or compensations since she does not accept the male demands on her. She has little vested interest in maintaining the present political system since all of its institutions -- church, state, media, health, schools -- work to keep her down. If she understands her oppression, she has nothing to gain by supporting white rich male America and much to gain from fighting to change it. She is less prone to accept reformist solutions to women's oppression.

Economics is a crucial part of woman oppression, but our analysis of the relationship between capitalism and sexism is not complete. We know that Marxist economic theory does not sufficiently consider the role of women or Lesbians, and we are presently working on this area.

However, as a beginning, some of the ways that Lesbians threaten the economic system are clear: In this country, women work for men in order to survive, on the job and in the home. The Lesbian rejects this dividson of labor at its roots; she refuses to be a man's property, to submit to the unpaid labor system of housework and childcare. She rejects the nuclear family as the basic unit of production and consumption in a a capitalist society.

The Lesbian is also a threat on the job because she is not the passive/part-time woman worker that capitalism counts on to do boring work and be part of a surplus labor pool. Her identity and economic support do not come through men, so her job is crucial and she cares about job conditions, wages, promotion, and status. Capitalism cannot absorb large numbers of women demanding stable employment, decent salaries, and refusing to accept their traditional job exploitation. We do not understand yet the total effect that this increased job dissatisfaction will have. It is, however, clear that as women become more intent upon taking control of their lives, they will seek more control over their jobs, thus increasing the strains on capitalism and enhancing the power of women to change the economic system.

Lesbians form movement to fight male supremacy:

Feminist-lesbianism, as the most basic threat to male supremacy, picks up part of the Women's Liberation analysis of sexism and gives it force and direction. Women's Liberation lacks direction now because it has failed to face class and race as real differences in women's behavior and political needs. As long as straight women see Lesbianism as a bedroom issue, they hold back the development of politics and strategies which would put an end to male supremacy and they give men an excuse for not dealing with their sexism.

A Lesbian means ending identification with, allegiance to, dependence on and support of heterosexuality. It means ending your personal

stake in the male world so that you join women, individually and collectively, in the struggle to end your oppression.

Lesbianism is the key to liberation and only women who cut their ties to male privilege can be trusted to remain serious in the struggle against male dominance. Those who remain tied to men, individually or in political theory, cannot always put women first. It is not that heterosexual women are evil or do not care about their sisters. It is because the very essence, definition, and nature of heterosexuality are men first. Every woman has experienced that desolation when her sister puts her man first in the final crunch: heterosexuality demands that she do so. As long as women still benefit from heterosexuality, receive its privileges and security, they will at some point have to betray their sisters, especially Lesbian sisters who do not receive those benefits.

Women in women's liberation have understood the importance of having meetings and other events for women only. It has been clear that dealing with men divides us and saps our energies and that it is not the job of the oppressed to explain our oppression to the oppressor. Women also have seen that collectively, men will not deal with their sexism until they are forced to do so. Yet, many of these same women continue to have primary relationships with men individually and do not understand why Lesbians find this oppressive.

Lesbians cannot grow politically or personally in a situation which denies the basis of our politics: that Lesbianism is political, that heterosexuality is crucial to the maintaining of male supremacy.[28]

---

[28] Charlotte Bunch (1972), "Lesbians in Revolt", For the Furies collective, The Furies: Lesbian / Feminist Monthly,

Lesbians must form our own political movement in order to grow. Changes which will have more than token effects on our lives will be led by woman-identified Lesbians who understand the nature of our oppression and are therefore in a position to end it.

Honoured Women at Home

There it goes again. Our well meaning but terminally goofy government has come up with yet another curious proposal. Apparently it is now thinking of ways to get husbands to pay wages to their stay-at-home wives. Oh well, not a salary, said Krishna Tirath, Union minister for women and child development (WCD). "What can you call it, may be honorarium or some other name."

The discomfort is obvious. Do you, the majestic lady of the house, the imagined goddess of your husband's heart, the awesome superwoman-cum-good-witch to your children, the difficult-but-dutiful daughter-in-law, and the benevolent-but-demanding memsa'ab, wish to be reduced to a salaried domestic employee of your husband? Perhaps, it is not.

But, to be fair, the proposal isn't really for people like you. It is for the millions of disempowered housewives who dedicate their lives solely to their family, keeping house and raising children, and get nothing in return. Who are neglected when old and infirm, have no savings, nowhere to go, often having gifted their property to the very children who shoo them away.

So yes, financial independence, as we all know by now, goes a long way in empowering women. There have even been attempts in India to establish a housewives' trade union. But the general demand for

---

January 1972, pp 8-9, Special collection Library, Duke University

salaries for wives is not new. In 1925, the silent Hollywood comedy Wages for Wives showed how much work a housewife does and why demanding half her husband's salary is quite justified. Besides, for decade's women's rights activists have been demanding salaries for housewives.

So why shouldn't we be delighted with this proposal?

How to empower women?

First, because a wife is supposed to be an equal partner in a marriage, reducing her to a paid domestic help is not just insulting, it seriously changes the power relations in the family. Moreover, she does not even have the freedom that a maid has. She is more like bonded labour — who can't quit, can't shop around for better options, and whose fate is inextricably entwined with her master's family.

Second, a wife is entitled to half the earnings and property of her husband, as an equal partner in a marriage. So giving her just a fraction of the husband's earnings would be cheating.

Third, in India, earnings do not ensure freedom or empowerment for women. Husbands routinely appropriate the wife's earnings. And the wife still has no decision-making authority even within the home. According to a 2005-06 survey of the National Family Health Survey (NFHS), only 20 to 24 per cent of married women control their own earnings. For the rest, that is almost four out of five women, her earnings are controlled either solely or largely by the husband or others.

Fourth, the very idea of getting the husband to pay a part of his earnings to his wife for services rendered is flawed. When the husband retires, the wife's salary stops, but her work continues. Now she is older, working is that much more difficult. In a salary structure, the wages cannot arbitrarily stop (or dwindle dramatically if you take a fraction of the husband's pension as her salary) while the expectation of the work continues exactly as before.

Fifth, a market-driven approach to non-marketable commodities is unfair. How does one monetize the dedication, affection, the overwhelming sense of ownership of a wife and mother? Calculating the cost of buying domestic services is hugely flawed, and even opportunity costs for women who have given up jobs to become homemakers would be grossly inadequate. These would not take into account the full scope of her duties. The emotional and mental effort that goes into the physical work that wives and mothers do would never be addressed.

Sixth, by definition the wife would never be able to earn as much or more than her husband, or as much as she would have in say, a corporate job. So while assuming that all is fair and square, we would be actually keeping homemakers forever squished under a low, home-made glass ceiling. She would be forever inferior to her husband, forever underpaid, forever unpaid for the host of intangibles that she offers as a good wife or mother.

Seventh, for financial independence of women their dependence on husbands needs to be reduced, not increased. There fore, income to women must be ensured for their safety and happiness.

So were the feminists demanding wages for wives all wrong? Let's get some clarity. The feminists' hollering about monetization came out of a desperate need to be recognized as useful contributors to society and the family. The need to be seen counted and respected. A woman's work is never done, yet it is never acknowledged either. It was about entitlement, about legitimacy, not about money per se. It was a fight against invisibility, denial of rights and social neglect. It was about money only so far as money gets you dignity and the freedom to make choices that affect yourself and your family.

For financial empowerment of married women we need to ensure that she has equal right — and access — to the husband's money, investments and property. And the same goes for the husband of an earning wife. Marriage is about equal sharing, where the family earns as a whole, one partner holds up the backend and the other the front office.

The government could help by improving the situation of women in general. It is possible by raising awareness of equal rights, by ensuring equal pay for equal work by men and women; by pushing women's literacy; by ensuring that laws to protect women are used efficiently.

For example, why is it that of the almost 15,000 cases of domestic violence registered in New Delhi, there has not been a single conviction?

For a monetary push, the government could offer tax benefits for joint accounts of spouses, or investments of housewives. It could even suggest that salaries of a married person, man or woman, would be paid into their joint account with their spouse. The focus should be on equal rights and equal access.

But more importantly, we could revive the once accepted "honorarium" for vital unpaid services, like the role of the wife or mother as an enabler and partner in social and economic activity. It was called gratitude. It involved appreciation, respect, honour, dignity and a place among the family's decision makers. In short, we could side-step monetization and relearn to value stuff that makes life worth living.[29]

Women's education 'Smartest Global investment'

UN Secretary-General Mr. Ban Ki-moon has called on business leaders at the World Economic Forum in Davos to increase their investment in women's education and health to ensure their well-being and encourage their participation in the world economy.

Mr. Ban said at an event organised by the Every Woman Every Child initiative, a global effort launched in 2010 to mobilise and intensify global action to save the lives of 16 million women and children and improve the lives of millions more.

Mr. Ban said: **Investing in the health of women and girls is the right thing to do and the smart thing to do for national economies and global stability. The business community can help and your partnership is crucial in preventing unnecessary suffering for women and girls everywhere.**

Mr Ban said, adding that despite recent progress, much remained to be done.

Mr. Ban underscored the need to boost maternal health efforts so that women everywhere could give birth safely. "Last year, more than 300,000 women died giving birth. The vast majority of those deaths could have been prevented." He also stressed the need to provide education for girls so they could lead productive lives, contribute to the economy and start families when they decided to do so. He emphasised the role that the business community could play to help them succeed. "The private sector is uniquely

---

[29] Antara Dev Sen (2012), " Maid of Honour", The Deccan Chronicle, September 15, 2012

positioned to deliver a better life for women and children around the world" he said.

"Telecommunication companies are harnessing their networks to bring mobile health solutions to women living in the countryside. Corporations are using their technological strengths to develop affordable healthcare equipment for remote areas. Pharmaceutical companies are making essential drugs available to those most in need."

Mr. Ban also urged business leaders to continue to support the global fight against HIV/AIDS, tuberculosis and malaria. "For the first time, the number of people falling ill with tuberculosis each year is declining. And malaria has been cut by more than half in 43 countries," Mr Ban said at an event to mark the tenth anniversary of the Global Fund for AIDS, Tuberculosis and Malaria.

"The Global Fund has contributed to international efforts to scale up prevention. And it has helped create a world where nearly seven million people lived longer, healthier lives thanks to antiretroviral treatment for HIV," Mr Ban said. He said countries needed to "raise the volume" of their efforts as the threat still remained high in many countries.[30]

Top TEN Most Powerful Women in the World in 2013

It's been just a few days after International Women's day and we already have an article dedicated to Women power. Women! The fairer sex or as some call them the weaker sex are one of the most beautiful creation of god. Ever though why do we refer all the beautiful creations of god as feminine? Why mother nature? Why is a river referred as she and not he?

---

[30] The United Nations Press Release, The Statesman January 31, 2012

That is because beauty equals womanhood. But then again there are misogynists and patriarchs who have always made an effort to subdue the opposite sex. What is it that makes them so insecure of women? Is it their ego or is it some deep rooted mindset. It is quite difficult to get to the crux of the problem as this is an international problem. Everywhere you see, the virility of stubborn and arrogant men waylays women. But till when you can keep them from having that respect they deserve and power they can have. So this article is homage to all those women who have the balls in their courts or are struggling to turn the circumstances in their favor, and women who control the world. Take a look at these 10 most powerful women in the world.

1. **Angela Merkel**: The German chancellor is the most powerful lady in the world. She heads the 27 member European Union and also carries the burden of future of Euro on her shoulders. The first woman chancellor of Germany is also the party leader of Christian Demographic Union. She was earlier a physical chemist who entered politics during 1989 Revolutions, i.e. at the time of fall of Berlin Wall. But her biggest challenge lies in reviving her government's now declining popularity before next elections and also overcoming the challenges of her hard line austerity prescriptions for solving European debt crisis which are opposed by both the concerned parties. She is also the second woman to head G8 and preside over European Council. She is not only the most powerful woman but also the second most powerful person in the world, according to Forbes magazine.

2. **Hillary Clinton**: Hillary Clinton is the Secretary of state, US and second most powerful woman in the world. The wife of former president of US – Bill Clinton, she has the reputation of being a no-nonsense diplomat. Earlier, from 2001 to 1009, she was United States Senator for New York. During the

2008 elections, she was a leading candidate for the Democratic Presidential Nomination but ultimately lost to Barack Obama. She has been spending her final months as a secretary visiting countries, one after the other. Her last 12 months have been quite formidable probably because Wikileaks released sensitive diplomatic cables in November where she urged Syrian president Bashar Assad to leave power and warned North Korean leader to take a different route than his militant father. In fact, she faced ridicule after it went viral and there were meme ridiculing her which went viral.

3. **Dilma Rousseff:** The third most powerful lady in the world is the president of World's 6th largest economy which is Brazil. She is 36th president of Brazil and only woman to hold office. From 2005 to 2010 she served as chief of staff under former president. She was a socialist during her youth and after 1964 coupe she joined left wing and Marxist urban guerilla groups who revolted against military dictatorship. She was jailed for 2 years where she is said to have been tortured. She was later elected as the first woman president of Brazil.

4. **Melinda Gates:** The American philanthropist is the 4th most powerful woman and wife of Bill gates whom she met while working at Microsoft. She has a Masters in Business Administration from Duke University and she heads World's most generous and wealthiest organization. Shortly after graduating, she worked for Microsoft in development of its multimedia products such as Publisher, Microsoft Bob, Expedia and Encarta. She recently hit headlines for challenging Vatican to reverse its stance against birth control. The Catholic lady donated $650 million to improvement in accessing contraception in poor countries. She is also the co founder of Bill and Melinda Gates Foundation.

5. **Jill Abramson**: She is first woman to head a 161 year old publication and the 5th most powerful woman ranked by Forbes. The executive editor of New York Times has completely transformed it by shuffling senior editorial staff and bringing in digital transformation. She has a B.A. in History and Literature from Harvard University. While in college, she worked as the Arts Editor of The Harvard Independent. She later worked for Time magazine from 1973 to 1976. For next ten years she worked as a reporter for The American Lawyer and was later appointed as editor in chief of Legal Times.

6. **Sonia Gandhi:** The only Indian woman to feature in a list full of American women. She was ranked as the 6th most powerful woman by Forbes magazine. She is an Italian born Indian politician who is the president of Indian National Congress since 1998. The head of ruling political party in India holds the control of world's tenth largest economy. She is the widow of former prime minister of India-Rajiv Gandhi. After her husband's assassination in 1991, she was offered to join the party but she refused and publicly stayed away from politics. She was finally elected as the president of Congress in 1998. She has also served as the chairperson of UPA in Lok Sabha since 2004. She is also the longest serving president in the history of Congress party.

7. **Michelle Obama:** She is the first Afro- American First Lady of the United States. Michelle Obama is the wife of 44th president of the US- Barack Obama. She is a graduate from Princeton University and Harvard Law College and then worked with a law firm- Sidley Austin where she first met Barack Obama. She then worked for Chicago mayor Richard m. Daley and for the University of Chicago Medical Centre. During 2007 she helped campaign for her husband's presidential campaign and played a vital role in the re-election too. She was the keynote speaker at the 2008 Democratic National Convention. Her popularity

is more than her husband's probably because of her stylish fashion picks and mission to end child obesity and focusing on healthy eating habits.

8. **Christine Lagarde:** The 57 year old woman has been ranked 8th most powerful woman by Forbes magazine. Christine Lagarde is the Managing Director at International Monetary Fund since July 2011. The French national is the first woman to run the 188 country financial organization. She is a well known antitrust and labor lawyer and became the first chairperson of international law firm- Baker and McKenzie. Previous to working for IMF, she has held various positions in French government such as Minister of Economic Affairs and Minister of Trade among other posts she has held. She is also the first woman to become the Finance Minister of a G8 economy, as well as first woman to head IMF. In November 2009, she was ranked the best Minister of Finance in Euro-zone by Financial Times. She definitely has a lot of honors for being the first everywhere.

9. **Janet Napolitano:** The 9th most powerful woman in the world serves as Secretary to United Nations Homeland Security and the only female to hold this post. The Democrat joined office in 2009 and now serves in the administration of President Barack Obama. She took over this post after serving as a governor of Arizona from 2003 to 2009. The third female governor of Arizona is now at the top of third largest Department in US politics. Prior to serving as a governor, she served as Attorney General of Arizona from 1999 to 2002. In March 2009, she received the Council on Litigation Management's Professionalism Award for her unique abilities to lead in the highest order of her profession. She also battled with cancer and later credited her friends and family for standing up for her while she was battling cancer.

10. **Sheryl Sandberg:** She is the 10th most powerful woman in the world, at the age of 43. She is the Chief Operating Officer of Face book since 2008. In June 2012, she was elected by board of directors thus becoming Face book's first female board member and also owns around $1 billion stock of the company. The US citizen is a graduate from Harvard College with an A.B. in economics for which she was awarded with John h. William prize. She also has an MBA from Harvard Business School with a distinction. Previous to Face book, she has worked with Google as its vice president of Global Online sales and operations. She also had a hand in launching Google.org. Prior to Google, she worked at United Stated Department of Treasury as its chief of staff.[31]

No Women No Peace

7 October 2011 will mark the 10-year anniversary of the US-led international intervention in Afghanistan. Since then there have been some significant advances in women's rights and gender equality, however, women continue to suffer discrimination and violence.

Hard won gains could be seriously compromised as the Afghan government and its international partners (including the UK government) proceed with talks without ensuring mechanisms to guarantee women's rights are respected. Find out more about this issue here. Download the petition and gather signatures here.

The Afghan Women's Network, a network of women and women's NGOs working to empower Afghan women and ensure their equal participation in Afghan society, is asking the international community to:

[31] Rakhi Bansal (2013), "Top 10 Most Powerful Women in the World 2013", Top on Lists, Home Celebrities

1) Use their influence to ensure women have an effective voice and role in all levels of the peace process: at the national, provincial and district levels.

2) Work with the Afghan government to ensure that all the human rights in the constitution are upheld in any peace settlement. These include women's right to an education and the right to participate in political life with a guaranteed 30% female quota in parliament.

3) Increase support to development programmes that promote women's rights and wellbeing in political, social and economic spheres.

ACT NOW:

On 5th December 2011, the UK Government will be represented at the Bonn Conference on Afghanistan, at which the peace process will be an important focus of discussion.

We call on the UK government to ensure that the voices of Afghan women are heard at the Bonn Conference, including the recommendations of the Afghan Women's Network, and that any agreements made at Bonn explicitly call for women's rights in Afghanistan to be protected not undermined.

We will submit this petition to William Hague later this autumn, along with signatures gathered by our member organisations.[32]

Conclusion

---

[32] http://www.nowomennopeace.org/sign-our-petition-and-support-afghan-women

The government must provide women with higher education facilities free of cost to equip them with degrees, knowledge and expertise for employment, empowerment and state's progress.

The women and children must improve their mind and thinking process, as human mind is a seat of perception where information from all the senses is gathered and processed. The mind does not say anything on its own, it just reflects what we believe.

Women must attend YOGA classes and be physically strong. They cannot compete in this world if they accept sufferings and they have to achieve laurels in life. They must read more and compete with the opposite sex in knowledge, strength and aspirations.
Women should find time to pray God and avail strength in mind.

They should prefer health services, educational services and computer engineering to do justice to the society, but they should specialize in that branch of education which attract them most.

Women have achieved success in politics. They have occupied the posts of Presidents, Prime Ministers, and Speakers in many countries. They have proved successful in foreign affairs too.

Women are successful in cinema, drama, sports and singing. Women have achieved Nobel Prizes in research and peace. A woman has proved as a successful astronaut. So it is time, all women should work to achieve more successes in life as compared to men in all fields.

World Peace is possible when both men and women acquire advanced knowledge, faith, cooperation, sacrifice and will power. They must work in harmony.

+++++

Chapter IV

HEALTHCARE SUPPORT TO WOMEN AND CHILDREN

The greatest destroyer of peace is abortion because if a mother can kill her own child, what is left for me to kill you and you to kill me? There is nothing between. -- Mother Teresa

Women have health issues that deserve special consideration- everywhere. Women's health related issues and problems cover a vast range of topics - from reproductive health to mental health. Moreover, there are major health concerns for women. Their health problems are many, such as "how to keep your heart and bones healthy?" They should know on 'reproductive health and sexual health including breast health'. They should decide to make healthier choices for better lifestyle which will give them more opportunity to enjoy more aspects of life for longer.

Of course steps for healthcare need high expenditure. And this is possible for rich families residing in cities.

Women suffer from a number of diseases such as: Headache, Migraine, Epilepsy, Eye Care, Dental Care, Thyroid Disorders, Asthma, Heartburn, Back Pain, Gall Stones, Constipation, Hepatitis, Urinary Tract Infection, Overactive Bladder, Hemorrhoids IBS,

Some of the women are always tired. It is because, they suffer from: Metabolic Disorders, Anemia, and Insomnia. They might suffer from: Obesity, Swine Flu, and Dengue.

Women are easy prey of reproductive health, breast health, heart health, bone health and mental health.

These are as follows:

(a) Reproductive Health: Reproductive Organs, PMS Periods, PID Endometriosis, Polycystic Ovaries, Uterine Fibroids, Vaginal Discharges, Pelvic Pro-lapse, Sexual Dysfunction, STD Coping With Infertility, Managing Menopause, Medical Causes of Infertility
(b) Breast Health: Basics of Breast Health, Breast Conditions, Breast Pain, and Breast Self Examination, Mammograms
(c) Heart Health: Heart Disease, Hypertension, Cholesterol Facts
(d) Bone Health: Bone Health Basics, Osteoporosis, Exercise for Bones
(e) Mental Health: Depression, Eating Disorders, Conquering Phobias, Anxiety Moods and Irritability, Somatization, Disorders, Balancing Work and Family Life

So it is really difficult to award healthcare facilities to all women. So there is need to ask for assistance from World Health Organization, developed countries and philanthropic institutions for medicines. But distribution of medicines is possible if the rural doctors are sincere to their duties. It is reported that most of the rural hospitals are managed by pharmacists or nurses. The doctors have their clinics in cities or towns.

The present world is suffocated by air pollution, water pollution, climate change, violence everywhere, manipulation of state laws, fear of war, and lawlessness. The worst sufferers are women in developing countries. Unless they are taken care of by the state laws in principle and practice, the aim of creating permanent WORLD PEACE would be a dream rather than a reality. Let us try to save the women and children for a happy future to all. In this chapter healthcare activities are discussed in different countries,

New Global Plan

To save mothers and children from AIDS-related deaths

The world leaders met at the UN to unveil a Global Plan on June 9, 2011 designed to eliminate new HIV infections among children by 2015 and to keep their mothers alive. UN Secretary General Ban Ki-moon, Nigerian President Good luck Jonathan, former US President Bill Clinton, UNAIDS Executive Director Michel Sidibé and United States Global AIDS Coordinator Ambassador Eric Goosby launched the Plan along with UNAIDS Goodwill Ambassadors Annie Lennox and Naomi Watts. The plan brings together 30 countries and 50 civil society, private sector, networks of people living with HIV and international organizations in a consolidated effort to realize a world with zero new HIV infections, zero discrimination against people living with HIV, and zero AIDS-related deaths. While the plan will focus on all low and middle income countries, it will particularly focus on 22 with the highest prevalence of HIV-positive pregnant women.

"We are here to launch 'Countdown to Zero,' the Global Plan to eliminate new HIV infections among children and keep their mothers alive," said Ki-moon.

"This is no fantasy. Developed countries already do this. But we cannot rest until this is true for our whole world... As the developed world shows, there is every reason to believe that we can save millions of lives across the developing world." Sidibé echoed this enthusiasm, telling the room, "We believe that by 2015 children everywhere can be born free of HIV and that their mothers can remain healthy."

Success stories were highlighted from around the world. Jonathan shared some of the progress which recently emerged from Nigeria, including efforts to end stigma and the recently passed health bill which will free up additional resources to scale up HIV treatment centers at the local level, with an emphasis on reaching the poor and vulnerable. Clinton looked to Cambodia, where in 2007 just 10 percent of HIV positive mothers received treatment to prevent mother-to-child transmission of HIV (PMTCT). Less than four years later, over 60% of mothers are receiving this treatment, largely due to service linkages and the scaling-up of health systems. Clinton called for mothers to have access to the drugs they need for effective PMTCT, and for an increase in funding for evidence-based interventions.

In response to the Plan's call to action, the United States President's Emergency Plan for AIDS Relief (PEPFAR) announced an additional US$ 75 million for PMTCT efforts. The Bill & Melinda Gates Foundation pledged US$ 40 million, Chevron committed to US$ 20 million and Johnson & Johnson pledged US$ 15 million. These investments will be crucial in transforming the Plan's goals into reality.[33]

"Helping pregnant women to protect their babies is really important. Like all mothers, I would do

---

[33] New Global Plan launched to save the lives of mothers and children from AIDS-related deaths" Women Deliver, Democracy in Action. Org, June 30. 2011

anything to give my child a healthy start in life—and this prevention should be available to women everywhere." said HIV-positive mother Babalwa Mbono.

G8 Leaders Recommit to Improve **Maternal Health and Reduce Child Mortality**

The 37th G8 Summit was held in Deauville, France from May 26-27, 2011. The three priorities of the French Presidency of the G8 Summit were the internet and green growth, international peace and security and partnership with Africa. Though health was not a priority of the G8 this year, the Deauville Statement reaffirmed a commitment to improving maternal health and reducing child mortality, most notably through the Muskoka Initiative for Maternal, Newborn and Child health launched in 2010.

The Muskoka Initiative is aimed at supporting developing countries in reducing deaths of women in pregnancy and childbirth, reducing deaths of children fewer than five, and at increasing access to family planning. In June 2010, Prime Minister Stephen Harper announced at the G-8 summit in Muskoka, Canada's commitment of US $2.85 billion over five years to help save the lives of mothers, children and newborns in developing countries. Of that, $1.1 billion was new funding for the Muskoka Initiative on Maternal, Newborn and Child Health, while the remaining $1.75 billion maintained current funding levels for similar initiatives through the Canadian International Development Agency (CIDA).

Overall, the G-8 committed to provide $10 billion for the Muskoka Initiative by 2015, and made an initial commitment of $5 billion. A report released by the G8 last week gave a first glimpse into these commitments. It appears that collectively the G8 may have already surpassed the initial $5 billion commitment by about $2.656 billion, roughly 53%. Since the G-8 Summit, Canada and its global partners have committed nearly $7.3 billion to the Muskoka Initiative.

In the Deauville statement, the G8 also committed to support the recommendations of the Commission on Information and Accountability for Women's and Children's Health. They will implement them, and urge others to do so.

The Muskoka Initiative was the G8 contribution to the Global Strategy for Women's and Children's Health launched in September 2010 by the UN Secretary-General and over 90 stakeholders, with US $40 billion in commitments. G8 leaders committed to implement and monitor their Muskoka commitments in coordination with other stakeholders in the Global Strategy.

According to the 2011 G8 Accountability Report, G8 member commitments to Muskoka are as follows:

(a) Canada - C$ 1.1 billion;
(b) France - € 500 million;
(c) Germany - €400 million;
(d) Italy - US$ 75 million;
(e) Japan - US$500 million;
(f) Russia - US$ 75 million;
(g) United Kingdom - £ 2.1 billion;
(h) US - US$ 1.346 billion;
(i) EU - $ 70 million.[34]

The United States of America

Inquiries of Pregnancy Related Deaths and Complication

Lawmakers, researchers, advocates, and survivors of maternal complications gathered on Capitol Hill in

[34]The 37th G8 Summit was held in Deauville, France from May 26-27, 2011. Quoted from Women Deliver, Democracy in Action Org, June 30, 2011

2011 to call attention to the deteriorating state of maternal health in the United State —as well as a new bill that could help answer why so many women die during pregnancy and childbirth in one of the world's most developed nations.

Maternal health in the United States:
A worsening outlook

The United States in 2010 ranked behind 49 countries on maternal mortality - meaning that U.S. women are at a greater risk of dying from pregnancy and childbirth-related complications than women in 49 other nations. While this figure is staggering enough, it marks a sharp decline from last year, when the country ranked 41st. This slip in performance comes just as the global community is paying unprecedented attention to the issue of maternal health.

For example, 2010 saw the launch of the United Nations's Global Strategy for Women's and Children's Health, the hosting of the second Women Delivery conference, and the establishment of the U.N. Commission on Information and Accountability for Wmen's and Children's Health, which featured Women Deliver President Jill Sheffield as a commissioner.

As the world makes a collective effort to achieve safe motherhood for all, maternal mortality in the United States is marked by a long history of stagnation. Maternal deaths have not decreased in the last 20 years, with the maternal mortality ratio lagging far behind the government's stated goal, according to an Amnesty International report called Deadly Delivery. In 2010, the maternal mortality ratio was 12.7, three times higher than the government's 4.3 deaths per 100,000 live births goal.

Disaggregating this number shows a wide disparity based on race and ethnicity, location, and income.

For example, the risk of maternal mortality has remained three to four times higher among black women than white women during the last 60 years. In addition, states where more than 18 percent of people live below the poverty level were found to have 77 percent higher maternal mortality ratios. The geographic variance in maternal mortality ratios reflects "significant differences in health care access, funding, policies, and staffing," from a low of 1.4 deaths per 100,000 live births in Maine to 41.6 deaths per 100,000 live births in the District of Columbia, according to Deadly Delivery. With a maternal mortality ratio of 26 deaths per 100,000 live births, Michigan is a state in need of the type of funding proposed in Conyers' recently introduced " Maternal Health Accountability Act of 2011" or H.R. 894.

The bill proposes providing $10 million in grant funding for states to establish Maternal Mortality Review Committees focused on examining pregnancy and childbirth-related deaths and complications. The objective of the legislation is to reduce preventable maternal mortality and morbidity and eliminate disparities in maternal health outcomes. To discuss the need for the legislation, Convers convened a hearing with U S and international experts—all of whom affirmed the need for research to identify the underlying causes and social determinants of deteriorating maternal health outcomes in the country.

Amnesty International's Deadly Delivery—which informs much of the proposed bill—highlights Illinois as one state that routinely reviews maternal morbidity and mortality data and uses this research to improve care. All birthing hospitals in the state are required to report any cases of obstetric patients admitted to the ICU or who receive more than three units of blood. Based on the cases the Maternal Mortality Review Committee have led to state-wide postpartum hemorrhage education program and the creation of rapid response teams to address hemorrhage cases.

The largely partisan bill was introduced in March and has 41 co-sponsors, including one Republican, Rep. Andy Harris (Md.) who is also a physician. [35]

Feed mom extra for a healthy baby

A million infants die every year as they are born too early, accounting for 28 percent of total newborn deaths. A recent report by the March of Dimes Foundation (MODF) said 10 percent of all births worldwide, 13 million babies, are premature. And a major cause of premature and undernourished babies are their malnourished mothers.

There's clear evidence that what mothers eat from the time they get pregnant to the time of delivery greatly decides how healthy the child will be: even as an adult. In India, of the 2.6-crore births annually, 23% of babies are low weight (below 2.5 kg). According to the National Institute of Nutrition (NIN), "pregnancy is physiologically and nutritionally a highly demanding period." Extra food is required to meet the foetus's requirements as a woman prepares herself to meet the nutritional demands by increasing her own body fat deposits during pregnancy.

A child's under-nourishment occurs in a window that spans the 1000 days from conception to its second year. Poor nutrition during pregnancy has critical consequences throughout the child's life. "Optimal nutrition during the first 1000 days after conception is critical both for the mother and child. During this period good nutrition not only helps fight common childhood diseases but also ensures proper mental

---

[35] Women Deliver, Democracy in Action. Org, June 9th, 2011 / June 30. 2011

development of the child as he grows up," said Dr Sunita Mittal, gynecologist at Delhi's AIIMS.

Such evidence prompted The Times of India and Nestle to jointly launch an initiative to promote healthy nutrition in the crucial first 1,000 days.

A lactating mother requires extra food to secrete adequate quantity/ quality of milk. Dr D Raghunatha Rao, member of India's dietary guidelines committee says a normal adult woman requires 2200 calories per day. But when pregnant, she requires an additional 350 calories. Some micronutrients are required in extra amounts, like folic acid, which if taken throughout pregnancy, reduces the risk of congenital malformations and increases birth weight. "The mother as well as the growing foetus needs iron to meet the high demands of red blood cell formation. Calcium is essential, both during pregnancy and lactation, for proper formation of bones and teeth, for secretion of breast-milk rich in calcium and to prevent the mother's osteoporosis," NIN's guidelines say.

Dr Kaushiki Dwivedee, gynecologist at Max hospital suggests a sample diet. "A normal pregnancy diet should include 6-11 servings of grains, 3-5 servings of vegetables, 2-4 servings of fruit, 3-4 servings of dairy, 2-3 servings of meats, beans or nuts and a serving of sweet." Dr Veena Bhat, director, obstetrics and gynecology, Artemis Health Institute cautions pregnant women from popping random pills as drugs can cross the placenta and enter fetal circulation adversely affecting the growing baby.

For the baby, pediatrician Dr Anjali Saxena says the ideal situation is 'exclusive breastfeeding for first 6 months of life'. "Thereafter, solid foods can be introduced in a step wise manner. Complementary foods are an important source of nutrients after six months in breastfed infants," she said, adding that home-made cereal preparations may be used.

"Seasonal fruits can be mashed or stewed. The preferred order to start foods is rice cereal, followed by fruits and vegetables. Lean meat and eggs are next and lastly red meat. Water should be initiated during this period," Dr Saxena added.

Zulfiqar A Bhutta, professor and head of women and child health division at Aga Khan University says preconception care during adolescence and before and between pregnancies can impact 136 million women who give birth each year and ensure that newborns receive the healthiest start possible. Preconception care is any intervention provided to women and couples of childbearing age. "Preconception care also means women's education and empowerment and more targeted healthcare interventions such as vaccination and micronutrient supplementation," Dr Bhutta said.[36]

International Confederation of Midwives

At the opening ceremony of the International Confederation of Midwives 29th triennial Conference in Durban, South Africa on Sunday, a hall full of midwives joined voices to sing "One Love," Bob Marley's anthem of compassion for humankind. As a witness, I can report that you have not heard the power of a collective voice until you've heard 3,000 midwives singing about their love and commitment to mothers and babies: "Hear the children crying... let's get together and feel all right."

Today, women all over the world are giving birth and listening for the joyful squawk of their newborns crying for the first time. But many of these mothers will hear only heartbreaking silence – as many as one out of 10 babies may have difficulty breathing at birth, and asphyxia (or lack of oxygen) is responsible for more than 20 percent of newborn deaths. With

---

[36] Times of India, Mumbai, March 23, 2012

their unique access to women and children at a critical moment, midwives may hold the key to ending this tragedy.

Interventions performed by a midwife, like stopping a hemorrhage and administering antibiotics to prevent infection during birth, can have an immediate impact on women's lives. But their role doesn't end there. We have heard here at ICM about the importance of the Continuum of Care, a model that extends the reach of midwives to the health and survival of newborns. As midwives continue to gain recognition as a sustainable resource to support women's health, they are also gaining the knowledge and skills to protect the lives they help bring into the world.

At a standing-room-only workshop for the Helping Babies breathe program at the conference, I was reminded why it is so important to engage midwives in the Continuum of Care. As the presenters shared stories and best practices for combating newborn asphyxia – for example, an estimated 42,000 newborns a year could be saved simply by having a birth attendant dry the baby and stimulate it to breathe – the midwives in the packed room responded with gasps, vocal approval and excited murmurs. At a work station, crowds of midwives surrounded the infant-sized mannequins used for practicing newborn resuscitation.

In a partnership with Save the Children, the American Academy of Pediatrics and USAID, Johnson & Johnson is supporting Helping Babies Breathe training in Malawi and Uganda over the next five years. But there is more work to be done. In some countries, more than 80 percent of women still give birth without a skilled birth attendant, a number that is tied closely to rates of maternal and infant mortality. As part of the conference this week, The State of World's Midwifery 2011, Delevering Health Saving Lives was released by UNFPA, providing the first comprehensive analysis of the role of midwives in the parts of the world with the greatest need. The report names nine countries that need to increase their midwifery workforce by 6 to 15 times, just to meet the current need.

This week, here in Durban, South Africa, those 3,000 midwives from more than 120 countries will again join voices to talk about how midwifery can change the way we address global maternal and child health. These women save lives, and as their role expands to take on more responsibility, midwives deserve the respect and support of health systems and local governments and the legitimacy of true health professionals. After all, they may be our best shot at giving more mothers a chance to hear that first beautiful cry.[37]

Healthcare Awards for Children Fund

ViiV Healthcare announced today that it has awarded £1 million to 82 projects in 21 countries across the globe aimed at improving the health and welfare of women, children, and families affected by HIV in small grants from the possible action for Children's fund. With this large number of smaller community grants, the Positive Action for Children Fund hopes to stimulate grassroots community action in support of global PMTCT (Preventing Mother to Child Transmission) community efforts to eliminate vertical transmission of HIV. Such work is closely aligned with the World Health Organisation's vision for addressing mother-to-child transmission of HIV and works toward achieving the Millennium Development Goals set to reduce child mortality, improve maternal health and combat spread of HIV.

---

[37] Joy Marini (2011), "Midwives Can Be the Voice Heard Around the World" Women Deliver, Democracy in Action. Org, June 22. 2011

This announcement is directly supportive of the Global Plan towards the Elimination of New HIV infections among Children by 2013 and Keeping Their Mothers Alive as set out by the UNAIDS convened Global Task Team, announced on June 08 2011. The plan sets out the following key principles for success: women living with HIV are at the center of the response, country ownership – i.e. responses designed, developed and delivered by local communities, leveraging synergies linkages and integration for improved sustainability and shared responsibility and specific accountability–between families, communities and countries.

This new call for proposals aims to support a broader mix of organisations with a focus on the priority issues in the priority countries to address mother to child transmission of HIV. In particular they have prioritized 14 countries for PMTCT interventions: Nigeria, Democratic Republic of Congo, Uganda, Ethiopia, Cameroon, Mozambique, Zimbabwe, Zambia, Malawi, Angola, Burundi, Chad, Tanzania and India. Projects range from £3000 to £20,000.[38]

ViiV Healthcare's Positive Action for Children Fund is committed to fund $48 million on community based PMTCT interventions through 2015 and will have a targeted spending pattern -- at least 80 percent will support projects focused on sub-Saharan Africa, while up to 20 percent may be dispersed to projects focused elsewhere. To qualify, at least 85 percent of the project's budget must be spent in the targeted country.

ViiV Healthcare is a global specialist HIV company established by GlaxoSmithKline and Pfizer to deliver advances in treatment and care for people living with HIV.

---

[38] Women Deliver, Democracy in Action. Org, June 30. 2011

Celebrate Solutions: INDIA

Community mobilization guide to improve the health of mothers and babies

The infant mortality rate in India is estimated at about 39 deaths per 1,000 live births. And nearly double that in rural areas -- so it's notable when a new project results in a 45 percent drop in newborn deaths. That's precisely what has happened with a community mobilization effort in India and Bangladesh.

Using the reach and know-how of local women's groups, a community mobilization project called Saving Mothers and Children has found great success in improving the health of mothers and their babies. In addition to the 45 percent reduction in newborn deaths in India, it helped moderate maternal depression to fall 57 percent and increased the uptake of health services in Bangladesh. Both countries saw an improvement in hygienic delivery practices, such as the use of delivery kits and exclusive breastfeeding.

The community mobilization approach is rooted in targeting women of reproductive age and focusing meetings on topics that are relevant to the target audience (to eliminate the need for a financial incentive for participation). Working in collaboration with community health workers and facilities is also important, both to strengthen community links and to improve services when possible.

Existing organizations familiar with a participatory approach were found to be more effective and efficient than newly-formed organizations. The approach has greater success in rural communities, where people are more likely to participate and cooperate in group action, than in urban areas, where people are more transient and communities less cohesive.

Being able to effectively reach women, first physically and then intellectually and/or emotionally, is the key to success for community mobilization efforts like the one implemented by Saving Mothers and Children.

Documenting Good Practices:

UK-based Women and Children First, which helped to implement the project, has developed a Good Practice Guide based on the approach used in Bangladesh and India that can be adapted elsewhere to yield similar improvements in child and maternal health. The Saving Mothers and Children project was focused in tribal and rural areas in India and Bangladesh.

The Good Practice Guide details the participatory learning and action cycle used in the community mobilization, and describes the four phases of the cycle as follows: "assessing the situation and identifying maternal and newborn health problems; identifying strategies to address these problems; taking action; and measuring progress and impact. Each phase includes a series of women's group meetings that cover different topics. Completing the whole cycle takes around two years."

One woman in the project area, quoted in the guide, summarizes the potential impact of the community mobilization approach for so many other women around the world who do not realize the risks they face during pregnancy and childbirth: "Perhaps my daughter and I would not be alive today if our group members hadn't convinced my family to admit me in the hospital. I will be grateful to our Women's Group members forever."[39]

---

[39] Rachel Cernansky (2011), "Celebrate Solutions: Community mobilization guide to improve the health of mothers and babies" Women Deliver, Democracy in Action. Org, June 30. 2011

Miscarriage of healthcare:
Counterfeit Drugs and Irrational Medication

INDIA is fast becoming the epicenter of counterfeit drugs, sale of expired medicines, doctors and nurses with dubious qualifications, unlicensed hospitals, nursing homes and pathologists, and unapproved medical, paramedical and nursing colleges. The common man is not in a position to differentiate between horses and mules. The Central Drugs Standard Control Organisation (CDSCO), the Medical Council of India and the Ministry of Health and Family Welfare have not been able to rectify the malaise.

The World Health Organisation had advanced several cautionary measures relating to the manufacture and sale of banned chemical substances in drugs. It had also tried to stop the export of counterfeit drugs from India. The entire system of controls is plagued by corruption, lethargy, and red tape.

Healthcare programmes must be comprehensive, covering the manufacture and sale of approved drugs, their easy availability and at the right price, proper storage as specified by the drug manufacturer, disposal of hazardous bio-medical waste, and a crackdown on fake, counterfeit and banned drugs. The current state of affairs is awful and might persist if the monitoring agencies continue to be ineffective. Not that the authorities are unaware; it is corruption that pervades the system.

India boasts a trillion dollar economy. Yet the highest number of people dies every day either due to wrong diagnosis or counterfeit drugs or without any treatment at all. The health of the stock market does not reflect the people's health and the nation cannot be a global power without a 'total healthcare' system. The issue is terribly critical in the US, Europe, Japan, and many developed countries in South-east Asia and the Australasia region. Unfortunately, the few good and honest people are like bonsai trees. They just don't grow.

Drugs that have been globally discarded are still produced, sold within the country and also exported out of the country. What attract the common man is the brand name and not just the chemical composition. For instance, Furazolidone, Nitrofurazone, Phenolphthalein are some of the banned chemical substances for use in drugs. Lomofen, Furacin and Agarol are banned as they might lead to cancer as a side-effect. 'Quinidochlor' is a banned substance in drugs, but people continue to use the anti-diarrhoea enteroquinol which is one and the same. Analgin, Furazolidone and Nitrofurazone are even banned for veterinary use in the United States, but people consume it in India. Who will rectify this in a nation where copyright denotes 'right to copy' and where intellectual property is considered 'public property'?

It is shocking that doctors continue to prescribe banned substances such as Phenylpropanolamine and Nimesulide which are basically Vicks Action-500 and Nimulid respectively. Even Bangladesh has banned the use of Nimulid by both adults and children, but it is widely prescribed and is available across the counter in this country. Analgin sold here as Novalgin and Baralgan, is banned abroad. Bone marrow depression could be one major side-effect.

India is a signatory to the World Health Organisation regulations on counterfeit drugs and the rational use of medicines. "Rational use" implies that patients should receive medication suitable to their clinical needs and in doses that meet their own personal requirements, for sufficient time and at the lowest cost. The common forms of irrational use are: excessive medicines per patient, improper use of anti-microbials, and injections when oral medicines would suffice. The inability to get access to medicines and incorrect dosage can result in morbidity and mortality, especially during childhood infections.

Several well-established structured procedures are available to measure the extent of irrational use. A perverse sense of financial incentives is the prime reason behind such use. Those who prescribe such use earn more money by selling more than the requirement per patient. It serves to convey the impression that for health, one needs wealth. To ensure rational consumption of medicines, the activities of the stakeholders must be monitored and curbed. If regulations and warnings by the government are to have any effect, they must be backed by strong and honest monitoring agencies, including the judiciary.

The other serious issue is counterfeit medicines. Their identity and source are fraudulently mislabeled. This applies to both branded generics and counterfeits, including medicines with correct active substances but insufficient strength, wrong ingredients or with fake packaging. Like counterfeit currency, the patients are unable to detect or differentiate between genuine and counterfeit drugs. In general, it is not the chemists who try to push the sale of the drug; it is the doctors who prescribe such medicines to the patients.

The regulatory authority in India feels that it is not necessary that a drug banned in other countries should automatically be banned in India. A lot needs to be done by the national pharmaco vigilance commission. There are many doctors who are aware of the ban on certain drugs; equally, many others lack awareness and do not keep track of new developments. Professional knowledge can be updated by reading the British Medical Journal or the New England Journal of Medicine.

Transportation, storage of medicines and safe disposal of hazardous hospital waste is also vital to 'total health care'. Many antibiotics need to be stored at temperatures below 25 deg C, but a large number are exposed to the peak summer heat without any facility of either an AC or a temperature regulated system. As a result, such antibiotics possibly lose their efficacy. Yet patients keep buying such drugs which do not work. It is the doctor or the pharmaceutical company or the state authorities who must ensure that the medicine reaches the patient in a manner and condition as printed on the packaging label.

Widespread is the illegal dumping of hazardous bio-medical hospital waste. Very few hospitals ensure incineration of the waste. This can either spread disease or even create a new symptom that may be difficult to diagnose.

The Union ministry of health needs to team up with all state health departments, municipalities and the pollution control boards and take action accordingly. To put in place a 'total health care' system, both civil society and students, irrespective of political affiliation, must take the initiative to set things right. They may be disappointed if their efforts fail, but doomed if they don't try.[40]

Female infanticide

Female infanticide has come to Britain. In India there are copious statistics available as to which castes, communities, regions and religions abort foetuses because, like Lady Macbeth they want to "bring forth men children only". (One must interpose on

[40] Chandan K Bhattacharjee (2012), "Miscarriage of healthcare:;Counterfeit Drugs And Irrational Medication", The Statesman , February 3, 2012

Shakespeare's behalf and insist that it wasn't a cause he espoused. He made Lady M say it because the Elizabethans though much concerned with the burdens of dowry, also believed that men had stouter hearts than women and Lady M was crying out for a world in which murder in the service of personal ambition would be emotionally OK).

Several Indian forums gather data on the communities and castes which have an imbalance of males to females. I imagine that it would be, as in the tossing of coins, a 50-50 split and so over time and a large sample one would assume a balance of gender in any population. I have absolutely no biological knowledge or qualification and cannot with any certainty say that there aren't in particular collections of population some physiological preponderance which makes the birth of males more likely than that of females. I suspect though that there's no such thing, that the imbalance in numbers can be accounted for by choice, preference, abortion or murder.

A recent expose in the British national press didn't provide this sort of statistic but it did entrap a few clinics and individual consultant (senior) doctors who offered abortions on the grounds of gender — female gender in the main. The expose recorded and photographed a senior doctor telling an enquiring client that she didn't care why the client wanted to abort her child — it wasn't within the realm of her concerns — but she could arrange for a termination of the pregnancy. She was subsequently recorded phoning her colleague with a request for such an abortion with the express caveat that no questions were to be asked. It was a purely commercial transaction.

The consultant doctor who was so entrapped happened to work for a clinic and also happens to be female of Asian origin. She will undoubtedly be investigated and judged by the British Medical Council and even by Her Majesty's Courts.

One can't conclude that her being Asian meant that she was approached by a largely Asian clientele who may have thought that she would in some sense "understand" their decision to demand an abortion based on the gender of the foetus. I must admit I was tempted to come to such a conclusion based on the area in which her clinic was situated and the wording of the recorded conversation, but have to admit here that such a conclusion has to be resisted as there is no evidence that female infanticide in its modern form, the data of amniocentesis, has been imported to Britain by Asian immigrants, albeit of the third generation. The termination that the doctor proposed or agreed to arrange and her recorded conversation about it not being her business why it was required are both illegal in Britain. She may face being struck off and even face criminal charges.

Abortion is not illegal but can be legitimately performed if a medical practitioner certifies that it is being done in the interests of the mother's or the unborn child's physical or psychological health. The choice of the gender of your baby falls outside this definition.

I recently read a book by an Indian writer in which a rural community in a part of India murdered newborn female infants by feeding them crushed glass in their first forced dose of bottled milk — as soon as they are born. The monstrous contention of the murderers is that they are administering a painless death to the girl child.

The practice originated in this community's centuries-old feudal tradition of a refusal to give away a parcel of land as dowry with the grown girl child on her betrothal. It decimated the land of the village. Boy-children gained land, girl-children lost it — not because God or Darwin decreed it, but because of the settlements of feudal agricultural production. Britain today has no feudal agricultural production.

Western societies did indeed do dowries. Shakespeare's King Lear starts the play by handing or not handing them out. A famous dowry is that of the "islands" which now form Mumbai gifted to Charles II on his marriage to the Portuguese Infanta Catherine of Braganza. The dowry tradition, destroyed in Europe by capitalism and the growing political and social equality of the sexes as citizens and as wage-earners in the family, has almost disappeared. Two girls of my family, a daughter and very close niece are to be married this year and (fingers crossed) the young men, both British, to whom they are affianced have made no demands on the family. The prospect of them doing so would be an absurdity.

The thought has crossed my mind that the beauty, education and accomplishments of my daughter and niece merit reverse dowries, but their young men are equal in most or "different" respects to them and social evolution has made its deals.

So it is with most communities of these scepter isles, except for the Asian immigrants, the Greek and Chinese immigrants and perhaps the tiny Romany population. Traditions linger. Land and money in Punjab, Mirpur, Gujarat or even Birmingham and the local Southall bank, change hands in the arrangements which precede marriage.

Consider China where the liabilities attached to a girl child have been abolished by the communist order. And still the one-child policy of the government has resulted in the not-so-mysterious preponderance of male births.[41]

---

[41] Farrukh Dhoni (2012), " Female Foeticide is not an Asian import", The Deccan Chronicle, Saturday March 10, 2012

That should worry India as the shortage of women in China in a generation may lead to them pouring over the Himalayas in quest of what they will no doubt classify as a "natural resource".

Catholic View of Abortion

The death of Savita Halappanavar has brought into sharp focus the Catholic view of abortion. It also offers an opportunity to explore the Hindu perspective on this much debated issue.

The medically avoidable, gut-wrenchingly painful death of Savita Halappanavar in an Irish hospital on October 28, 2012 brought thousands of Irish citizens, most of them born Catholics, to the streets in heart warming solidarity with the family of an unknown Indian. Halappanavar was denied an abortion though she was miscarrying, on grounds that it was illegal in the Catholic nation. She protested that she was not a Catholic and her husband pointed out that there was no chance of saving the foetus. Yet the doctors refused and did not shift her to neighbouring England; she suffered untold agony for a few days before death ended her misery.

Her tragedy shocked the world, especially Christians who bear the brunt of such unreason in many countries. The problem, which most Westerners do not realise, is a compact between church and polity, which privileges church ideology over the free choice of adults and erects barriers difficult for ordinary mortals to surmount.

Her case is doubly tragic because a person of one faith from another country was forcibly subjected to the religious prejudices of another faith in another country and allowed to suffer to death. This raises complex issues of religious morality, medical ethics, and international law, which call for deep introspection.

For the Vatican, which has for decades conducted Interfaith Dialogue, even as Christian scholars have penetrated non-Christian societies to understand their internal dynamics, this is the moment to show respect for the religious beliefs and practices of other world traditions. Western Christian clergy must clarify if their self-claimed mandate to convert the world to their faith includes imposing Christian law upon non-believers who fall into their custody in unforeseen circumstances.

To promote a larger understanding on the issue within and outside the country, a brief exposition of the multi-layered Hindu view on abortion may be in order. Hinduism or Sanatana Dharma as it is properly called upholds certain universal values, but it is not static or captive to absolutism. The tradition maintains that dharma must be understood in a time and space (place) context, else there is danger of distortion or perversion. The Sanatana Dharma is a formal religion and a living civilisation. Like a river, it flows through the ages, constantly replenishing its waters (contents) and altering its course, while appearing changeless (giving continuity). This dynamism has enabled Hindus to adapt to change without losing their sense of religious identity.

Dharma (religion) deems human life to be the highest form of life, which is attained after innumerable cycles of birth wherein the spirit evolves through densest matter towards ever higher forms of consciousness. Human birth is a unique gift, and gives the soul the opportunity to realise the Self and merge with the Atman and attain release from the cycle of birth and rebirth.

The question arises — if human birth is so critical to self-realisation, may we legitimately interfere with human birth? The answer lies in dharma's notion of life and death, which are seen as parts of a cycle and not as linear opposites. In the Hindu worldview, human birth is not a once-only occurrence but an incessant cycle that affords the individual the chance to negate the effects of bad karma and eventually neutralise both good and bad karma. Death is not the end of the story; nor is it equated with sin and suffering. Death is a new beginning.

Conception involves divine intervention. The ancient Charak Samhita states: The combination of sperm, ovum and life-principle (embodied soul) implanted in the womb is known as embryo. It is the aggregate of the five mahabhutas (elements) being the seat of consciousness which is regarded as the sixth constituent of embryo. This imparts the unborn life with spiritual continuity.

Thus, physical and spiritual Life enters the human embryo at the moment of conception itself; there is never a pure state of matter alone. The soul enters the body along with its past karma (which determines factors like choice of parents), and this gives each embryo its unique identity. The karmic inheritance invests the unborn with moral qualities and entitles it to care and protection. Having said this, it must be pointed out that Hindu thought rejects absolutism and can tackle a hierarchy of competing rights and values, a rare intellectual characteristic that has received less attention than it deserves.

Thus, in pregnancies where the mother risks grave injury or even death (as was the case with Halappanavar), the Charak Samhita clearly accords greater weightage to maternal life over that of the foetus. This remains the Hindu position to this day — because the adult human being is karmically more evolved than the unborn child, has existing obligations to family and society, and has far more at stake for her spiritual destiny. Simply put, the life and health of the mother and the integrity of her family weigh more than the esoteric demands of faith, even though the unborn life does not lose its intrinsic significance. Moreover, being incomplete, it will certainly be born again.

This is the well-considered position of Hindu tradition. The Susruta Samhita (another ancient treatise mainly devoted to surgery) recommends abortion in difficult cases where the foetus is irreparably damaged or defective and chances of normal delivery negligible. Susruta says that in such cases the surgeon should not wait for nature to take its course, but should intervene by performing craniotomic operations to remove the foetus.

As Irish society now grapples with the need to help pregnant girls, women with deformed babies, and victims of rape-pregnancy, the clergy and medical community would do well to take a cue from Hindu tradition. This profound civilisational view has influenced modern India's Medical Termination of Pregnancy Act, 1971, which offers virtually on-demand abortion to adult women.

Unsurprisingly, while the Vatican and Irish Church have maintained stoic silence over Halappanavar's death, in India, the Catholic-Christian Secular Forum has jumped into the fray, circulating gruesome pictures of aborted foetuses and vigorously proclaiming 'abortion is murder'. [42]

Disregarding the fact that Halappanavar was not a Catholic, CSF's Joseph Dias insists that her death "is hardly any justification for Vatican to change its doctrine into one to suit deviants from the faith". People who work abroad must follow the law of the land, he says, just as Indians expect foreigners to obey Indian law, as in the case of the Italian marines! A command performance, if ever there was one.

---

[42] Sandhya Jain (2012), "Faith is fine, but life is precious", the Pioneer, November 20, 2012

Beyond Yoga

Yogic lifestyle is more than just a technique or a daily exercise routine; it is a way of living and experiencing life to its fullest.

Yoga is the Sanskrit word for connection or union of the body, mind, emotions and soul. Over time, *yogis* have lent their interpretations, evolving new forms to fit various lifestyles. Of these, the ones that have gained popularity over the past few years are Ashtanga vinyasa yoga or power yoga, Iyenger yoga or instrument yoga, sahaj yoga or easy yoga, Sivananda yoga, dance yoga, gymnastic yoga and aqua yoga. These forms are diverse enough to allow an individual to choose the one that suits his/her personality type.

But more important is adopting the essence of *yogic* lifestyle, one that provides us the correct way to lead a life. If followed sincerely, it permeates deep into our consciousness and psyche and nourishes our body, mind and soul.

Early to bed, early to rise

Sleep is a rhythmic change in activity during which a state of withdrawal and relative unconsciousness occurs. *Yogis* know the trick of going to sleep voluntarily and wake up at the exact moment they had determined they would. It involves power and mind control that does not come easy to most of us. This is best known as Yoga Nidra and is effective for bringing the mind and body to a state of rest while the mind maintains awareness. Translated in the modern context, our lifestyle and creature comforts come in the way of attaining such a disciplined state. The only way we can get there perhaps is by following the basic tenets of nature.

For one, ancient Hindu wisdom believes in following the sun — to sleep at sundown and wake up at sunrise. The sun is symbolic of the ultimate victory over darkness (night). The Eastern philosophy believes in training and slowly gaining control over your sleep. By doing so, you automatically take your body and mind from lethargy to momentum. This pattern helps greatly in meditation — a state that takes us into deeper realms of consciousness and relaxes our being. The underlying idea is to shun forgetfulness and waft in that bliss of ultimate relaxation.

Eat fresh and on time

Stick to *shakahaari* or vegetarian food. This means consume only that which is pure, simple and natural. Light meals mean faster digestion and better assimilation of food. Only take care that your diet is balanced. An ideal food chart would contain vegetables and fruits for vitamins, legumes, lentils, grains and dairy products for proteins and rice and roots for carbohydrates.

Satvik food promotes clarity and calmness of mind. Ancient Hindu wisdom calls for a yogi to be an *alpahari* (one who eats half of his actual hunger). Science has it that your brain takes 20 minutes to register the food or glucose levels. So, eat half of what you really require. That way you'll not feel bloated and be active and fresh throughout the day.

It is equally important to know how and when to eat. Do not eat late at night. There should be a gap of at least two, preferably three hours, between supper and sleep.

Food should be freshly prepared and must be consumed with attention, respect and gratitude. Eat to live rather than live to eat. The attitude of the person preparing the food is of paramount importance. It is said that the mood of the cook permeates into the cooking. Food prepared with love and positive energy takes on that energy.

Breathe right

Yoga teaches us how to use lungs to their maximum capacity and how to control breath. Breathing should be deep, slow and rhythmic. This increases vitality and mental clarity.

The breathing practice or *pranayam* is the main tool of yoga. A balanced *prana* leads to balance endocrine functions and hormone secretions. By balancing the *prana* through exercises, one learns to align one's breath, thereby controlling thoughts and emotions. *Pranayam* helps calm our emotions and brings about serenity and equanimity in life. For instance, a woman is asked to control her breathing during labour in order to calm down and relax; sportsmen are trained to breathe in a certain way while playing and exercising. Likewise, in day-to-day life, we can deal with stress if we practise *pranayam* before leaving for work and after coming back. *Pranayam* like Bhastrika and Kapalbhati are especially designed to get rid of the excess baggage of memory, emotions and thoughts while Ujjai and Anulom vilom are designed for deep relaxation and are beneficial for blood pressure patients and pregnant women.

The art of meditation

To meditate is to concentrate and focus the mind on a particular point with undivided attention. It helps one conquer the subconscious, unconscious and conscious mind. Put differently, meditation is deep observation of one's body and its silent language — reading one's thoughts, emotions; sleep patterns, aches and pains.

In order that your mind can function with awareness,

one's thoughts must be balanced and positive. By abstaining from criticism (of oneself and others) and by being forgiving, we slowly train our mind to be positive, thereby bringing about a major change in our body language. Emotions are food for the soul. If one learns to differentiate between being compassionate, sensitive and being sentimental, we will find true peace within. This could take us from attachment to liberation, from possession and ownership to detachment.

In short, a yogic lifestyle works upon all the layers and nourishes one's soul with spiritual food. This wholesome approach to a better lifestyle will help us through our journey of life.[43]

Ethiopia

Fostering Husband's Involvement and Support in Ethiopia

A few months ago I wrote about a program that works to empower young woman in Guatemala by providing essential health, education, and social services to an underserved population. Today I'd like to highlight the flip side: a gender project that works with men in rural Ethiopia.

In Ethiopia, the lifetime risk of maternal death is 1 in 40 and the contraceptive prevalence rate is just 15 percent. HIV prevalence in the Amhara region is significant. The Addis Birhan (meaning "new light" in Amharic) program seeks to promote HIV prevention by changing attitudes and promoting equitable relationships through educating and engaging husbands in issues related to reproductive health, including HIV prevention, family planning, gender

---

[43] Exotica, the wellness and lifestyle magazine from The Pioneer Group / Krishna S Semwal, " Beyond Yoga", The Sunday Pioneer, July 31, 2011

violence, alcohol and drug abuse, and domestic responsibilities.

The program follows on the success of previous Population Council programs for vulnerable girls in Ethiopia, including married adolescents. As the programs for married girls became increasingly popular, demand for a support program arose from their husbands.

The curriculum spans roughly three months and was adapted for rural Ethiopia from previous materials from Population Council India, Engender health, and Promundo. Groups of married men attend meetings with trained male mentors on a weekly basis. Mentors range in age from 25 to 40 and must have at least six years of education. The meetings consist of 25 to 30 men and promote dialogue, self-exploration, and expression in a casual setting, and use pictures as teaching aids, as many of the participants cannot read.

The program continues to expand, recently to 11 new project sites where 33 male mentors were recruited and trained. Members range in age from 18 to 85 years, with the majority aged 25-39 years. Since Addis Birhan was established in 2008, nearly 30,000 men have participated.

Participants and their families have described changes resulting from participation in Addis Birhan, such as increased communication among couples and more two-way rather than directive dialogue. This is especially important for families as they discuss issues of family planning and make sexual and reproductive health choices together. Men report that they share what they have learned from the group meetings at home with their wives and children.

They also report that they have started to change the way they think about distribution of labor at home, with many men now undertaking traditionally female roles, such as fetching water. Many members reported that they changed risky behavior, such as drinking.[44]

Pakistan

Reproductive Health for Women in the Workplace

Across the developing world, women workers are a rising force in manufacturing industries, yet many of these women don't have access to adequate healthcare or knowledge of their health-related rights in the workplace. The HER project, founded by BSR (Business for Social Responsibility), is working to change that with a peer-driven health education initiative that focuses specifically on women workers in factories in Pakistan.

In Pakistan, women comprise the majority of the workforce in the manufacturing of textiles, home goods, and apparel. The need is staggering: In Pakistan, for example, the lifetime risk of maternal death is 1 in 93 and the contraceptive prevalence rate is just 30 percent. For many women, the workplace is the only venue where they can access reproductive and maternal health services. To address this need, The HER project began working in 2007 in Bangladesh, China, Egypt, India, Kenya, Pakistan, and Vietnam. Through a series of partnerships with 13 companies, 50 factories, local organizations, clinics, hospitals, and population health departments, BSR and its partners are working to give women the services and information they need to stay healthy.

---

[44] Mariko Rasmussen (2011), "Fostering Husbands' Involvement and Support in Ethiopia" Women Deliver, Democracy in Action. Org, June 20. 2011

Some of the major issues affecting the reproductive and maternal health of female workers are lack of family planning access, lack of knowledge about health-related rights, minimal understanding of HIV/AIDS prevention and pre- and post-natal care, and unhealthy personal hygiene behaviors during menstrual periods. The HER project curriculum addresses these issues through peer-led seminars.

At the Levi Strauss & Co. textile factory in Pakistan, nearly 72 percent of female workers had difficulty achieving production targets during their menstrual periods. During the health needs assessment conducted at the start of the program, the team revealed that not one female worker of the 3,567 in four factories was using menstrual pads. Seventy-five percent of female workers had never seen a condom before and only 30 percent of the women knew the importance of prenatal nutrition and getting a tetanus toxoid immunization.

In a partnership with Aga Khan University's Department of Community Health Science, Aahung, (a sexual and reproductive rights organization in Karachi, Pakistan), the Family Planning Association of Pakistan, Green Star Social Marketing, and Ipas, Levi Strauss and the HERproject team developed trainings in pre-natal nutrition, health-related rights, HIV/AIDS, family planning, and domestic violence Workers learned about their rights to be assigned easier duties during pregnancy, to go on maternity leave and to access on-site factory childcare. The women in all four factories were also linked directly with health service providers and menstrual products.

What were the results? After the 18-month training, the HER project team tracked a number of successes:

(a) Female worker absenteeism was 11 percent lower;
(b) Women worked an average 2.5 hours more per month during their menstrual periods;
(c) Knowledge of essential immunizations, pre- and post-natal care increased from 30 to 86 percent among female workers;
(d) Women reported better work-manager relations because the workers felt valued by the company and could better communicate with their managers; and
(e) The company experienced increased interest and recruitment from the local community due to their improved reputation for workplace health and welfare.

The HER project continues to be a leader in women's workplace health initiatives spreading the message that companies can do business while doing good, and that investing in women is a sure path to a better world.[45]

Yemen:

Community educators change perceptions of child marriage

Nearly one-half or 48 percent of girls in Yemen are married by the age of 18 years old, with 14 percent married by the time they turn 15 years old. In addition, it is common for girls in remote areas to be betrothed as young as 9 years old and for 57 percent of girls living in poverty to be married age 18.

Institutionalized child marriage "deprives young girls of a childhood, enhances their risk of domestic abuse, and entraps them in a cycle of abuse," according to USAID. The health consequences are severe and long lasting for girls and their babies. Child marriage

---

45 Madeline Taskier (2011), "Reproductive Health for Women in the Workplace Women Deliver", Democracy in Action. Org, June 30. 2011

increases the prevalence of depression, sexually transmitted infection, cervical cancer, obstetric fistulas, and maternal mortality among girls as well as the likelihood of premature birth and infant death. To prevent child marriage and the negative impact it has on communities, USAID in 2009 partnered with the Yemeni Women's Union to launch the Safe Age of Marriage program. The pilot program has educated more than 40 community educators and leaders to help alter social norms about child marriage and to promote girls' education. Not only does education improve girls' abilities and confidence, keeping girls in school longer is one of the most effective ways for avoiding child marriage.

Specifically, community leaders come from and work in the isolated and mountainous Al Sawd and Al Soodah districts in Amran province. Amran has some of the worst child marriage and early birth levels in the country, with 71 percent of mothers and 21 percent of fathers married by age 18. The community educators lead health affairs, movie screenings, plays, quiz shows, health and religious lectures, and mobile health visits. During these awareness-raising sessions, the educators discuss the causes of child marriages in Yemen, including socio-cultural reasons, such as tribal customs, and economic factors, such as minimizing dowries.

These sessions especially focuses on the concept of "model families," which both delay their daughters' marriages and also educate them through the twelfth grade. The concept has gained such popularity that the governor of Amran recognized twelve families, who are protecting their daughters as well as increasing their opportunities.

Community educators have reached 29,000 people and been critical in preventing 53 girl-child and 26 boy-child marriage in the first year of the program. A household survey of 400 families in the program area also suggests that the peak age marriage for girls has increased from 14 years old to 18 years old in the two regions.

As part of the effort, the Ministry of Endowment and Guidance in Amran has called on all religious leaders to speak about the negative impact of child marriages during sermons. In addition the entire Al Soodah community has taken an oath against participating in child marriages, defined as involving girls and boys younger than 18 years old. Yemen currently has no law declaring a minimum age of marriage.

Community educators and traditional leaders continue to be instrumental in spreading information and acting as role models about child marriage. According to USAID Senior Gender Adviser Leah Freij, one community educator is changing perceptions not only through her words but her actions of being a married woman, who has completed college with her husband and family's support. Freij adds, "Girls used to think you had to choose between an education and marriage. Now they see they can have both."[46]

Health of Girls and Women

GBC Health, formerly known as the Global Business Coalition on HIV/AIDS, Tuberculosis, and Malaria, announced that it will expand its mission to a broader public health mandate, including a focus on girls' and women's health, education, and empowerment. The announcement came during the GBC Health 10th Anniversary Conference held in New York, NY on June 1-2, 2011. For more than a decade, GBC Health has been working to engage the private sector in the fight against HIV/AIDS, tuberculosis, and malaria, to increase the number of corporate health programs,

---

[46] Rati Bishnoi (2011), "Community educators change perceptions of child marriage" Women Deliver, Democracy in Action. Org, June 30. 2011

and to improve partnerships with civil society and governments. And now, GBC Health will not only take on a new name, but it will take on new responsibility in the fight for better global health.

In fact, girls' and women's health, education, and empowerment were important and prominent themes at the conference. Many of the speakers spoke about how health, including girls' and women's health, is the anchor of corporate social responsibility, about the importance of engaging the private sector in global health issues, about the power of business to affect social change, and about how now is the time for companies to step up to the plate and take action. No matter what the motivation—a workforce made up of mostly women or a primarily female-consumer base—it is clear that many companies are engaged, or are ready to be engaged, in issues affecting girls and women.

Mark Kramer refers to a company's policies and operating practices that enhance its competitiveness while simultaneously advancing the economic and social conditions in the communities in which it works. In short, shared value means doing business and doing good—terms that are no longer mutually exclusive. And, many companies, like GE and Anglo American, are working to adopt and implement this concept into their business and to use it to address some of the world's most pressing global health issues.[47]

Women Deliver welcomes the input and excitement of these corporate partners to join the fight for girls and women around the world. We cannot change the world alone, and we need all partners, from the public to private sectors and from local to global

[47] Kristin Rosella (2011), "The Power of Business to Impact the Health of Girls and Women" Women Deliver, Democracy in Action. Org, June 30. 2011

organizations, to come together under the same message: Invest in women – it pays. Companies are recognizing that investing in girls and women is not only the right thing to do, it is smart business.

Mothers Facing Famine in Horn of Africa

The United Nations Population Fund (UNFPA) is intensifying its efforts to assist mothers affected by famine and displacement in the Horn of Africa.

UNFPA Executive Director Dr. Babatunde Osotimehin said in an agency release, "We call upon the international community to urgently look after the unique needs of pregnant women and mothers whose families' survival are particularly at risk."

After two poor rainy seasons, the east African region is experiencing one of the worst droughts since 1950 and 1951, according to the U.N.'s Food and Agriculture Organization. The famine has already killed tens of thousands of people and risks having long-lasting damage on a generation of children, the U.N.'s World Food Program states. Hunger and exhaustion can cause complications during pregnancy and childbirth and increase the risk of maternal deaths. Poor nutrition can also cause infant illness, disabilities, and even death. In addition to the wide-spread famine, the military group al-Shabab is blocking the World Food Program from providing emergency food to starving people.

With 80 percent of refugees in the region being women and children, UNFPA is focusing on caring for pregnant women and lactating mothers. The agency is distributing reproductive health care supplies, medical equipment, and 3,500 "dignity kits" to women in famine-affected areas. Dignity kits are designed to meet women's unique needs and include hygiene items such as sanitary pads, underwear and soap. They also include headscarves to ensure that women can travel in public to food distribution centers while still abiding by the strict dress code for women in Somalia.

Sexual violence and exploitation are a very real danger for women and girls traveling to and living in refugee settlements, such as Dabaab refugee settlement in Kenya. The camp has a population of nearly 380,000 people, making it the largest refugee settlement in the world. "While a short-term and immediate response is urgently needed," explained Osotimehin, "UNFPA is working on a strategy for long-term support to the region."[48]

MALI

Family Planning and Child Immunizations

In Mali, the lifetime risk of maternal death is 1 in 22 and the national contraceptive prevalence rate (CPR) is just 8.2 percent. For women living in Mali, especially the capital, Bamako, the CPR has decreased in the last ten years from 19 to 16 percent. Unmet need for family planning is most significant among new mothers just after childbirth at 79 percent. The Family Planning Child Immunization Program seeks to link new mothers in Bamako with family planning counseling, services, and long-acting methods while they get their new babies immunized. The program puts emphasis on reaching postpartum women to encourage birth spacing.

In 2009, this program was born out of Population Services International (PSI/Mali), which aimed to expand its existing family planning programs to include promotion and delivery of long-acting contraceptive methods. PSI/Mali saw a unique opportunity to catch its target audience at immunization clinics where new mothers were

48 Rati Bishnoi, Special Projects Intern, July 26th, 2011

regularly bringing their babies. Fortunately, the waiting area where mothers spent hours waiting for a five minute immunization appointment proved to be an ideal spot for presentations, counseling, and service provision.

Long-acting reversible contraception (LARC) has many benefits for women. Compared to oral contraceptives (a short acting method), LARC has significantly lower unintended pregnancy rates associated with one year of use (0.8 percent compared with 8 percent). A LARC, such as an intrauterine device (IUD) or a contraceptive implant, requires little to no action from the woman for extended periods of time—up to 5 years for implants and 12 for IUDs. These methods are generally hidden on the body which allows women to keep their contraceptive use private. Among Malian woman, LARC use is less than 1 percent.

The program operates in series of events that are scheduled during immunization days at local clinics to ensure maximum turnout of postpartum women. Starting in 5 out of 53 private ProFam clinics in Bamako, PSI midwives and clinic staff conduct a 30-45 minute presentation on the importance of family planning, maternal and child health for those mothers waiting to get their children immunized.

After the presentation, the midwives engage the women in a Q&A period, dispelling myths and concerns about contraceptives and long-acting methods. Women who are interested in receiving family planning are able to do so on site while they wait for their baby to be immunized. Women who opt into the program receive counseling, a physical exam to determine eligibility, and the application of a long-acting method. PSI/Mali provides an implant or IUD at a subsidized rate of about $1 (500 CFA).

Since its inception, the family planning presentation has reached 35,800 women in the clinics, resulting in 20% of the women selecting long-acting methods. In 2009 alone, the program provided 3,997 implants and IUDs to women attending the clinics. The projections for 2010 and 2011 are higher as PSI/Mali has expanded to program to include events days at public sector clinics.[49]

NIGERIA

Preventing Mother-to-Child Transmission of HIV

When I put myself in their shoes, I imagine one of the most difficult feelings experienced by any one of the 200, 000 Nigerian pregnant women living with HIV is knowing that the deadly virus could be transmitted to their child without the right care.

An estimated 56,000 infants of the 85,450 at-risk infants contract HIV through mother-to-child transmission annually. HIV can be transmitted to a child during pregnancy, delivery, or breastfeeding. Combinations of using antiretroviral and other drugs, safe infant feeding practices, and other interventions, however, can help stop the spread.

The state of maternal health in Nigeria further complicates mothers' abilities to protect their children from contracting HIV. Only 58 percent of pregnant women received any antenatal care and 39 percent had deliveries assisted by skilled birth attendants in 2008. Unsurprisingly, it is often poor and rural women who receive the least—if any—care. As a result, Nigeria has one of the highest maternal mortality rates in the world (840 deaths for every

---

[49] Madelina Taskier (2011), "Celebrate Solutions: For New Moms, Linking Long-Acting Family Planning with Child Immunizations", Partnership Coordinator at Women Deliver, July 25th, 2011

100,000 live births) and fails at preventing 50,000 maternal deaths annually.

More pregnant women living with HIV are obtaining services that could help prevent transmission and make them healthier mothers after delivery. The number of health care centers offering services to prevent mother-to-child transmission has increased from 67 in 2004 to 684 in 2010. These health care centers seek to provide voluntary counseling and testing, offer antiretroviral treatment, advise on infant feeding options, and safe deliveries, although quality remains an issue. According to a government survey, the number of pregnant women counseled and tested from HIV has also grown from 18,554 in 2010 to 1.7 million in 2010.

Despite this expansion in coverage, antiretrovirals to prevent transmission reached only 22 percent of pregnant women with HIV in 2009—a long way from the government's goal of ensuring that 80 percent of all eligible women and men and children receive antiretroviral treatment by 2015. Antiretroviral treatment keeps HIV or AIDS in the body at a low level and can keep a person from becoming ill for many years if a treatment regimen of taking a combination of drugs daily is followed closely. Adhering to an antiretroviral treatment regimen can help a mother keep her immune system from weakening.

I believe Nigeria needs to do better and reach more pregnant women and mothers living with HIV. I hope the recent shift in government will help improve maternal health services for all women in my country.[50]

---

[50] Toyin Ajao (2011), "Local Perspectives: Preventing Mother-to-Child Transmission of HIV in Nigeria", Winner of Women Bloggers Deliver Contest, July 14, 2011

MOROCCO

Reduction of Maternal Mortality in Morocco

The Moroccan Ministry of Health last week hosted a scientific meeting to share lessons on its success in reducing maternal mortality by 60 percent since 1990—a success that has won it the distinction of being "one of a small group of countries 'on track' to achieve MDG 5 by 2015," according to UNFPA.

The meeting was held in Rabat from June 29 to July 1 and convened national and regional researchers, policymakers, and administrators, including representatives from Tunisia, Djibouti, Palestine, Egypt, Sudan, Morocco, and Yemen.

At the meeting, leaders in the maternal health field where able to explore the Moroccan government's multi-sectoral and "whole-of health-systems" approach that has helped make the right of safe motherhood a reality for increasing numbers of Moroccan women. Currently, the maternal mortality ratio in Morocco is estimated at 112 deaths per 100,000 live births.

Although there have been some efforts to improve maternal and child health since the 1970s, maternal mortality became a top priority in political discourse in 2008. In the same year, the Minister of Health appointed a commission charged with accelerating the reduction of maternal mortality and undertook several key measures to improve the functioning of the health care system for obstetric and neonatal emergencies. The commission brought together the academic community, professional associations, and public health officials and was backed by 1.4 billion dirham (U.S. $1 = 8 dirham) across five years.

The commission's national strategy focused on three intervention areas:

(a) Reducing physical and financial barriers to emergency obstetric care;
(b) Improving the quality of care; and
(c) Improving governance.

To reduce barriers to access and improve the availability of qualified personnel, policymakers removed fees for all emergency obstetric care, including caesarean sections, and newborn care, providing obstetric ambulances for women in rural areas, increasing the training of doctors and midwives, offering ongoing training for existing providers, and using mobile medic units to identify and manage high-risk pregnancies in rural areas.

The commission also used nearly 30 percent of its budget on upgrading the physical equipment of maternity hospitals. An audit of all maternal care facilities across Morocco had shown that only 28 percent of 90 maternal hospitals and 518 health centers with maternity units provided the basic functions of emergency obstetric and neonatal care. Now, these facilities offer "privacy, respect, and comfort" and allow mothers to receive 48 hours of mandatory post-partum care and families members can stay in reception and waiting areas.

More midwives, obstetrician-gynecologists, and anesthetists have also been trained under the commission's plan. For example, midwifery students have increased from 168 in 2007 to 530 in 2010. In addition, continuing education for health care providers has included an annual one-week course on managing labor and delivery complications for midwives and general practitioners, twice yearly visits by obstetricians to coach midwives in health centers, and refresher courses on new World Health Organization clinical guidelines.

In addition, a national maternal mortality surveillance system for maternal deaths has been established to monitor progress. The system uses a confidential inquiry to track all maternal deaths irrespective of where they occur and requires the reporting of deaths of women ranging from 15 years old to 49 years old. In just the course of one year, the system has already provided valuable information. For example, in 2009, the system captured data on 3,814 deaths of women aged 15 to 49 years old, 436 of which were maternal deaths. A total of 313 maternal deaths were analyzed and showed the main causes of death to be post-partum hemorrhage (33 percent), pre-clampsia and eclampsia (18 percent), infection (8 percent), and uterine rupture (7 percent). The analysis also showed that 77 percent of these deaths could have been prevented with timely access to care (42 percent) and appropriate treatment (44 percent).

More than 800 community liaison volunteers currently work with communities to raise awareness of the benefits of delivering in health care facilities and connect community members to midwives at birthing homes, ambulances, and hospitals. These advocacy efforts and better services have helped the proportion of births attended by skilled personnel rise from 61 percent in 2004 to 83 percent in 2009. According to UNFPA, Morocco's success shows that dramatic reduction in maternal mortality can be achieved within a decade. In particular, lessons learned from Morocco's experience show that strong political engagement, mobilizing funding, and collaboration can help improve an entire health system.[51]

God of awful things

In the name of God, hapless girls are still being made to become devadasis, which in stark terms means being raped by the priests, secretly auctioned to

---

[51] Rati Bishnoi (2011), " Celebrate Solutions: Accelerating the Reduction of Maternal Mortality in Morocco" Special Projects Intern at Women Deliver, July 5th, 2011

brothels and finally dying of AIDS. A few of these unfortunate women who died everyday of their life for a farce called service of the God.

I was nine when I got married to my village deity Yellamma. The mahajan, after presenting me with the mangalsutra, tied me to a pole near the temple where worshippers could come and pay obeisance. At night, I was taken to the big kothis where the men of the house would take turns in raping me. At first it used to hurt and I would bleed profusely. But after a few nights, I became used to the pain. When I was 19, I was taken to a city and handed over to a madam who runs a brothel. Since then, my life has only revolved around customers and the money I made. I have two children. I have told them that they are children of God," Lakhmiamma, who is now in her 50s, recalls how she was forced to become a jogini by her parents.

Like Amma, many lower caste girls in the country are forced to go through the horrific fate. "Often upper caste families influence the farmers (from lower castes) to dedicate their daughters to them in the name of God. The landlord suggests that the girl can continue serving his family and the local goddess throughout her life and offers `2,000 to `3,000 to the father for this arrangement.

Some poor families force their physically challenged girls to become joginis. Some families offer their eldest daughter. When a girl has copper-coloured hair, which is due to malnutrition, the villagers believe that she is born to be a jogini. In many areas, a sick baby girl is abandoned outside a temple in the night. If she is still alive in the morning, the family believes she is born for the goddess," Grace Nirmala tells you, adding that according to an estimate by Aashray, her home for such distraught women, there are about 27,000 joginis in Andhra Pradesh today.

"What is more painful is the self-perception of these girls. They believe they are tender buds meant for God. It is the ultimate offering in worship. And when they grow up, they rarely mingle with outsiders, so the joginis do not perceive sex work as prostitution but as service to society," says Grace.

In Andhra Pradesh alone, 95 per cent of the joginis belong to the Scheduled Castes (Mala and Madiga) and Scheduled Tribes and a small percentage to the Backward Castes like Telaga and Chakali. The joginis are concentrated in the districts of Chittoor, Anantapur, Nellore, Prakasham, Warangal, Mahboobnagar and Nizamabad.

"It is basically feared of diseases, curses and superstition that force parents to dedicate their daughters to the goddess. A Devadasi is not allowed to marry, but is expected to satisfy the lust of any man, for, that is her religious duty. Hundreds of young women have been devastated by a system that forces them into prostitution. The children of devadasies have no one they can call father," Asha Triplani Patnaik, another activist who has started a home for the children of these women in Odisha, tells you. At present, there are over 50 children and 35 women who have taken shelter at Jai Kalia, Patnaik's initiative in Puri.

Fiftyseven-year-old Purivamma from Nellore got a second lease of life when she was bought to Ashray earlier this year. "I had a very lavish marriage ceremony and it was the happiest day for my family. I was getting married to goddess Yellamma and that was supposed to be the most auspicious wedding. There was food for everyone. When the senior jogini tied that mangalsutra around my neck I was scared. In a few weeks time I was asked to go to the home of the head priest to perform some ritual to appease the gods. Villagers believed that my communion with the priest would ward off a deadly disease, which had struck my village. Mahajana raped me that night and for the rest of the week. But when this did not have any impact and the disease started spreading like wild fire, I was beaten up by priests in the temple premises. They thought I had angered the Lord. When I fainted, they left me alone. The next day I woke up at this ashram in the city," Purviamma, a jogini at 12, tells you her story amid hysteria.

Purviamma has a daughter whom she wants to dedicate to the service of the local deity. "We are born to be dasis. We are anyways not treated any better. At least as a dasi my daughter will get some respect from villagers," Purviamma says.

While the Government has a 1988 Jogini Abolition Act in place, activists rubbish it as toothless. "The Act is there, but it is not a very stringent one. According to this Act, those found encouraging the practice will be punished. But how can you punish the entire community, including political heads of the village and the parents of the girl? Villagers regard this as a ritual that must be carried out to appease the Gods. And the parents of the girl comply willingly, as a result of which these cases don't even get registered. We are demanding multiple developments. The Government has to see everything, their income etc. If we implement the schemes, the girls will come out of the vicious system. The village administration, political parties and the sarpanch (head of a Gram Panchayat) should bear the responsibilities of doing away with this heinous ritual," Grace tells you.

For other activists, it is the lawmaker who abuses the system. "The law works to the disadvantage of women because it criminalizes their actions and not the actions of their patrons. The police sometimes go as far as to demand sex as bribe. They will threaten to file charges under the act if the woman rebuffs them. Their perceived status in society, as women who are supposed to serve men sexually, also makes it more difficult for the devadasis to approach the police for help. When a devadasi is raped, it is not considered rape. She can be had by any man, any time," Aparna Singhdeo, co-founder for Jai Kalia, says.

The devadasi practice is rampant in Andhra Pradesh and Karnataka as also in some temples in Maharashtra and Orissa. Once dedicated, the girl can't get married, is forced to become a prostitute to serve the upper castes and eventually auctioned to an urban brothel.

The age-old practice continues to legitimise sexual violence and discrimination that have come to signify the intersection between caste and gender.

"The patrons of the devadasis are generally from higher castes because those from the devadasis' own castes cannot afford the rituals. In earlier days, the patron kept these devadasis at home and the number of girls used to be a yardstick of the status of that man. This system of patronage has given way to commercial prostitution in cities," Patnaik explains

"When I was pregnant with Raju's child, he refused to marry me. Instead, he offered me a solution — he wanted me to abort the child and dedicate my life to the deity at a local temple. He promised to continue his relationship with me if I became a devadasi. The next day I hung a mangalsutra around my neck and declared to the villagers that I was married to God. I was expecting Raju to fulfill his promise and spend the rest of his life with me. Instead, he introduced me to many landlords in our village and the nearby ones. In the name of service to God, I was made to satisfy their sexual desires. I had spent 12 years of my life with other men, serving as their object of pleasure. I have had to undergo seven abortions," recalls Meera of Pathanipata village near Jajpur district in Orissa.

Meera is 44-years-old now and childless. She was rescued from her village earlier this year and still has hoped that Raju will be back. "Meera's condition was unstable when we found her. She had not been fed properly. She was paid a pittance as compensation, but her parents feel proud that she has served the Gods. They have been blessed with better farm produce and they are leading a better life," Patnaik tells you with a hint of sarcasm.

In 1992, the Karnataka Government passed the Karnataka Devadasi (Prohibition of Dedication) Act, which called for their rehabilitation. Like many laws aimed at protecting women and lower castes, the Act suffered from lack of enforcement. Moreover, as local activists ask, when the cops themselves are known to use devadasis for their sexual fantasies, how will the Act be implemented?

In September 2010, Radhamayee was rescued from the Khandoba temples premises in North Karnataka. "I will never let my children go through what I did. I was forced to marry the deity because my parents wanted a son to take their legacy forward. My mother thought, by sacrificing me to the service of God, she will be blessed with a son. I had been a jogini for 20 years and every day was killing. Now, I don't remember anything that I went through. I can barely recognise my son. He is taken care of by the NGO members," she tells you. Radhamayee was brought to Pannah a rehabilitative NGO that works for the betterment of joginis in Mangalore.

Activists involved in the Dalit women's emancipation movements explain that the nexus between caste and forced prostitution is strong and that the devadasi system is no exception. Most Indian girls and women in India's urban brothels come from lower-caste, tribal, or minority communities. Like other forms of violence against women, ritualised prostitution, activists believe, is a system "designed to kill whatever vestige of self-respect the lower castes have in order to subjugate them and keep them underprivileged."

Ram Dayal, member of the Centre for Justice and Peace says: "Thousands of untouchable girls (between 6 and 8 years) are forced to become maidens of God. They are taken from their families, never to see them again. They are later raped by the priest and auctioned secretly into prostitution and ultimately die from AIDS. According to current statistics, 5,000 to 15,000 girls are auctioned secretly every year."And, we are in the 21st century with ambitions to become superpower!

The bad and worse of system

The eldest woman of the devadasi community ties the mangalsutra. In some ceremonies, the girl is made to march to the temple. The audience welcomes her with garlands and sweets. The mahajana then performs a havan. Vows are recited and the girl is declared wedded to the Lord.

Every Tuesday and Friday, joginis are required to go around the village, carrying a slate in their hands, which says that they are slaves of the Lord and beg for food. During weddings, death ceremonies and religious fairs, joginis are invited to bless the event. They are made to keep a fast when there is a death in a particular family. During a wedding, they walk along with the groom and bride around the pandal.

Polepally jatara (falr): A jogini is made to sit in a cradle hung to a hydraulic crane. As the cradle rotates, she throws flowers and turmeric powder over the crowd below. The cradle rotates so fast that the women very often land up with fractured ribs and many have not survived the ordeal.

Once the girls attain puberty, they are trained to become courtesans, catering to villagers. The girls undergo an elaborate ceremony at which liquor flows freely and some influential villagers initiate them into the profession.[52]

World Bank Evaluation Report

In a newly released evaluative report[53], the International Planned Parenthood Federation commends the World Bank for its commitment to sexual and reproductive health as shown through its implementation of the first year of the Reproductive Health Action Plan. However, it also calls on the bank to more closely monitor reproductive health (RH) indicators and increase collaboration with countries to better integrate RH into health systems strengthening programs and national policies.

The Scorecard: Monitoring, Evaluating the Implementation of the World Bank's Reproductive Health Action Plan 2010 - 2015 assesses the first year of the action plan, which focuses on reducing high fertility, improving pregnancy outcomes, and reducing sexually transmitted diseases. The plan also outlines the activities the bank will take to help countries borrowing from the International Development Association (IDA) and the International Bank for Reconstruction and Development (IBRD) improve reproductive health outcomes. The scorecard is part of an ongoing effort to monitor the plan's progress and was conducted in collaboration with reproductive health experts from the bank's Health, Nutrition, and Population division.

---

[52] Deebashree Mohanty (2011), " God of awful things", the Sunday Pioneer, August 28, 2011

[53] IPPF Releases One-Year Evaluation of World Bank's Reproductive Health Action Plan, July 19th, 2011

Recommendations for further integrating sexual and reproductive health into the policy, programming, and lending including having the Bank:

(a) Align the action plan's reproductive health indicators with those in existing, high-level frameworks, such as the health-related Millennium development Goals and the Global Strategy for Women's and Children's Health
(b) Support the goals of regional policy frameworks, such as the Maputo Program of Action
(c) Ensure that the action plan is used to shape health systems strengthening programs
(d) Advocate with national policy makers to include the action plan's indicators in Country Assistance Strategies, which seek to focus World Bank development support for all borrowing countries
(e) Report regularly on the action plan's overall and regional progress
(f) Ensure "policy coherence" on reproductive health across the World Bank

Conclusion

The government should prioritise to start 'Health Clubs for Women' in each government hospitals, CD Blocks, Panchayats (elected body in a group of villages) to look after ailing women and distribute medicines and medical aid and advices to the patients.

In each government hospitals three rooms should be provided for Homeopathic medicines, Ayurvedic medicines (Medicines prepared from plants, seeds or leaves) and for physical fitness training in YOGA. There are doctors or specialists in these categories. All rural hospitals should be updated and full-fledged. Red Cross vehicles should be provided for mobility of delivery patients at a cost.

Doctors' ratio to total population should be looked into. Hence, more number of medical colleges should be created by the government. The states need more doctors, medical advices and right medicines.

Crimes against women can be linked with falling gender ratio of women. Hence, female infanticide must be treated at par with homicide. Doctors indulged in 'abortion of girl foetuses' must be booked for criminal activity.

Gender crimes are caused because all TV serials, Cinema and advertisements of news papers advertise on beautiful picture of beautiful heroines.

Women health cannot be improved unless their economy improves and they get their proper diet and live in peace. Better health of of all people would bring 'Peace to all'.

However, it is not desirable to award reservations for women in elections for Parliament, Assembly or Senate. Let they prove their merit and efficiency as political leaders in Elections.

The NGOs associated in health camps, rural health awareness and blood group camps are doing more business than services. The NGOs are also cheating the donors, governments and the patients which are associated with 'women welfare schemes'. If the governments are corrupt and managed by corrupt officials, all government programs and activities would be paralyzed.

There should not be 'quota system' in service sector for women, tribals and Scheduled castes in India. The Constitution should be amended that all voters have equal rights in the country.

+++++

Chapter V

WOMEN AS AMBASSADORS OF PEACE

While I know myself as a creation of God, I am also obligated to realize and remember that everyone else and everything else are also God's creation. --- Maya Angelou

The Nobel Peace Prizes at their best set before us an array of great human spirits. The nine women Prizewinners clearly belong in this list. They come from a variety of backgrounds and represent a variety of forms of peace making.

The earliest of these heroines of peace was the Austrian baroness who inspired the Prize, while the most recent was the Indian from Guatemala who rose to leadership overcoming poverty and oppression. They include the woman regarded as the greatest of her generation in the United States; the scholar and reformer who was the acknowledged intellectual leader of the American peace movement; two Northern Irish advocates of nonviolence who made a dramatic effort to resolve the longstanding violent conflict in their land; a saintly missionary working in the slums of Calcutta; a Swedish social reformer who became a cabinet minister and ambassador; and a Burmese intellectual who led the opposition to a brutal military dictatorship.

They were not only of different nationalities and different classes, but also of different faiths; among them were Catholics and freethinkers, a Buddhist and a Quaker. They worked against war in peace societies and in political life, as humanitarians and defenders of human rights. This small group of nine Laureates represents the diverse paths to peace, which the Norwegian Nobel committees have recognized over the years. But they are most interesting in themselves; each has a fascinating story to tell.

Let us consider the lives and peace efforts of these nine laureates, picturing them as the members of the Nobel Committee described them in presenting them with their prizes at the award ceremonies. Thereafter we shall reflect on what, if anything they had in common. Moreover, the contributions of other women, the wives and mothers of other Nobel laureates who won the Prize also need mention.

In this chapter topics like Baroness Bertha Von Suffer, Jane Addams, Emily Greene Bakh, Betty Williams and Mairead Corrigan, Mother Teresa, Alva Mydral, Aung San Suu Kyi, Rigoberts Menchu Tum, Ms. Jody Williams, Shriin Ebadi, List of Womem Nobel Peace Prize laureates are included as they are equally capable as the opposite male people have achieved laurels in life. Women are the real ambassadors of peace. Their role in 'World Peace' assumes more importance in the Twenty-first century.

Baroness Bertha von Suttner (1905)

It is all the more remarkable that Baroness von Suttner won an international reputation at the beginning of the twentieth century. On a lecture tour of the United States in 1904 she was even received at the White House by President Theodore Roosevelt.

Not the least of her achievements was her break with the military and aristocratic traditions of her family, first by deciding to earn her living as a governess and later by writing the anti-war novel Die Waffen Nieder (Lay down Your Arms), which brought her into the peace movement. Eloping with the brother of the young ladies she was tutoring and going off with him to the Caucasus to become a writer was also not quite what a well-bred countess was expected to do.

The Baroness was not able to come to Norway when her prize was announced in 1905 on the traditional day, December 10, and there was no presentation speech. The following April, she was introduced by Bjørnstjerne Bjørnson who spoke of her "real influence on the growth of the peace movement and how in one of the most militaristic countries of Europe she had continued to cry, "Down with arms." Although laughed at first, her words received a hearing because a person of noble character uttered them and because they proclaimed humanity's greatest cause.

Jane Addams (1931)

The Norwegian Nobel Committee had waited so long to give the Prize to Jane Addams, that she was ill and unable to go to the award ceremony or to come later to present a Nobel lecture. In fact, on the very day of the award, December 10, 1931, she was being admitted to the hospital in Baltimore.

Jane Addams had opposed the First World War. She held fast to the ideal of peace even during the difficult hours when other considerations and interests obscured it from her compatriots and drove them into the conflict. Toiling for peace during the war and for a true peace afterward, she spoke for the pacifist women of the world. She continued to lead the Women's International League for Peace and Freedom. Even when her views were at odds with public opinion, she never gave in, and in the end she regained the place of honors she had had before in the hearts of her people. She was the greatest woman who ever lived.

Addams herself wrote that as a life-giver and a life-nurturer, woman has a special feeling about war and peace. She combined all the best feminine qualities, which would help us to develop peace on earth. She possessed the highest and purest moral standards of society. Women have a special role as peacemakers with love and warm maternal feeling which renders murder and war so hateful to every woman.

Without superlatives, perceptive observers, in whose hearts Addams may not have lost a place of honor, have given her the highest praise. She inhabited reality and she was not only good, but also great.

Emily Greene Balch (1946)

Emily Greene Balch was a colleague of Jane Addams' in the effort to stop the First World War, her partner in the work of WILPF, and successor as its leader. In 1946 she herself shared a prize with the YMCA leader, John Mott. It came to her as the result of a successful campaign organized at the request of WILPF by its member, Mercedes Randall, who did a remarkable job of bringing Balch's indisputable qualifications before the Nobel committee and securing a large number of prominent supporters.

Committee Chairman Gunnar Jahn gave a far fuller description of Balch's activities than Koht had devoted to Addams. He told of her landmark research on Slav immigrants to the U.S., of her twenty-year teaching of social economics at Wellesley College, which ended when she was dismissed because of her pacifist activities during World War I. In her next career, she was at the center of WILPF's international work, serving for a time as its secretary-general in the Geneva headquarters, and continuing to be a familiar figure at the League of Nations.

Jahn was impressed with her practicality, her effort to improve international political relations by promoting international cooperation in other fields, and by her control of the facts in all her proposals. As an example he referred to her work to secure the withdrawal of the U. S. troops from Haiti in 1926 after eleven years of occupation. She went to Haiti with a delegation, showed great skill in investigating the situation, wrote most of the report, and fought to get the recommendations accepted by the government. Eventually they were all carried out and the troops withdrawn.

Jahn referred to Balch's difficult decision in World War II, as an absolute pacifist who had joined the Quakers, to support the U.S. war effort to vanquish the evil, which Hitlerism represented. She could not be unaffected by the fate of her WILPF colleagues and Jewish friends. Jahn commended Balch for her gradualism, as compared with the Utopianism of less patient peace workers.

She continued to develop imaginative proposals for slow international progress through functional cooperation and came to be regarded by American peace activists as their intellectual leader.

Betty Williams and Mairead Corrigan (1977)

When Egil Aarvik, vice-chairman of the committee presented the postponed 1976 prize to Betty Williams and Mairead Corrigan in 1977, he began his speech with a graphic description of the tragic accident that had occurred the previous August on a street in Belfast in Northern Ireland. A car out of control, its driver an Irish Republican Army (IRA) gunman shot dead fleeing from British soldiers, smashed into a family out for a walk. Two of the children were killed outright, the third was mortally injured, and the mother critically injured.

This senseless killing of innocent children produced a wave of revulsion against the violence which had been sweeping Northern Ireland, with Catholic IRA members using murder and terror to drive out the British, Protestant extremists doing the same in response, and many innocent victims killed as a consequence. Betty Williams, a housewife who came upon the scene after she heard the shot, and Mairead Corrigan, the young aunt of the dead children, led the movement. Aarvik told how the two women led marches in which Protestants and Catholics walked together in demonstrations for peace and against violence. That so many people in Northern Ireland had recognized that violence couldn't bring social justice. Aarvik declared:

This could be the dawn of a new day bringing lasting peace to the sorely tried people of Ulster.

Williams and Corrigan "have shown us what ordinary people can do to promote peace." They had the courage to take the first step. "They did so in the name of humanity and love of their neighbour; someone had to start forgiving. Love of one's neighbor is one of the foundation stones of the humanism on which our western civilization is built."

It is vitally important that it "should shine forth when hatred and revenge threaten to dominate." Theirs was "a courageous unselfish act that proved an inspiration to thousands that lit a light in the darkness..."

Unfortunately, that light was dimmed in Northern Ireland until very recently. The Peace People, the organization, which emerged from the movement, declined in numbers and influence. Betty Williams immigrated to the United States, where she teaches in a university and has become a stirring lecturer on peace. Mairead Corrigan Maguire has continued to work with the Peace People in Belfast and has also effectively carried her message of nonviolence into other countries. Quakers in the seventeenth century thought of themselves as "God's ordinaries." When ordinary people rise to face challenge, they may go far beyond the ordinary.

Mother Teresa (1979)

Professor John Sanness, who chaired the committee, gave the speech of presentation for the 1979 prize to Mother Teresa. After speaking of the many paths to peace, which had been recognized in previous awards, he explained what was special in this one:

Can any political, social, or intellectual feat of engineering, on the international or on the national plane, however effective and rational, however idealistic and principled its protagonists may be, give us anything but a house built on a foundation of sand, unless the spirit of Mother Teresa inspires the builders and takes its dwelling in their building?

Sannes explained that this spirit is rooted in the Christian faith. She sees Christ in every human being, and this in her eyes makes man sacred... The hallmark of her work has been respect for the individual and the individual's worth and dignity. The loneliest and the most wretched, the dying destitute, the abandoned lepers, have been received by her and her Sisters with warm compassion devoid of condescension, based on this reverence for Christ in Man.

Mother Teresa was born into a Roman Catholic Albanian family living in Skopje, capital of the Yugoslav republic of Macedonia. At the age of twelve she had felt the call to help the poor, and a few years later decided to work in India. At the age of eighteen she joined the Irish order of Loreto and went to teach in their girls' school in Calcutta. After sixteen years she felt a new call, to work in the Calcutta slums. There she started a new order, the Missionaries of Charity, committed to serve the poorest of the poor, which soon spread to many other countries.

Mother Teresa worked for people who were not of her race, religion or nationality. She had transcended all barriers. "With her message she is able to reach through to something innate in every human kind---if for no other purpose than to create a potential, a seed for good. She promotes peace in the most fundamental manner, by her confirmation of the inviolability of human dignity."

Alva Myrdal (1982)

Chairman Egil Aarvik of the committee gave the presentation speech at the award ceremony when the 1982 prize was shared between Alva Myrdal and Alfonso García Robles of Mexico. Aarvik explained that in recognizing two prominent leaders in the disarmament movement the committee wanted at the same time to give that movement a helping hand. Myrdal had headed the Swedish delegation to the U.N. Disarmament Committee from 1962 to 1973 and had produced one of the best books on the disarmament race.

Her social commitment went back to the 1930s, when she played a prominent part in developing the Swedish welfare state. She was a staunch champion of women's liberation and equal rights. Alva Myrdal's name became a rallying point for men and women that in the last resort mind is bound to triumph over matter. Myrdal was not only a champion of reason but in her writing and in all her activities one of its most brilliant practitioners.

She was the first woman to be appointed head of a department in the United Nations Secretariat, and she had served her country with distinction as a cabinet member and as ambassador to India. So glowing was her record in all her assignments, so many honors had been heaped upon her. She held her first important position after the age of forty. The career of her husband, Gunnar Myrdal, had taken priority at times when she had been offered high positions.

Of all the honors she had received, Myrdal regarded the Nobel Peace Prize as "the peak." She confided to Chairman Egil Aarvik that the Norwegian People's Prize was "dearer to my heart." In 1981 when she had been nominated once again for the Nobel and the committee had given the prize to the U.N. High Commissioner for Refugees, there was such an outcry of criticism in Norway that a popular movement arose, which raised sixty thousand dollars to be presented to her as the Norwegian People's Prize. The ceremony at the Oslo city hall in February 1982 had touched her deeply.

Myrdal had said in accepting the first Einstein Peace Prize: Despite all disillusionment, I had never allowed myself to feel like giving up. This is my message today; it is not worthy of a human being to give up.

Aarvik emphasized this message, no doubt thinking of the failure of the U.N. disarmament session earlier that year. He said that the committee intended the 1982 peace prize to go to "people who are not satisfied merely to draw attention to alarming trends, but who also devote their energy and their ability to turning the tide." Certainly such a one was Alva Myrdal.

Aung San Suu Kyi (1991)

At the ceremony for Aung San Suu Kyi in December 1991, she was still being held in detention by the military dictatorship in Myanmar (Burma) and could only be represented by her two sons, her husband and her picture facing the audience. In his speech presenting the prize to her sons, Professor Francis Sejersted, chairman of the committee, declared, "Her absence fills us with fear and anxiety," but he felt we could also have confidence and hope. He went on to sum up the meaning of her prize:

In the good fight for peace and reconciliation, we are dependent on persons who set examples, persons who can symbolize what we are seeking and mobilize the best in us. Aung San Suu Kyi is just such a person. She unites deep commitment and tenacity with a vision in which the end and the means form a single unit. It's most important elements are: democracy, respect for human rights, reconciliation between groups, non-violence, and personal and collective discipline.

The sources of her inspiration, Sejersted explained, were Mahatma Gandhi, about whom she had learned when her mother was ambassador to India, and her father, Aung San, the leader in Burma's struggle for liberation. She was only two when he was assassinated, but she had made his life a center of her studies. From Gandhi she drew her commitment to nonviolence, from her father the understanding that leadership was a duty and that one can only lead in humility and with the confidence and respect of the people to be led. Both were examples for her of independence and modesty, and Aung San represented what she called "a profound simplicity."

We must add that under girding her political philosophy in spirit and deed has always been her Buddhist faith, which is also the foundation for her belief in human rights. In championing human rights in her political opposition to the military dictatorship, she needed to be fearless. Sejersted referred to the incident during her election campaigning when she courageously faced a detachment of soldiers, whose officer lined them up in front of her, prepared to fire if she continued to walk down that street, which she did.

Several times in his speech Sejersted cited the collection of her essays, entitled Freedom from Fear, which her husband, Michael Aris, edited and published before the ceremony, so that her voice could be heard beyond the reach of her oppressors. The title essay begins, "It is not power that corrupts but fear. Fear of losing power corrupts those who wield it and fear of the scourge of power corrupts those who are subject to it." Fearlessness is the best response to governmental violence. In conclusion she writes "truth, justice and compassion... are often the only bulwarks against ruthless power." These are the teachings of Buddha.

Sejersted told how Suu Kyi spent many years abroad, first when with her diplomat mother in her younger years, then studying at Oxford, working at the United Nations in New York, marrying Aris, a British Tibetan scholar, starting a family when they were in Bhutan, finally ending up in England, after scholarly assignments in Japan and India. Burma was always on her mind and heart, however, especially after the military seized power in 1962. When she married Aris, she told him that one-day she must return to Burma when she was needed.

It was to nurse her dying mother that she returned from England, but as the daughter of Aung San, she could not stay aloof when she saw the government brutally repressing a popular movement in opposition. She headed a political party in the elections which the military permitted, but she was so successful that even before Election Day, she was ordered confined to her home. Nevertheless, her party won by a great majority, after which it's other leaders were jailed.

"We ordinary people, I believe," Sejersted declared, "feel that with her courage and her high ideals, Aung San Suu Kyi brings out something of the best in us... The little woman under house arrest stands for a positive hope. Knowing she is there gives us confidence and faith in the power of good."

As of this writing Suu Kyi is still under detention, separated from her family, despite efforts of many governments and the United Nations to secure her liberation. A group of Nobel peace laureates only got as far as Thailand in an attempt to bring their petition to the military dictators who hold her. In 1994, however, a U.S. congressman was permitted to see her, and, as a result of mediation by a Buddhist monk, she had a conference with members of the government. There is now more hope. Suu Kyi was under detention or house arrest for about two decades.

Rigoberta Menchú Tum (1992)

It was announced in October 1992 that the prize would go to Rigoberta Menchú, a Mayan Indian of Guatemala "in recognition of her work for social justice and ethno-cultural reconciliation based on respect for the rights of indigenous peoples."

The decision was generally applauded, but conservative critics charged that Menchú had taken part in violent actions of the Guatemalan guerrillas against the government. Previous Nobel prizes for champions of human rights had been given only to those who used nonviolent methods, like Aung San Suu Kyi of Burma. It was true that Menchú had every provocation to take up arms, and two of her sisters had indeed joined the guerrillas. Government soldiers had brutally murdered their mother and brother because their father opposed the landowners, and finally the soldiers had set fire to the Spanish embassy where the father and other compesinos were making a peaceful protest and burned them all to death.

Menchú tells this terrible story in *I, Rigoberta Menchú, An Indian Woman in Guatemala,* a book composed of a series of reminiscences she dictated in Spanish to the anthropologist Elisabeth Burgos-Debray. That Menchú did not turn to violence, but to political and social work for her people is the reason why she received the prize. She became an active member of the Committee for Campesino Unity and then helped found the Revolutionary Christians. Menchú explained, "We understood revolutionary in the real meaning of the word 'transformation.' If I had chosen the armed struggle, I would be in the mountains now."

Committee Chairman Sejersted in his presentation speech emphasized the meaning of Menchú's decision. He spoke of "the brutalizing effect of the use of violence. Whoever commits an act of violence will lose his humanity. Thus, violence breeds violence and hate breeds hate." How one break out of this circle, especially when one could is confronted with the blind violence of the other side?

An answer can be found in "the shining individual examples of people who manage to preserve their humanity in brutal and violent surroundings, of persons who for that very reason compel our special respect and admiration. Such people give us a hope that there are ways out of the vicious circle."

Even in the most brutal situations, one must retain one's faith that there is a minimum of human feelings in all of us.

Her whole life story represents a remarkable achievement. Born in abject poverty among a suppressed people, working since the age of eight --- "I never had a childhood" --- she managed to get some minimal education in her church, where she first showed her potential ability, taught herself Spanish so that she could tell the world of the sufferings of her people, and, driven into exile in Mexico in fear of her life because of her political activities, she developed the skills of leadership and diplomacy until, as the prize announcement states, "Today, Rigoberta Menchú stands as a vivid symbol of peace and reconciliation across ethnic, cultural and social dividing lines, in her own country, on the American continent and in the world."[54]

Three more illustrated women namely Jody Williams (1997). Shirin Ebadi (2003) and Wangari Maattai (2004) have received Nobel Peace Prize for their outstanding and humanitarian performances to award peace to people of world.

Ms. Jody Williams (1997)

Ms. Jody Williams (born October 9, 1950, in USA) is an American teacher and aid worker who received the 1997 Nobel Peace Prize jointly with the campaign she worked for. She is the founding coordinator of the International Campaign to Ban Landmines (ICBL), which was formally launched by six nongovernmental organizations (NGOs) in October of 1992. Ms. Williams has overseen the growth of the ICBL to more than 1,000 NGOs in more than sixty countries. She has served as the chief strategist and spokesperson

---

[54] Irwin Abrams (1997), "Heroines of Peace – the Nine Nobel Women", Nobel Prize Org, 22 September, 1997

for the campaign. Working in an unprecedented cooperative effort with governments, UN bodies and the International Committee of the Red Cross, the ICBL achieved its goal of an international treaty banning antipersonnel landmines during the diplomatic conference held in Oslo in September 1997.

In her capacity as ICBL coordinator, she has written and spoken extensively on the problem of landmines and the movement to ban them. In recognition of her expertise on the issue, Ms. Williams was invited to serve as a technical adviser to the UN's Study on the Impact of Armed Conflict on Children, led by Ms. Graca Machel, former first lady of Mozambique.

Prior to beginning the ICBL, Ms. Williams worked for eleven years to build public awareness about U.S. policy toward Central America. From 1986 to 1992, she developed and directed humanitarian relief projects as the deputy director of the Los Angeles-based Medical Aid for El Salvador. From 1984 to 1986, she was co-coordinator of the Nicaragua-Honduras Education Project, leading fact-finding delegations to the region. Previously, she taught English as a Second Language (ESL) in Mexico, the United Kingdom, and Washington, D.C.

Ms. Williams has a Master's Degree in International Relations from the Johns Hopkins School of Advanced International Studies (Washington, D.C., 1984), a Master's Degree in Teaching Spanish and Emglish as a Second Language (ESL) from the School for International Training (Brattleboro, Vermont, 1976), and a Bachelor of Arts degree from the University of Vermont (Burlington, Vermont, 1972).

In her capacity as ICBL coordinator, she has written and spoken extensively on the problem of landmines and the movement to ban them. She has spoken in various fora, including at the United Nations, the

European Parliament, and the Organization of African Unity. Ms. Williams co-authored a seminal study, based on two years of field research in four mine-affected countries, detailing the socioeconomic consequences of landmine contamination. She has written articles for journals produced by the United Nations and the ICRC, among others. Papers and publications include: After the Guns Fall Silent: The Enduring Legacy of Landmines, Shawn Roberts and Jody Williams, Vietnam Veterans of America Foundation, Washington, D.C., 1995.

The organization ultimately achieved its goal in 1997 when an international treaty (Ottawa Treaty) banning antipersonnel landmines was signed in Ottawa in 1997 (though some nations, notably the United States, People's Republic of China (PRC), and Russia refrained).

One broader aspect of Williams' work was her pioneering use of People Power: massively distributed collaboration in trans-national political action, initially via fax and eventually via email—Williams' own explanation, Imagine trying to get hundreds of organizations – each one independent and working on many, many issues – to feel that each is a critical element of the development of a new movement. I wanted each to feel that what they had to say about campaign planning, thinking, programs, actions was important. So, instead of sending letters, I'd send everyone faxes. People got in the habit of faxing back. This served two purposes – people would really have to think about what they were committing to doing before writing it down, and we have a permanent, written record of almost everything in the development of the campaign from day one.

Williams continues to serve the ICBL as a campaign ambassador and editor of the organization's landmine report, and, since 2003, has held a faculty position of distinguished professor of social work and global justice at the University of Houston, Graduate College of Social Work.

In 2006, Williams was one of the founders of The Nobel Women's Initiative along with sister Nobel Peace Laureates rigoberta Menchu Tum, Shirin Ebadi, Wangari Maathai, Betty Williams and Mairead Corrigan Maquire. Six women representing North America and South America, Europe, the Middle East and Africa decided to bring together their experiences in a united effort for peace with justice and equality. It is the goal of the Nobel Women's Initiative to help strengthen works being done in support of women's rights around the world.

She was the Head of Mission of the High-Level Mission dispatched by the Human Rights Council to report on the situation of human rights in Darfur and the needs of Sudan in this regard (established at the 4th special session of the Human Rights Council in decision S-4/101). The Mission issued its report on March 7, 2007.[55]

Shirin Ebadi:

Nobel Peace Prize laureate 2003

Shirin Ebadi (born 21 June 1947) is an Iranian lawyer, a former judge and human rights activist and founder of Defenders of Human Rights Center in Iran. On 10 October 2003, Ebadi was awarded the Nobel Peace Prize for her significant and pioneering efforts for democracy and human rights, especially women's, children's, and refugee rights. She was the first ever Iranian, and the first Muslim woman to have received the prize.

In 2009, Ebadi's award was allegedly confiscated by Iranian authorities, though this was later denied by the Iranian government. If true, she would be the first person in the history of the Nobel Prize whose

---

[55] Nobel Prize Org and Wikipedia

award has been forcibly seized by state authorities. Ebadi lives in Tehran, but she has been in exile in the U.K. since June 2009 due to the increase in persecution of Iranian citizens who are critical of the current regime.

Ebadi was born in Hanadan from an ethnic Persian family, Iran. Her father, Mohammad Ali Ebadi, was the city's chief notary public and a professor of commercial law. Her family moved to Tehran in 1948.

She was admitted to the law department of the University of Tehran in 1965 and in 1969, upon graduation, passed the qualification exams to become a judge. After a six-month Internship period, she officially started her judging career in March 1969. She continued her studies in University of Tehran in the meanwhile and received a master's degree in law in 1971. In 1975, she became the first woman to preside over a legislative court.

Following the Iranian Revolution in 1979, conservative clerics insisted that Islam prohibits women from becoming judges and Ebadi was demoted to a secretarial position at the branch where she had previously presided. She and other female judges protested and were assigned to the slightly higher position of "law expert." She eventually requested early retirement as the situation remained unchanged.

As her applications were repeatedly rejected, Ebadi was not able to practice as a lawyer until 1993, while she already had a law office permit. She used this free time to write books and many articles in Iranian periodicals, which made her widely known.

Ebadi now lectures law at the University of Tehran and is a campaigner for strengthening the legal status of children and women, the latter of which played a key role in the May 1997 landslide presidential election of the reformist Mahammad Khatami.

As a lawyer, she is known for taking up cases of dissident figures that have fallen foul of the judiciary. She has represented the family of Dariush Forouhar, a dissident intellectual and politician who was found stabbed to death at his home. His wife was also killed at the same time.

The couple was among several dissidents who died in a spate of grisly murders that terrorized Iran's intellectual community. Suspicion fell on extremist hard-liners determined to put a stop to the more liberal climate fostered by President Khatami, who championed freedom of speech. The murders were found to be committed by a team of the employees of the Iranian Ministry of Intelligence, whose head, Saeed Emami, allegedly committed suicide in jail before being brought to court.

Ebadi claimed that she had only videotaped Amir Farshad Ebrahimi's confessions in order to present them to the court. This case was named "Tape makers" by hardliners who questioned the credibility of his videotaped deposition as well as his motives. Ebadi and Rohami were sentenced to five years in jail and suspension of their law licenses for sending Ebrahimi's videotaped deposition to Islamic President Khatami and the head of the Islamic judiciary. The sentences were later vacated by the Islamic judiciary's Supreme Court, but they did not forgive Ebarahlml's vldeotaped confession and sentenced him to 48 months jail, including 16 months in solitary confinement. This case brought increased focus on Iran from human rights groups abroad.

Ebadi has also defended various child abuse cases and a few cases dealing with bans of periodicals. She established two non-governmental organizations in Iran with western funding, the **Society for**

Protecting the Rights of the Child (SPRC) and the **Defenders of Human Rights Center** (DHRC).

She also helped in the drafting of the original text of a law against physical abuse of children, which was passed by the Iranian parliament in 2002.

Political Views

In her book **Iran Awakening**, Ebadi explains her political/religious views on Islam, democracy and gender equality

In the last 23 years, from the day I was stripped of my judgeship to the years of doing battle in the revolutionary courts of Tehran, I had repeated one refrain: an interpretation of Islam that is in harmony with equality and democracy is an authentic expression of faith. It is not religion that binds women, but the selective dictates of those who wish them cloistered. That belief, along with the conviction that changes in Iran must come peacefully and from within, has underpinned my work. At the same time, Ebadi expresses a nationalist love of Iran and a critical view of the Western world. She opposed the pro-Western Shah, initially supported the Islamic Revolution, remembers the CIA's 1953 overthrow of prime minister Mahammad Mosaddeq with rage.

At a press conference shortly after the Peace Prize announcement, Ebadi herself explicitly rejected foreign interference in the country's affairs:

The fight for human rights is conducted in Iran by the Iranian people, and we are against any foreign intervention in Iran.

Subsequently, Ebadi has openly defended the Islamic regime's nuclear development programme: Aside from being economically justified, it has become a cause of national pride for an old nation with a glorious history. No Iranian government, regardless of its ideology or democratic credentials, would dare to stop the program.

Ebadi also expressed indirectly her views on Israeli – Palestinian conflict. In April 2010, Associated Students of the University of California passed A Bill to "In Support of UC Divestment From War Crimes", calling UC to break ties with companies providing technology to the army of Israel. Shirin Ebadi, together with three other Peace Prize laureates, supported the bill.

Nobel Peace Prize

On 10 October 2003, Ebadi was awarded the Nobel Peace Prize for her courageous efforts for democracy and human rights, especially for the rights of women and children. The selection committee praised her as a "courageous person" who "has never heeded the threat to her own safety". Now she travels abroad lecturing in the West. She is against a policy of forced regime change. Her husband, Javad Tavassolian, was an advisor to President Khatami.

The decision of the Nobel committee surprised some observers worldwide – then Pope John Paul II was the bookies' favourite to scoop the prestigious award amid feverish speculation that he was nearing death.

Some observers, mostly supporters of Pope John Paul II, viewed her selection as a calculated and political one, along the lines of the selection of Lech Walesa and Mikhail Gorbachev, among others, for the Peace Award. They claimed that none of Ebadi's previous activities were directly related to the stated goals for the award of the Nobel Peace Prize, as originally stated by Alfred Nobel, and that according to his will the prize should have been awarded:

To the person who shall have done the most or the best work for fraternity between the nations, for the abolition or reduction of standing armies and for the holding and promotion of peace congresses.

She presented a book entitled, **Democracy, human rights, and Islam in modern Iran: Psychological, social and cultural perspectives (2003, Bergen: Fagbokforlaget)** to the Nobel Committee.

The volume documents the historical and cultural basis of democracy and human rights from Cyrus and Darius, 2,500 years ago to Mohammad Mossadeq, the popular Prime Minister of modern Iran who nationalised the oil industry.

In Iran, officials of the Islamic Republic were either silent or critical of the selection of Ebadi, calling it a political act by a pro-western institution and were also critical when Ebadi did not cover her hair at the Nobel award ceremony. IRNA reported it in few lines that the evening newspapers and the Iranian state media waited hours to report the Nobel committee's decision—and then only as the last item on the radio news update. Reformist officials are said to have "generally welcomed the award", but "come under attack for doing so."

Reformist president Mohammad Khatami did not officially congratulate Ms. Ebadi and stated that although the scientific Nobels are important, the Peace Prize is "not very important" and was awarded to Ebadi on the basis of "totally political criteria". Vice President Mohammad Ali Abtahi, the only official to initially congratulate Ebadi, defended the president saying "abusing the President's words about Ms. Ebadi is tantamount to abusing the prize bestowed on her for political considerations".

Post-Nobel prize:

Ebadi has lectured, taught and received awards in different countries, issued statements and defended people accused of political crimes in Iran. She has traveled to and spoken to audiences in India, the United States, and other countries; released her autobiography in an English translation; participated in the Nobel Women's Initiative along with five other Nobel Laureates.[56]

The Iranian authorities seized Ebadi's Nobel medal together with other belongings from her safe-deposit box in November 2009. Her relations are also tortured by the police without any cause. Ebadi is active in doing justice to the poor women and children in many countries. She is a mass puller and takes up cases where ever there is violation of human rights. Ebadi is an eloquent speaker and addresses professors and students in reputed universities; undertakes frequent tours in foreign countries to lobby international leaders against the Islamic regime's human rights abuses. She criticized the British government's foreign policy on the Islamic regime's nuclear programme and for attending President Ahmadinejad's inauguration. She strongly emphasizes that human rights were being neglected in many countries.

In short, Ebadi emphasizes on:

(a) Undemocratic countries are more dangerous than a nuclear bomb. It is undemocratic countries that jeopardize international peace.
(b) She calls for the downgrading of Western embassies, the withdrawal of ambassadors and the freezing of the assets of Iran's leaders.

---

[56] Wikipedia and the Green Voice Freedom

(c) She is a specialist on 'women empowerment, human rights, democracy, and Baha'i Faith and Islam religion'.

In short, what did all these women peace Laureates have in common? They were all women of high ideals, prepared to work and sacrifice to bring something better into being, and they labored in the certainty that their objectives would eventually be realized. They all carried within that sacred flame, which inspired them to struggle against odds, to withstand disappointments and defeats, to resolve never to give up.

They shared a faith in humanity, whether born of religious conviction or humanism. Most displayed remarkable courage.

In the good fight for peace and reconciliation, we are dependent on persons who set examples, persons who can symbolize what we are seeking and mobilize the best in us. All the women Laureates have faith in the power of good. The best feminine qualities could definitely help us to develop peace on earth. Above all, these Nobel Women are and would be the torchbearers of the human spirit to achieve WORLD PEACE. They would be the guides to all peace workers, women and men in years to come.

Women Nobel Laureates (1903 – 2011)

1903 Marie Curie-Skłodowska - Chemistry
1905 Bertha von Suttner - Peace
1909 Selma Lagerlof (1908) - Literature
1911 Marie Curie-Skłodowska - Chemistry
1926 Grazia Deledda - Literature
1928 Sigrid Undset - Literature
1931 Jane Addams - Peace
1935 Irène Joliot-Curie - Chemistry
1938 Pearl S. Buck - Literature
1945 Gabriela Mistral - Literature

1946 Emily Greene Balch - Peace
1947 Gerty Theresa Cori - Physiology or Medicine
1963 Maria Goeppert-Mayer - Physics
1964 Dorothy Crowfoot Hodgkin - Chemistry
1966 Nelly Sachs - Literature
1976 Betty Williams - Peace
1976 Mairead Corrigan - Peace
1977 Rosalyn Sussman Yalow - Physiology or Medicine
1979 Mother Teresa – Peace
1982 Alva Myrdal - Peace
1983 Barbara McClintock - Physiology or Medicine
1986 Rita Levi-Montalcini - Physiology or Medicine
1988 Gertrude B. Elion - Physiology or Medicine
1991 Nadine Gordimer - Literature
1991 Aung San Suu Kyi - Peace
1992 Rigoberta Menchú - Peace
1993 Toni Morrison - Literature
1995 Christiane Nüsslein–Volhard: Physiology/ Medicine
1996 Wisława Szymborska - Literature
1997 Jody Williams - Peace
2003 Shirin Ebadi - Peace
2004 Elfriede Jelinek - Literature
2004 Wangari Maathai - Peace
2004 Linda B. Buck - Physiology or Medicine
2007 Doris Lessing - Literature
2008 Françoise Barré-Sinoussi – Physiology /Medicine
2009 Elizabeth Blackburn -Physiology or Medicine
2009 Carol W. Greider - Physiology or Medicine
2009 Ada E. Yonath - Chemistry
2009 Herta Müller - Literature
2009 Elinor Ostrom - Economics
2011 Ellen Johnson Sirleaf - Peace

Conclusion

It is a fact that women are yet to achieve justice as compared to male dominated society. Women have been awarded only 44 Nobel prizes out of 549 Nobel Prizes awarded till 2011. The illustrated women have received Nobel prizes: 15 in Peace, 12 in Literature,

10 in Physiology/Medicine, 4 in Chemistry, 2 in Physics and 1 in Economics.

But women have achieved laurels in music, dance, cinema, literature, and politics. An educated woman is an asset to the family and to the nation. It is said that if all women are educated, the whole world would be educated because an educated mother would make the family educated.

Let us hope that the world is free from hunger, illiteracy, and injustice. Achieving World Peace is not a utopian thought. It is possible.

+++++

Chapter VI

WOMEN IN POLITICS

Every country deserves to have the best possible leader and that means that women have to be given a chance to compete. If they're never allowed to compete in the electoral process then the countries are really robbing themselves of a great deal of talent.

– Madeleine K. Albright, NDI Chairman

History speaks that men underestimated females for generations. Even many countries did not allow them voting rights and did not permit them to enter into politics.

Even the kings and emperors practiced polygamy. Marco Polo has reported that king of Mabar had 500 wives and king of Calicut had 300 wives and both territories were in the kingdom of Pandya (India). But Suryamati, queen of Kashmir rose to be the de facto ruler of Kashmir and royal princesses of south India became governors of provinces. Moreover, queen Balamahadevi of south Kannada district took a masculine title and ruled the kingdom for about 14 years. The Kakatita queen Rudramba ruled the kingdom for nearly 40 years.

In the nineteenth century, Laxmi Bai, the queen of Jhanshi could challenge the British administration for the freedom of the country and she died in the battlefield.

In this chapter, women's roles in politics have been analyzed to assess their performances and short-comings.

Women's Suffrage

World Chronology of the Recognition of Women's Rights to Vote and to Stand for Election

Women till 1788 women were not treated at par with men in all countries in politics, but they were treated as equal only in social, religious and family functions. They were treated as an appendage to males. The Islam religion permitted that a man can marry four women, but not permitted that a woman can marry four males. Today even, man supersedes a woman in politics, authority, or as family head in all religions. It is because they are mostly engaged in family welfare, child rearing and cooking.

The twenty-first century witnesses both males and females are marching ahead with their rights and duties. It has become possible because of education, politics and media coverage. In some cases the women have advanced as compared to their partners.

Let us compare the rights of women as in all other countries that are protected by law. Whether they have same values as human beings? The women folk belonging to royal families had achieved their rights in the past. But housewives in the societies were not even allowed to take part in deliberations in public meetings.

The women were allowed their rights to vote and to contest in elections in democracies. This constitutes a history of only two centuries only. Women were granted right to vote and /or to contest in election in different countries in the year as mentioned against the country. For example, women were allowed to contest in election in the year 1788 in the USA.

Women Suffrage

1788: USA (to stand in election)
1893: New Zealand (to vote)

1902: Australia
1906; Finland
1907: Norway (to stand for election)

1913: Norway
1915: Denmark, Iceland

1917: Canada (to vote), Estonia, Georgia, Germany, Hungary, Ireland, Kyrgyz Stan, Latvia, Lithuania, Poland, Russian Federation, United Kingdom

1918: Austria, Canada (to vote), Estonia, Georgia, Germany, Hungary, Ireland, Kyrgyz Stan, Latvia, Lithuania, Poland, Russia federation, united kingdom

1919: Belarus. Belgium (to vote), Luxembourg, Netherlands (to vote), New Zealand (to stand for election), Sweden, Ukraine

1920: Albania, Canada (to stand for election), Czech Republic, icc land, Slovakia, United States of America (to vote)

1921: Armenia, Azerbaijan, Belgium (to stand for election), Georgia, Sweden

1924: Kazakhstan, Mongolia, Saint Lucia, and Tajikistan

1927: Turkmenistan
1928: Ireland, United Kingdom
1929: Ecuador, Romania
1930: South Africa (Whites), Turkey (to vote)
1931: Chile, Portugal, Turkey (to stand for election)
1932: Brazil, Maldives, Turkey (to stand for election)
1934: Cuba, Portugal, Turkey (to stand for election)
1935: Myanmar (to vote)
1937: Philippines
1938: Bolivia, Uzbekistan
1939: El Salvador
1941: Panama
1942: Dominican Republic
1944: Bulgaria, France, and Jamaica

1945: Croatia, Guyana (to stand for election), Indonesia, Italy, Japan, Senegal, Slovenia, Togo

1946: Cameroon, D. P. R. of Korea, Djibouti (to vote), Guatemala, Liberia, Myanmar (to stand for election), Panama, Romania, The F Y R of Macedonia, Trinidad, and Tobago, Venezuela, Vietnam and Yugoslavia

1947: Argentina, Japan, Malta, Mexico (to vote), Pakistan, Singapore

1948: Belgium Israel, Niger, Republic of Korea, Seychelles, and Suriname

1949: Bosnia and Herzegovina, Chile, China, Costa Rica, Syria Arab Republic (to vote),

1950: Barbados, Canada (to vote), Haiti and India

1951 Antigua and Barbuda, Dominica, grenade, Nepal, Saint Kitts and Nevis, Saint Vincent and the Grenadines

1952: Bolivia, Cote d'Ivoire, Greece, Lebanon

1953: Bhutan, Guyana (to vote), Mexico (to stand for election), Syrian Arab Republic

1954: Belize, Colombia, and Ghana
1955: Cambodia, Eritrea, Ethiopia, Honduras, Nicaragua, and Peru

1956: Benin, Comoros, Egypt, Gabon, Mali, Mauritius and Somalia

1957: Malaysia, Zimbabwe (to vote),
1958: Burkina Faso, Chad, Guinea, Lao P D R, and Nigeria (South)

1959: Madagascar, San Marino (to vote), Tunisia, United Republic of Tanzania,

1960: Canada (to stand for election), Cyprus, Gambia and Tonga

1961: Bahamas, Burundi, El Salvador (to stand for election), Malawi, Mauritius, Paraguay, Rwanda and Sierra Leone

1962; Algeria, Australia, Monaco, Uganda, and Zambia

1963: Afghanistan, Congo, Equatorial Guinea, Fiji, Iran (Islamic Republic of), Kenya, morocco, Papua New Guinea (to stand for election)

1964: Bahamas, Libyan Arab Jamahiriya, Papua New Guinea (to vote) and Sudan

1965: Botswana, Lesotho
1967: Democratic Republic of Congo (to vote), Ecuador, Kiribati, Tuvalu, Yemen (D P R)

1968: Nauru, Swaziland

1970: Andorra (to vote). Democratic Republic of Congo (to stand for election), Yemen (Arab Republic)

1971; Switzerland
1972: Bangladesh
1973: Andorra (to stand for election), Bahrain, San Marino (to stand for election)
1974: Jordan, Solomon Islands
1975: Angola, Cape Verde, Mozambique, Sao Tome and Principe, Vanuatu

1976: Portugal
1977: guinea Bissau
1978: Nigeria (North), Republic of Moldova, Zimbabwe (to stand for election)
1979: Marshall Islands, Micronesia (Fed states), Palau

1980: Iraq, Vanuatu
1984: Liechtenstein, South Africa (Coloured + Indians)

1986: Central African Republic, Djibouti (to stand for election)
1989: Namibia
1990: Samoa
1993: Kazakhstan, Republic of Moldova
1994: South Africa (Blacks)
2005: Kuwait[57]

Women in leadership

There have always been female rulers since time immemorial. Egyptian Queens are believed to have governed from around 3000 BCE, and the first to be named by the sources without any doubt is Ku-baba,

---

[57] Note: Some countries are shown repeatedly because changes in the state laws for election and voting rights. Changes of colonial rule to independence have caused changes in rules. A number of countries have taken years in granting rights. Source: Inter-Parliamentary Union

who ruled the Mesopotamian City-State of Ur round 2500 BCE.

However, it was not until during and just after the World War I that the first few women became members of the revolutionary governments in Ukraine, Russia, Hungary and Ireland. Nina Bang, Danish Minister of Education 1924-26, was the first woman to be minister in democratically elected parliamentary government.

First female Prime Ministers and President

In 1960 Sirivamo Bandaranaike of Sri Lanka became the world's first female elected Prime Minister and in 1974 Isabel Perón of Argentina became the first woman President - one woman had been Acting Head of Government and two women Acting Heads of State before that.

In 2009 Monaco became the last country in the world to have its first female member of government. 1999 Sweden became the first country to have more female ministers than male. 11 women and 9 men and in 2007 the Finish government had 60 percent women.

Female heads of state and Government

There are 192 member countries in the United Nations. Moreover, there are 2 independent states, a few self-declared de-facto independent states and many self-ruling decencies. There are 32 female leaders in 30 different countries or self-ruling territories in 2011.

Of the monarchies, there are reigning Queens in 3 countries: Denmark, The Netherlands and the United Kingdom. There are female Governor Generals in 3 countries; Antigua and Barbuda, Australia and Saint

Lucia. They function as their countries' de-facto Heads of State.

There are 12 female Presidents in Argentina, Brazil, Costa Rica, Finland, India, Ireland, Kosovo, Kyrgyzstan, Liberia, Lithuania, San Marino and Switzerland. And currently there are 12 woman Prime Ministers in Australia, Bangladesh, Croatia, Finland, Germany, Iceland, Mali, Peru, Slovakia and Trinidad and Tobago and in the self-governing territories of Bermuda, Sint Maartin and the Åland Islands.

There are female administrators, ambassadors, Members of Parliaments, Ministers, Chairpersons, female Bishops and Danish leaders and local leaders in each country.

Women in National Parliaments

The Inter-Parliamentary Union has calculated reported that the number of sovereign States having a Parliament has increased seven-fold during 1945 to 1995. The percentage of women MPs worldwide has increased four-fold during the same period. The record average level was reached in 1988 with 14.8 percent of women MPs.

The number of Parliaments increased from 26 in 1945 to 61 in 1955, 94 in 1965, 115 in 1975, 136 in 1985 and 176 in 1976.

Similarly percentages of women MPs increased from 3.0 percent in 1945 to 7.5 percent in 1955, 8.1 percent in 1965, 10.9 percent in 1975, and 12.0 percent in 1985 and decreased to 11.6 in 1995.

The percentage of women senators increased from 2.2 percent in 1945 to 7.7 percent in 1955, 9.3 percent in 1965, 20.5 percent in 1975, and 12.7 percent in 1985, but decreased to 9.4 percent in 1995.

As on April 30, 2011

There were 44, 771 MPs in the whole world as on April 30, 2011, But as per available data on gender analysis, it reported only 44, 447 MPs of which Men MPs were 35, 867 and women MPs were 8,560. So the percentage of women MPs was 19.3 percent. There has been a jump of number of women MPs in Parliament.

Single House or Lower House

(a) Total MPs: 37, 910
(b) Gender breakdown known for 37, 675 MPs
(c) Men MPs: 30, 332
(d) Women MPs: 7, 343
(e) Percentage of Women MPs: 19. 5 percent

Upper House or Senate

(a) Total MPs: 6, 861
(b) Gender breakdown known for: 6,772
(c) Men Mps: 5,535
(d) Women MPs: 1,237
(e) Percentage of Women: 18.3 percent

Regional Averages (as on April 30, 2011)

(a)There were 42.1 percent of women MPs in Nordic countries

(b) In Americas, the number of women MPs accounted for 22.3 percent in Lower House, 23.5 percent in Upper House and 22.5 percent in both Houses combined.

(c) In Europe, OSCE member countries including Nordic countries, the number of women MPs accounted for 22.0 percent in Lower House, 19.7 percent in Upper House and 21.5 percent in both Houses combined.

(d) In Europe, OSCE member countries excluding Nordic countries, the number of women MPs accounted for 20.1 percent in Lower House, 19.7 percent in Upper House and 20.0 percent in both Houses combined.

(e In Sub-Saharan Africa, the number of women MPs accounted for 19.8 percent in Lower House, 19.7 percent in Upper House and 19.8 percent in both Houses combined.

(f) In Asia, the number of women MPs accounted for 18.3 percent in Lower House, 15.3 percent in Upper House and 18.0 percent in both Houses combined.

(g) In Pacific, the number of women MPs accounted for 12.4 percent in Lower House, 32.6 percent in Upper House and 14.7 percent in both Houses combined.

(h) In Arab States, the number of women MPs accounted for 11.4 percent in Lower House, 7.3 percent in Upper House and 10.7 percent in both Houses combined.[58]

Women Speakers in Parliament

Austria is the first country in the world to elect a woman to the presidency of one of the Parliament's Chambers (the Bundesrat) in the year 1927. But during 1945 - 1997, 42 countries elected Women Speakers to preside over Parliament or a House of Parliament for 78 terms during the period. In other words, some Women Speakers were re-elected to the Chair for their efficiency and impartiality during business transactions.

---

[58] Note: Regions are classified by descending order of the percentage of women in the lower or single Houses. Source: Inter-Parliamentary Union

These countries are: 18 European countries, 19 countries of the Americas, 2 African countries, 1 Asian country and 1 country in the Pacific. 24 of the States concerned had bicameral Parliaments. Women are preferred for Presidency in Senate than in the lower House.

It is reported that there are 38 Women Speakers in different Parliaments and House of Parliaments to preside over one of the Houses of the 186 existing Parliaments as on April 30, 2011. There are also 75 bicameral Parliaments in these countries. Parliaments of different countries are known in different names in these 38 countries.

These are:

Albania (People's Assembly); Antigua and Barbuda (House of Representatives and Senate); Austria (National rat); Bahamas (Senate); Belize (Senate); Bosnia and Herzegovina (House of Peoples); Botswana (National Assembly); Bulgaria (Naradno Schranie); Czech Republic Poslanecka Snemovna); Dominica (House of Assembly); Estonia (Riigikogu); Gabon (Senate); Germany (Bundesrat); Ghana (Parliament); Grenada (Senate); Iceland (Althingi); India (Lok Sabha); Leo People's Democratic Republic (Saphs Heng Xat); Latvia (Saeima); Lesotho (National Assembly); Lithuania (Seimas); Mozambique (Assembleia da Republica); Netherlands (Twede Kamer der Staten Generaal); Pakistan (National Assembly); Romania (Chamber of Deputies); Rwanda (Chamber of Deputies); Saint Lucia (House of Assembly and Senate); San Marino (Consiglio grande e generale); Serbia (Narodna Skupstina); Suriname (Nationale Assemblee); Swaziland (Senate); Turkmenistan (Mejlis); United Kingdom (House of Lords); United Republic of Tanzania (Bunge); Uzbekistan (Legislative chamber); and Zimbabwe (Senate).

Women occupy only 13.4 percent of the total number of 268 posts of Presiding Officers (Speakers) of Parliament or of one of its Houses.

First Time Speakers (1927 - 2011):

Moreover, the occupancy of a WOMAN as a presiding officer in a Parliament or one of its Houses is possible in 82 countries till date, which occupied speaker's post in the following years for the first time.

These 82 countries are as follows: Austria (1927), Denmark (1950), Hungary (1963), Uruguay (1963), Germany (1972), Canada (1972), Argentina (1973), Iceland (1974), Switzerland (1977), Bolivia (1979), Italy (1979), Dominica (1980), Sao Tome and Principe (1980), San Marino (1981), Ireland (1982), Belize (1984), Jamaica (1984), Costa Rica (1986), Australia (1987), Luxemburg (1989). Grenada (1990), Nicaragua (1990), Finland (1991), Guatemala (1991), Sweden (1991), Trinidad and Tobago (1991), United Kingdom (1992), Croatia (1993), Japan (1993), Norway (1993), South Africa (1994), Antigua and Barbuda (1994), El Salvador (1994), Mexico (1994), Panama (1994), Ethiopia (1995), Latvia (1995), Latvia (1995), Peru (1995), Malta (1996), Poland (1997), Bahamas (1997), Suriname (1997), Netherlands (1998), Czech Republic (1998), Venezuela (1998), Spain (1999), Dominican Republic (1999), Lesotho (2000),

Republic of Moldova (2001), Georgia (2001), Chile (2002), Liberia (2003), Estonia (2003), Greece (2004), Belgium (2004), Saint Kitts and Nevis (2004), New Zealand (2005), Burundi (2005), Albania (2005), Zimbabwe (2005), Gambia (2006), Israel (2006), Swaziland (2006), Turkmenistan (2006), Saint Lucia (2007), United States of America (2007), Nigeria (2007), Uzbekistan (2008), Pakistan (2008), Serbia (2008), Rwanda (2008), Romania (2008),

Gabon (2009), Bosnia and Herzegovina (2009), Ghana (2009), India (2009), Bulgaria (2009), Lithonia (2009), Botswana (2009), Mozambique (2010), United Republic of Tanzania (2010) and Lao People's Democratic Republic (2011).

In other words, **104 countries** of the world are yet to find Women Speakers to preside over the Parliament in their countries.[59]

Present Prime Ministers and Presidents

(a) Isabel Peron, President, Argentina
(b) Julia Gillard, Prime Minister, Australia
(c) Angela Merkel, Chancellor of Germany
(d) A. Kim Cambell, President Canada
(e) Gro Harlem Brundtland, Prime Minister of Norway
(f) Cristina Fernandez de Kirchner, President, Argentina
(g) Dilma Rousseff, President, Brazil

(B)

In this chapter, the activities of a small number of powerful women politicians of the world are discussed because they have proved more capable than male politicians of their contemporary.

They are Indira Gandhi, Margaret Thacher, Benazir Bhutto, Aung San Suu Ki, Golda Meir, and Sirimavo Bandarnaike. Moreover, the incumbents of past and present Presidents, Prime Ministers, Speakers and Leaders of opposition parties have proved their successes in politics and in the male-dominated world.

---

[59] Inter-Parliamentary Union

INDIA

Indira Gandhi said:

(a) Forgiveness is a virtue of the brave.
(b) You cannot shake hands with a clenched fist.
(c) Martyrdom does not end something, it only a beginning.
(d) Even if I died in the service of the nation, I would be proud of it. Every drop of my blood... will contribute to the growth of this nation and to make it strong and dynamic.
(e) You must learn to be still in the midst of activity and to be vibrantly alive in repose.
(f) There are two kinds of people: Those who do the work and those who take the credit. Try to be in the first group because there is less competition there.

Best Known As: Prime Minister of India 1966-77 and 1980-84, Indira Amma (Indira Mother)

Indira Priyadarshini Gandhi (1917-1984), a prime minister of India, was the most effective and powerful politician of her day in that country. Sikh conspirators assassinated Indira Gandhi in 1984. Her son Rajiv Gandhi (1944-91) succeeded her as India's prime minister in 1984. Rajiv was killed in a 1991 bombing.

Indira Gandhi was the Prime Minister of India from 1966-77 and 1980-84 and one of the most famous women in 20th century politics. Her father was Jawaharlal Nehru, independent India's first prime minister (1947-64), and Indira spent her life amid Indian politics. In 1959 she was elected to the presidency of the Indian National Congress, and in 1964 she was elected to the parliament. When Prime Minister Lal Bahadur Shastri died in 1966, Gandhi was chosen as a compromise candidate to replace him. She was elected to the office in 1967 and advanced an ambitious program of modernization.

Indira was the only child of Jawaharlal Nehru, the first Prime Minister of India. She led the party to a fourth successive general election victory, though with a greatly reduced majority. In 1969 her nominee for President of India was successfully elected but precipitated a split within the Congress between the parliamentary and organizational wings. A radical left turn followed the split because of nationalization of banks and insurance companies.

INDIRA GANDHI
Ex- Prime Minister of India

In 1971 Gandhi went into a national election on a slogan of "eradicate poverty". Her appeal projected her as a national leader and undermined organizational opposition to her within the party. The successful execution of the Indo-Pak War (1971) under Gandhi's guidance led to the creation of Bangladesh. Her popularity was at an all-time high and was followed by Congress victories in the states.
After the 1973 global increase in oil prices, the opposition parties led a countrywide agitation against inflation and corruption. On 12 June 1975 the Allahabad High Court found Gandhi guilty of corrupt election practices.

On 25 June 1975, Gandhi, using article 352 of the constitution, imposed a **State of Emergency** in whole of India. It followed:

(a) Suspension of the constitution,
(b) Arrests of opposition leaders,
(c) Press censorship, and curtailment of the powers of the judiciary;
(d) 110,000 political activists were arrested.
(e) Twenty-point programme of economic and
(f) Social reforms

The State of Emergency was lifted in March 1977 and elections were held to the national parliament.

The 1977 elections led to a crushing defeat for the Congress, which won only 154 seats, and the election of a Janata government. Gandhi was tried for the excesses of the Emergency but prosecution backfired on the Janata government as it became raven with factional conflict. In 1980 when a national election was called, Gandhi campaigned on a platform of a government that works. She made a successful comeback, winning 351 seats.

Gandhi's final term as Prime Minister was marked by the centralization and personalization of power. Dissent within Congress was not tolerated. Opposition state governments were regularly undermined by the imposition of President's Rule. Following the defeat of Congress in Andhra Pradesh and Karnataka, Gandhi sought to consolidate her support among the Hindu community. Following the return to power in 1980, Gandhi dismissed the Akali Dal (Sikh Party) led state government in Punjab. This led to a statewide agitation by the Akali Dal for regional autonomy. Factions within Congress supported the more militant groups among the Sikhs in order to gain party advantage. Between 1981 and 1983 several rounds of negotiations took place between Sikh leaders and the central government, but Gandhi always blocked a deal. As violence in Punjab increased, central rule was imposed. On 4 June 1984 Gandhi ordered the Indian Army to eradicate militant resistance based in the Golden Temple. Operation Blue Star resulted in the deaths of 1,000 people and the permanent alienation of the Sikh community.

Although Operation Blue Star made Gandhi very popular among the Hindu community, it marked the first major use of the Indian army against civilians and was followed by a mutiny of soldiers. Sikh resentment continued to fester and her bodyguard assassinated her on October 1984. Her death was followed by massacres of Sikhs in Delhi in which 3,000 lost their lives.

Gandhi is often seen as the practitioner of real-politik. What she lacked in intellectual ability she compensated for by a ruthless streak gained from a long apprenticeship in politics. Gandhi began the process of de- institutionalization of Congress with her plebiscite politics in the early 1970s and the destruction of the old Congress Party. She is best contrasted with her father, Nehru, and is seen as a centralized that outmaneuvered more experienced contenders for power.

Gandhi became president of the Indian National Congress in 1959. The Congress had led the country to freedom and had then become its major political party. She had joined the Congress in 1938 and subsequently served as a member of its Youth Advisory Board and chairman of its Woman's Department. Prior to assuming the presidency of the organization, Gandhi was named to its 21-member executive Working Committee and was elected with more votes than any other candidate to the powerful 11-member Central Election Board, which named candidates and planned electoral strategy.

Split in Congress: The split was formalized when Gandhi's candidate for the presidency of India, V.V. Giri, won over the party's official nominee. Although Gandhi took 228 members of Parliament with her into the New Congress, this was not a majority in the

521-member house, and she held power only with support from parties of the left. In December 1970 when Gandhi failed to get the necessary support to abolish the privy purses and privileges of the former princes, she called on the President to dissolve Parliament. Midterm elections were set for March 1971, one full year ahead of schedule.

In the state elections held in India in March 1972, Gandhi's New Congress party scored the most overwhelming victory in the history of independent India; however, her opponent accused her of violating election laws, and a high court upheld the charge in 1975. Because of this development, as well as domestic unrest, Gandhi declared a state of emergency and postponed elections. In the 1977 elections Gandhi and her party suffered major defeats; Gandhi lost her seat and the premiership.

The following year she headed the Congress party faction as she returned to Parliament. In 1979 she again became Prime Minister. In efforts to prove India's no alliance in the global community, she visited both the United States and the USSR. Internally, riots broke out among Muslim, Hindu, and Sikh religious sects. Sikh separatists secured weapons within their sacred Golden Temple in Amritsar, assuming religious protection. Gandhi ordered government troops to storm the temple, leading to many Sikh deaths. This led to her assassination on the grounds of her own residence and office October 31, 1984, by her own Sikh security guards.

Bank Nationalization: Gandhi immediately set about reorganizing the party to make it a more effective instrument of administration and national development. Her goal was to achieve a wider measure of social and economic justice for all Indians. As her left-of-center policies became clear, the Congress party split, with the younger, more liberal elements coalescing around Gandhi and the older, more conservative party leaders opposing her. This division came to a head in July 1969 when she nationalized the country's 14 leading banks in a highly popular move meant to make credit more available to agriculture and to small industry.

Bangladesh Formation: The Pakistan army conducted widespread atrocities against the civilian populations of East Pakistan. An estimated 10 million refugees fled to India, causing financial hardship and instability in the country. The United States under Richard Nixon supported Pakistan, and mooted a UN resolution warning India against going to war. Nixon apparently disliked Indira personally, referring to her as a "witch" and "clever fox" in his private communication with Secretary of State Henry Kissinger as released by the State Departments). Indira signed the Treaty of Friendship and Cooperation, resulting in political support and a Soviet veto at the UN. India was victorious in the 1971 war, and Bangladesh was born.

Shimla Agreement: Gandhi invited the late Pakistani President Zulfikar Ali Bhutto to Shimla for a weeklong summit. After the near-failure of the talks, the two heads of state eventually signed the Shimla Agreement, which bound the two countries to resolve the Kashmir dispute by negotiations and peaceful means. Due to her antipathy for Nixon, relations with the United States grew distant, while relations with the Soviet Union grew closer.

She was criticized by some for not making the Line of Control (L o C) a permanent border while a few critics even believed that Pakistan-administered Kashmir should have been extracted from Pakistan, whose 93,000 prisoners of war were under Indian control. But the agreement did remove immediate United Nations and third party interference, and greatly reduced the likelihood of Pakistan launching a major attack in the near future. By not demanding total capitulation on a sensitive issue from Bhutto, she had allowed Pakistan to stabilize and normalize. Trade relations were also normalized, though much contact remained frozen (sealed) for years.

Nuclear weapons program: A national nuclear program was started by Gandhi in 1967, in response to the nuclear threat from the People's Republic of China and to establish India's stability and security interests as independent from those of the nuclear superpowers. In 1974, India successfully conducted an underground nuclear test, unofficially code named as Smiling Buddha near the desert village of Pokhran in Rajasthan. Describing the test as for peaceful purposes, India became the world's then youngest nuclear power.

Green Revolution: Richard Nixon and Indira Gandhi in 1971. They had a deep personal antipathy that coloured bilateral relations. Special agricultural innovation programs and extra government support launched in the 1960s finally transformed India's chronic food shortages into surplus production of wheat, rice, cotton and milk, the success mainly attributed to the hard working majority Sikh farmers of Punjab. That achievement, along with the diversification of its commercial crop production, has become known as the "Green Revolution". At the same time, the White Revolution was an expansion in milk production, which helped to combat malnutrition, especially amidst young children. 'Food security', as the program was called, was another source of support for Gandhi in the years leading up to 1975.

Eradication of Poverty Program: Lasting about ten years, the program was ultimately to bring about a tripling of wheat production, a lower but still impressive increase of rice; while there was little to no increase (depending on area, and adjusted for population growth) of such cereals as millet, gram and coarse grain, though these did, in fact, retain a relatively stable yield.

Indira's government faced major problems after her tremendous mandate of 1971. The internal structure of the Congress Party had withered following its numerous splits, leaving it entirely dependent on her leadership for its election fortunes. *Garibi Hatao* (Eradicate Poverty) was the theme for Gandhi's 1971 bid. The slogan and the proposed anti-poverty programs that came with it were designed to give Gandhi an independent national support, based on rural and urban poor. This would allow her to bypass the dominant rural castes both in and of state and local government; likewise the urban commercial class. And, for their part, the previously voiceless poor would at last gain both political worth and political weight.

Within a few months, President's Rule was imposed on the two opposition party ruled states of Gujarat and Tamil Nadu thereby bringing the entire country under direct rule. Indira Gandhi used the emergency provisions to grant herself extraordinary powers. Being the first woman Prime Minister of India, and an influential leader; in a prevalently male-dominated society, Indira Gandhi is a symbol of feminism in India.

The goodwill of the rural population earned by Gandhi still has its effects on the success of the Congress Party in rural India, as well as the popular support of the Nehru-Gandhi Family.

The Congress party uses her 'No Poor" slogan as political campaigns till date. The present president of the Indian National Congress, Sonia Gandhi, who is also the daughter-in-law of Indira Gandhi, is said to style herself in resemblance to her.

The United Kingdom

Margaret Roberts, the daughter of a grocer, was born in Grantham, Lincolnshire, on 13th October 1925. After graduating from Oxford University she worked as a research chemist. Later she studied law and eventually became a barrister.

On 13th December 1951 she married Denis Thatcher, a successful businessman. A member of the Conservative Party, Margaret Thatcher was elected to represent Finchley in October 1959. Two years later she joined the government of Harold Macmillan as joint parliamentary secretary for Pensions and National Insurance.

The Conservative Party was defeated in the 1964 General Election and Harold Wilson became the new prime minister. Edward Heath, the new leader of the Conservatives, appointed her as Opposition Spokesman on Pensions and National Insurance. She later held opposition posts on Housing (October 1965), Treasury (April 1966), Fuel and Power (October 1967), Transport (November, 1968) and Education (October, 1969).

Margaret Thatcher
Ex- Prime Minister, United Kingdom

Following the Conservative victory in the 1970 General Election, Thatcher became Secretary of State for Education and Science. In October 1970 she created great controversy by bringing an end to free school milk for children over seven and increasing school meal charges. Edward Heath, the prime minister, came into conflict with the trade unions over his attempts to impose a prices and incomes policy. His attempts to legislate against unofficial strikes led to industrial disputes. In 1973 a miners' work-to-rule led to regular power cuts and the imposition of a three-day week. Heath called a general election in 1974 on the issue of "who rules". He failed to get a majority and Harold Wilson and the Labour Party were returned to power.

In January 1975 Thatcher challenged Edward Heath for the leadership of the Conservative Party. On 4th February Thatcher defeated Heath by 130 votes to 119 and became the first woman leader of a major political party. Heath took the defeat badly and refused to serve in Thatcher's shadow cabinet. James Callaghan replaced Harold Wilson as prime minister on 16th March 1976. Thatcher gradually adopted a more right-wing political programme placing considerable emphasis on the market economy. In January 1978 she was condemned for making a speech where she claimed that people feared being "swamped" by immigrants.

In 1978 the Chancellor of the Exchequer, Denis Healey, controversially began imposing tight monetary controls. This included deep cuts in public spending on education and health. Critics claimed that this laid the foundations of what became known as monetarism. In 1978 these public-spending cuts led to a wave of strikes (winter of discontent) and the Labour Party was easily defeated in the 1979 General Election.

Thatcher now became the first woman in Britain to become prime minister. In November 1979 Thatcher attended a summit meeting of the European

Economic Community where she attempted to renegotiate Britain's contribution to the EEC budget.

Thatcher's government continued the monetarist policies introduced by Denis Healey. Inflation was reduced but unemployment doubled between 1979 and 1980. In 1981, Sir Geoffrey Howe, the Chancellor of the Exchequer, announced further public spending cuts. During this period public opinion polls suggested that Thatcher was the most unpopular prime minister in British history.

Thatcher's government also raised money by a programme of privatization. This included the denationalization of British Telecom, British Airways, Rolls Royce and British Steel.

On 2nd April 1982 Argentina invaded the Falkland Islands. The following day the United Nations passed resolution 502 demanding that Argentina withdrew from the Falklands. On 5th April the British Navy left Portsmouth for the Falklands. Britain declared a 200-mile exclusion zone around the Falklands and on 2nd May 1982 the Argentinean battleship General Belgrade was sunk. Two days later, an exnet missile hit HMS Sheffield.

British troops landed on the Falkland Islands at San Carlos on 21st May. Fighting continued until Port Stanley was captured and Argentina surrendered on 14th June 1982. Thatcher's personal popularity was greatly boosted by the successful outcome of the war and the Conservative Party won the 1983 General Election with a majority of 144.

Thatcher developed a close relationship with President Ronald Reagan. They both agreed to take a firm stance with the Soviet Union. This resulted in her being dubbed the Iron Lady. However, Thatcher was furious in November 1983 when the United States invaded the British dependency of Grenada without prior consultation.

Thatcher's government continued its policy of reducing the power of the trade unions. Sympathy strikes and the closed shop was banned. Union leaders had to ballot members on strike action and unions were responsible for the actions of its members. The government took a firm stand against industrial disputes and the miners' strike that began in 1984 lasted for 12 months without success.

At the funeral of K. Chernenko on 13th March 1985, Thatcher met the new leader Mikhail Gorbachev. Thatcher's views on the Soviet Union changed after Gorbachev announced his new policy of Perestroika (Restructuring). This heralded a series of liberalizing economic, political and cultural reforms, which had the aim of making the Soviet economy more efficient. Gorbachev also introduced policies with the intention of establishing a market economy by encouraging the private ownership of Soviet industry and agriculture.

At a meeting on 13th November 1985, Thatcher rejected the idea of entering the European Exchange Rate Mechanism. However, the following month she attended the Luxembourg European Council and during the meeting Thatcher agreed to sign the Single European Act.

In April 1986 Thatcher was widely criticized for giving permission for US bombers to take off from Britain to bomb Libya following a series of Libyan inspired terrorist attacks.

Thatcher was returned to power for a third time when she won the 1987 General Election with a majority of 102 seats. The following year she became Britain's longest serving prime minister for over a hundred years.

However, her popularity was severely damaged when the Community Charge (Poll Tax) was introduced in Scot land in April 1989 (the rest of Britain was to follow a year later). The new tax was extremely unpopular and led to public demonstrations.

In November 1990 Thatcher was challenged as leader of the Conservative Party. She won the first round of the contest but the majority is not enough to prevent a second round. On 28th November 1990, Margaret Thatcher resigned as prime minister and was replaced by John Major.

Pakistan

Benazir Bhutto (1953–2007) was a Pakistan -born politician, with Pakistani and Kurdish – Iranian origin, who chaired the Pakistan Peoples Party (PPP), a centre-left and the largest political party in Pakistan. Bhutto was the first woman elected to lead a Muslim State, having twice been Prime Minister of Pakistan (1988–1990; 1993–1996). She was Pakistan's first and to date only female prime minister and was the eldest child of former Prime minister of Pakistan Mr. Zulfikar Ali Bhutto and former First Lady of Pakistan Mrs. Nusrat Bhutto. She was sworn in as Prime Minister for the first time in 1988 at the age of 35, but was removed from office 20 months later under the order of then- President on the grounds of alleged corruption. In 1993 she was re-elected but was again removed in 1996 on similar charges, this time by her party's elected President Farooq Leghari. She went into self-imposed exile in Dubai in 1998.

Bhutto returned to Pakistan on October 18, 2007, after having reached an understanding with President Pervez Musharraf by which she was granted amnesty and all corruption charges were withdrawn. She was assassinated on 27 December 2007, after departing a PPP rally in the Pakistani city of Rawalpindi, two weeks before the scheduled Pakistani General Electiopn of 2008 in which she was a leading opposition candidate. The following year, she was named one of seven winners of the Education and personal life.

Benazir Bhutto
Ex- Prime Minister of Pakistan

After completing her early education in Pakistan, she pursued her higher education in the United States. From 1969 to 1973 she attended Radcliffe College at Harvard University, where she obtained a Bachelor of arts degree with cum laude honors in comparative government. Bhutto would later call her time at Harvard "four of the happiest years of my life" and said it formed "the very basis of her belief in democracy". Later in 1995 as Prime Minister, she would arrange a gift from the Pakistani government to Harvard Law Achool. In June 2006, she received an Honorary LL.D degree from the University of Toronto.

The next phase of her education took place in the United Kingdom. Between 1973 and 1977 Bhutto studied Philosophy, Politics and Economics at Lady Margaret Hall, Oxford, during which time she completed additional courses in International Law and Diplomacy. After LMH she attended St. Catherine's College, Oxford and in December 1976 she was elected president of the Oxford Union, becoming the first Asian woman to head the prestigious debating society.

On 18 December 1987, she married Asf Ali Zardari in Karachi. The couple had three children: two daughters, Bakhtawar and Asifa, and a son, Bilawal. When she gave birth to Bakhawar in 1990, she became the first modern head of government to give birth while in office.

Family:

Benazir Bhutto's father, Prime Minister Zulfikar Ali Bhutto, was removed from office following a military coup in 1977 led by the then Chief of Army General Muhammad Zia-ul-Haq, who imposed marital law but promised to hold elections within three months. Nevertheless, instead of fulfilling the promise of holding general elections, General Zia charged Bhutto with conspiring to murder the father of dissident politician Ahmad Raza Kasuri. Mr. Zulfikar Ali Bhutto was sentenced to death by the martial law court.

Despite the accusation being "widely doubted by the public" and many demency appeals from foreign leaders, Zulfikar Ali Bhutto was hanged on 4 April 1979. Appeals for clemency were dismissed by acting President General Zia. Benazir Bhutto and her mother were held in a "police camp" until the end of May, after the execution.

Struggle against martial law of General Zia-ul-Haq

After the overthrow of her father Prime Minister Zulfikar Ali Bhutto's government in a bloodless coup Benazir Bhutto spent the next eighteen months in and out of house arrest as she struggled to rally political support to force Zia to drop murder charges against her father. The military dictator ignored worldwide appeals for clemency and had Zulfikar Bhutto hanged in April 1979. Following the hanging of her father Bhutto was arrested repeatedly, however, following PPP's victory in the local elections Zia postponed the national elections indefinitely and moved Bhutto and her mother Nusrat Bhutto from Karachi to Larkana. This was the seventh time Benazir had been arrested within two years of the military coup. Repeatedly put under house arrest, the regime finally imprisoned her under solitary confinement in a desert cell in Sindhi province during the summer of 1981. She described the conditions in her wall-less cage in her book "Daughter of Destiny", which goes by the title of "Daughter of the East" in Commonwealth countries for copyright reasons:

"The summer heat turned my cell into an oven. My skin split and peeled, coming off my hands in sheets. Boils erupted on my face. My hair, which had always been thick, began to come out by the handful. Insects crept into the cell like invading armies. Grasshoppers, mosquitoes, stinging flies, bees and bugs came up through the cracks in the floor and through the open bars from the courtyard. Big black ants, cockroaches, seething clumps of little red ants and spiders entered to my room. I tried pulling the sheet over my head at night to hide from their bites, pushing it back when it got too hot to breathe."

After her six month imprisonment in Sukkur jail, she remained hospitalized for months after which she was shifted to Karachi Central Jail, where she remained imprisoned until December 11, 1981. She was then placed under house arrests in Larkana and Karachi eleven and fourteen months respectively.

Self-exile in London

In January 1984, after six years of house arrests and imprisonment, Zia succumbed to international pressure and allowed Bhutto to travel abroad for medical reasons. After undergoing a surgery she resumed her political activities and began to raise concerns about the mistreatment of political prisoners in Pakistan at the behest of Zia regime. The intensified pressure forced Zia into holding a referendum to give certain legitimacy to his government. The referendum held on 1 December 1984 proved a farce, and only 10% of the voters bothered to turn out despite the state machinery.

Further pressure from the international community forced Zia into holding elections, for a unicameral legislature on a non-party basis. The PPP thus announced a boycott of the election on the grounds that they were not being held in accordance with the constitution of Pakistan. She continued to raise voice against human rights violations by the regime and addressed the European Parliament in Strasbourg in 1985, "When the conscience of the world is justly aroused against apartheid and against human rights violations. Then that conscience ought not to close its eyes to the murder by military courts which takes place in a country which receives.. aid from the West itself." The Zia regime reacted to the speech by announcing death sentences for 54 PPP workers at a military court in Lahore.

Bhutto, who had returned to Pakistan after completing her studies, found herself placed under house arrest in the wake of her father's imprisonment and subsequent execution. Having been allowed in 1984 to return to the United Kingdom, she became a leader in exile of the PPP, her father's party, though she was unable to make her political presence felt in Pakistan until after the death of General Muhammad Zia-ul-Hak. She had succeeded her mother as leader of the PPP and the pro-democracy opposition to the Zia-ul-Haq regime.

The seat, from which Benazir contested for the post of Prime Minister, was the same one from which her father had previously contested, namely, NA 207. This seat was first contested in 1926 by the late Sardar Wahid Bux Bhutto, in the first ever elections in Sindh. The elections were for the Central Legislative Assembly of India. Sardar Wahid Bux won, and became not only the first elected representative from Sindh to a democratically elected parliament, but also the youngest member of the Central Legislative Assembly, aged 27. Wahid Bux's achievement was monumental as it was he who was the first Bhutto elected to a government, from a seat that would, thereafter always be contested by his family members. Therefore, it was he who provided the breakthrough and a start to this cycle. Sardar Wahid Bux went on to be elected to the Bombay Council as well. After Wahid Bux's untimely and mysterious death at the age of 33, his younger brother Nawab Nabi Bux Bhutto contested from the same seat and remained undefeated until retirement. It was he who then gave this seat to Zulfikar Ali Bhutto to contest.

On 16 November 1988, in the first open election in more than a decade, Bhutto's PPP won the largest bloc of seats in the National Assembly. Bhutto was sworn in as Prime Minister of a coalition government on December 2, becoming at age 35 the youngest person—and the first woman—to head the government of a Muslim-majority state in modern times. In 1989, Benazir was awarded the Prize for Freedom by the Liberal International. Bhutto's accomplishments during this time were in initiatives for nationalist reform and modernization that some conservatives characterized as Westernization.

Bhutto's government was dismissed in 1990 following charges of corruption, for which she was never tried. Zia's protégé Nawz Sharif came to power after the October 1990 elections. She served as leader of the opposition while Sharif served as Prime Minister for the next three years.

Second term (1993-96)

In October 1993 elections were held again and her PPP coalition was victorious, allowing her to continue her reform initiatives. According to journalist shyam

Bhatia, Bhutto smuggled CDs containing uranium enrichment data to North Korea on a state visit that same year in return for data on missile technology. In 1996, amidst various corruption scandals Bhutto was dismissed by then-president Farrooq Leghari, who used the Eighth Amendment discretionary powers to dissolve the government. The Supreme Court affirmed President Leghari's dismissal in a 6-1 ruling. Criticism against Bhutto came from the Punjabi elites and powerful landlord families who opposed Bhutto. She blamed this opposition for the destabilization of Pakistan. Shortly after rising to power in a 1999 military coup, Pervez Musharraf characterized Bhutto's terms as an "era of sham democracy" and others characterized her terms a period of corrupt, failed governments.

During her election campaigns, she promised to repeal controversial laws (such as Hudood and Zina ordinances) that curtail the rights of women in Pakistan. Bhutto was pro-life and spoke forcefully against abortion, most notably at the International Conference on Population and Development in Cairo, where she accused the West of "seeking to impose adultery, abortion, intercourse education and other such matters on individuals, societies and religions which have their own social ethos."

The Zina ordinance was finally repealed by a Presidential Ordinance issued by Pervez Musharraf in July 2006. Bhutto was an active and founding member of the Council of Women World Leaders, a network of current and former prime ministers and presidents.

Policy on Taliban

The Taliban took power in Kabul in September 1996. It was during Bhutto's rule that the Taliban gained prominence in afghanistann. She, like many leaders at the time, viewed the Taliban as a group that could stabilize Afghanistan and enable trade access to the Central Asia republics, according to author Stephen Coll. He claims that her government provided military and financial support for the Taliban, even sending a small unit of the Pakistani army into Afghanistan. More recently, she took an anti-Taliban stance, and condemned terrorist acts allegedly committed by the Taliban and their supporters.

Charges of corruption

After the dismissal of Bhutto's first government on August 6, 1990 by President Ghulam Ishaq Khan on the grounds of corruption, the government of Pakistan issued directives to its intelligence agencies to investigate the allegations. After fourth national elections, Nawaz Sharif became the Prime Minister and intensified prosecution proceedings against Bhutto. Pakistani embassies through western Europe, in France, Switzerland, Spain, Poland and Britain were directed to investigate the matter. Bhutto and her husband faced a number of legal proceedings, including a charge of laundering money through Swiss banks. Though never convicted, her husband, Asif Ali Zardari, spent eight years in prison on similar corruption charges. After being released on bail in 2004, Zardari suggested that his time in prison involved torture; human rights groups have supported his claim that his rights were violated.

A 1998 *New York Times* investigative report claims that Pakistani investigators have documents that uncover a network of bank accounts, all linked to the family's lawyer in Switzerland, with Asif Zardari as the principal shareholder. According to the article, documents released by the French authorities indicated that Zardari offered exclusive rights to Dassault, a French aircraft manufacturer, to replace the air force's fighter jets in exchange for a 5 percent commission to be paid to a Swiss corporation controlled by Zardari. The article also said a Dubai company received an exclusive license to import gold into Pakistan for which Asif Zardari received payments of more than $10 million into his Dubai-based Citibank accounts. The owner of the company denied that he had made payments to Zardari and claims the documents were forged.

Bhutto maintained that the charges levelled against her and her husband were purely political. An Audiitor General of Pakistan (AGP) report supports Bhutto's claim. It presents information suggesting that Benazir Bhutto was ousted from power in 1990 as a result of a witch hunt approved by then-president Ghulam Ishaq Khan. The AGP report says Khan illegally paid legal advisers 28 million rupees to file 19 corruption cases against Bhutto and her husband in 1990–92. Yet the assets held by Bhutto and her husband continues to be scrutinized and speculated about. The prosecutors have alleged that their Swiss bank accounts contain £740 million. Zardari also bought a neo- Tudor mansion and estate worth over £4 million in Surrey, England, UK. The Pakistani investigations have tied other overseas properties to Zardari's family. These include a $2.5 million manor in Normandy owned by Zardari's parents, who had modest assets at the time of his marriage. Bhutto denied holding substantive overseas assets.

Despite numerous cases and charges of corruption registered against Bhutto by Nawaz Sharif from 1996 to 1999 and Pervez Mussaraf from 1999 till 2008, she was yet to be convicted in any case after a lapse of twelve years since their commencement. The cases were withdrawn by the government of Pakistan after the return to power of Bhutto's Pakistan Peoples Party in 2008.

Early 2000s in exile

In 2002, Pakistan president Pervez Musharraf amended Pakistan's constitution to ban prime ministers from serving more than two terms. This disqualified Bhutto from ever holding the office again. This move was widely considered to be a direct attack on former prime ministers Benazir Bhutto and Nawaz Sharif. On 3 August 2003, Bhutto became a member of Minhai ul quran International (an international Muslim educational and welfare organization).

While living in Dubai, UAR, she cared for her three children and her mother Nusrat, who was suffering from Alzheimer's disease, traveling to give lectures and keeping in touch with the PPP's supporters. They were reunited with her husband in December 2004 after more than five years.

In 2006, Interpol issued a request for the arrest of Bhutto and her husband on corruption charges, at the request of Pakistan. The Bhuttos questioned the legality of the requests in a letter to Interpol. On 27 January 2007, she was invited by the United States to speak to President George W. Bush and Congressional and State Department officials. Bhutto appeared as a panellist on the BBC TV programme Question Time in the UK in March 2007. She has also appeared on BBC current affairs programme Newsnight on several occasions. She rebuffed comments made by Muhammad Ijaz-ul-Haq in May 2007 regarding the knighthood of salman Rushdie, citing that he was calling for the assassination of foreign citizens.

Bhutto had declared her intention to return to Pakistan within 2007, which she did, in spite of Musharraf's statements of May 2007 about not allowing her to return ahead of the country's general election, due late 2007 or early 2008. It was speculated that she may have been offered the office of Prime Minister again.

Nonetheless, by mid-2007, the U.S. appeared to be pushing for a deal in which Musharraf would remain as president but step down as military head, and either Bhutto or one of her nominees would become prime minister.

On 11 July 2007, the Associated Press, in an article about the possible aftermath of the Red Mosque incident, wrote:

Benazir Bhutto, the former prime minister and opposition leader expected by many to return from exile and join Musharraf in a power-sharing deal after year-end general elections, praised him for taking a tough line on the Red Mosque. "I'm glad there was no cease-fire with the militants in the mosque because cease-fires simply embolden the militants," she told Britain's Sky TV on Tuesday. "There will be a backlash, but at some time we have to stop appeasing the militants."

This remark about the Red Mosque was seen with dismay in Pakistan as reportedly hundreds of young students were burned to death and remains are untraceable and cases are being heard in Pakistani Supreme Court as a missing person's issue. This and subsequent support for Musharraf led Elder Bhutto's comrades like Khar to criticize her publicly.

Bhutto however advised Musharraf in an early phase of the latter's quarrel with the Chief Justice, to restore him. Her PPP did not capitalize on its CEC member, Aitzaz Ahsan, the chief Barrister for the Chief Justice, in successful restoration. Rather he was seen as a rival and was isolated.

2002 election: The Bhutto-led PPP secured the highest number of votes (28.42%) and eighty seats (23.16%) in the national assembly in the October 2002 General Election. Pakistan Muslim League (N) (PML-N) managed to win eighteen seats only. Some of the elected candidates of PPP formed a faction of their own, calling it PPP- Patriots, which was being led by Faisal Saleh Hayat, the former leader of Bhutto-led PPP. They later formed a coalition government with Musharraf's party,

PML–Q Benazir Bhutto's image: In mid-2002 Musharraf implemented a two-term limit on Prime Ministers. Both Bhutto and Musharraf's other chief rival, Nawaz Sharif, had already served two terms as Prime Minister.

In July 2007, some of Bhutto's frozen funds were released. Bhutto continued to face significant charges of corruption.

In an 8 August 2007 interview with the Canadian Broadcasting Corporation, Bhutto revealed the meeting focused on her desire to return to Pakistan for the 2008 elections, and of Musharraf retaining the Presidency with Bhutto as Prime Minister.

On 29 August 2007, Bhutto announced that Musharraf would step down as chief of the army.

On September 1, 2007, Bhutto vowed to return to Pakistan "very soon", regardless of whether or not she reached a power-sharing deal with Musharraf before then.

On September 17, 2007, Bhutto accused Musharraf's allies of pushing Pakistan into crisis by their refusal to permit democratic reforms and power-sharing.

A nine-member panel of Supreme Court judges deliberated on six petitions (including one from Jamaat-e-Islam, Pakistan's largest Isamic group) asserting that Musharraf be disqualified from contending for the presidency of Pakistan. Bhutto stated that her party could join one of the opposition groups, potentially that of Nawaz Sharf. Attorney-general Malik Mohammed Qayyum stated that, pendente lite; the Election Commission was "*reluctant*" to announce the schedule for the presidential vote. Bhutto's party's Farhatullah Babar stated that the Constitution of Pakistan could bar Musharraf from being elected again because he was already the chief of the army: "As Gen. Musharraf was disqualified from contesting for President, he has prevailed upon the Election Commission to arbitrarily and illegally tamper with the Constitution of Pakistan."

Musharraf prepared to switch to a strictly civilian role by resigning from his position as commander-in-chief of the armed forces. He still faced other legal obstacles to running for re-election. On 2 October 2007, Gen. Musharraf named Lt. Gen. Ashfag Kayani, as vice chief of the army starting October 8 with the intent that if Musharraf won the presidency and resigned his military post, Kayani would become chief of the army. Meanwhile, Minister Sheikh Rashid Ahmed stated that officials agreed to grant Benazir Bhutto amnesty versus pending corruption charges. She has emphasized the smooth transition and returns to civilian rule and has asked Pervez Musharraf to shed uniform.

On 5 October 2007, Musharraf signed the National Reconciliation Ordinance, giving amnesty to Bhutto and other political leaders—except exiled former premier Nawaz Sharif—in all court cases against them, including all corruption charges. The Ordinance came a day before Musharraf faced the crucial presidential poll. Bhutto's party, the PPP, and the ruling PMLQ, were involved in negotiations beforehand about the deal. In return, Bhutto and the PPP agreed not to boycott the Presidential election. On 6 October 2007, Musharraf won a parliamentary election for President. However, the Supreme Court ruled that no winner can be officially proclaimed until it finishes deciding on whether it was legal for Musharraf to run for President while remaining Army General. Bhutto's PPP party did not join the other opposition parties' boycott of the election, but did abstain from voting. Later, Bhutto demanded security coverage on-par with the President's. Bhutto also contracted foreign security firms for her protection.

Return to Pakistan and the assassination attempt:

While under house arrest, Benazir Bhutto speaks to supporters outside her house. Bhutto was well aware of the risk to her own life that might result from her return from exile to campaign for the leadership position. In an interview on September 28, 2007, with reporter Wolf Blitzer of CNN, she readily admitted the possibility of attack on herself.

After eight years in exile in Dubai and London, Bhutto returned to Karachi on 18 October 2007, to prepare for the 2008 national elections.

Two explosions occurred shortly after Bhutto had landed and left Jinha International reroute to Karachi airport. She was not injured but the explosions, later found to be a suicide-bomb attack, killed 136 people and injured at least 450. The dead included at least 50 of the security guards from her PPP who had formed a human chain around her truck to keep potential bombers away, as well as six police officers. A number of senior officials were injured. Bhutto, after nearly ten hours of the parade through Karachi, ducked back down into the steel command center to remove her sandals from her swollen feet, moments before the bomb went off. She was escorted unharmed from the scene.

Bhutto later claimed that she had warned the Pakistani government that suicide bomb squads would target her upon her return to Pakistan and that the government had failed to act. She was careful not to blame Pervez Musharraf for the attacks, accusing instead "certain individuals within the government who abuse their positions, who abuse their powers" to advance the cause of Islamic militants. Shortly after the attempt on her life, Bhutto wrote a letter to Musharraf naming four persons whom she suspected of carrying out the attack. Those named included Chaudhury Pervez Elahi, a rival PML-Q politician and chief minister of Pakistan's Punjab province, Hamid Gul, former director of the Inter-Service Intelligence, and Ijaz Shah, the director general of the Intelligence Bureau, another of the country's intelligence agencies. All those named are close associates of General Musharraf. Bhutto had a long history of accusing parts of the government, particularly Pakistan's premier military intelligence agencies, of working against her and her party because they oppose her liberal, secular agenda. Bhutto claimed that the ISI has for decades backed militant Islamic groups in Kashmir and in Afghanistan. She was protected by her vehicle and a "human cordon" of supporters who had anticipated suicide attacks and formed a chain around her to prevent potential bombers from getting near her. The total number of injured, according to PPP sources, stood at 1000, with at least 160 dead (*The New York Times* claims 134 dead and about 450 injured).

A few days later, Bhutto's lawyer Senator Farooq H. Naik said he received a letter threatening to kill his client.

2007: State of Emergency and response:

On 3 November 2007, President Pervez Musharraf declared a state of emergency, citing actions by the Supreme Court of Pakistan and religious extremism in the nation. Bhutto returned to the country, interrupting a visit to family in Dubai. She was greeted by supporters chanting slogans at the airport. After staying in her plane for several hours she was driven to her home in Lahore, accompanied by hundreds of supporters. While acknowledging that

Pakistan faced a political crisis, she noted that Musharraf's declaration of emergency, unless lifted, would make it very difficult to have fair elections. She commented that "The extremists need a dictatorship, and dictatorship needs extremists."

On 8 November 2007, Bhutto was placed under house arrest just a few hours before she was due to lead and address a rally against the state of emergency.

During a telephone interview with National Public Radio in the United States, Ms. Bhutto said "I have freedom of movement within the house. I do not have freedom of movement outside the house. They've got a heavy police force inside the house, and we've got a very heavy police force - 4,000 policemen around the four walls of my house, 1,000 on each. They've even entered the neighbors' house. And I was just telling one of the policemen, I said 'should you be here after us? Should not you be looking for Osama bin Laden?' And he said, 'I'm sorry, ma'am, this is our job. We're just doing what we are told.'"

The following day, the Pakistani government announced that Bhutto's arrest warrant had been withdrawn and that she would be free to travel and to appear at public rallies. However, leaders of other opposition political parties remained prohibited from speaking in public.

Preparation for 2008 elections

On 24 November 2007, Bhutto filed her nomination papers for January's Parliamentary elections; two days later, she filed papers in the Larkana constituency for two regular seats. She did so as former Pakistani Prime Minister Nawaz Sharif, following seven years of exile in Saudi Arabia, made his much-contested return to Pakistan and bid for candidacy.

When sworn in again on 30 November 2007, this time as a civilian president after relinquishing his post as military chief, Musharraf announced his plan to lift the Pakistan's state of emergency rule on December 16.

Bhutto welcomed the announcement and launched a manifesto outlining her party's domestic issues.

Bhutto told journalists in Islamabad that her party, the PPP, would focus on "the five E's": employment, education, energy, environment, equality.

On 4 December 2007, Bhutto met with Nawaz Sharif to publicize their demand that Musharraf fulfill his promise to lift the state of emergency before January's parliamentary elections, threatening to boycott the vote if he failed to comply. They promised to assemble a committee that would present to Musharraf the list of demands upon which their participation in the election was contingent.

On 8 December 2007, three unidentified gunmen stormed Bhutto's PPP office in the southern western province of Balochistan. Three of Bhutto's supporters were killed.

Assassination:

On 27 December 2007, Bhutto was killed while leaving a campaign rally for the PPP at Liaquat National Bagh, where she had given a spirited address to party supporters in the run-up to the January 2008 parliamentary elections. After entering her bulletproof vehicle, Bhutto stood up through its sunroof to wave to the crowds. At this point, a gunman fired shots at her and subsequently explosives were detonated near the vehicle killing approximately 20 people. Bhutto was critically wounded and was rushed to Rawalpindi General Hospital. She was taken into surgery at 17:35 local time, and pronounced dead at 18:16. Bhutto's body was flown to her hometown of Garhi Khuda Bakhsh in Larkana District, Sindh, and was buried next to her father in the family mausoleum at a ceremony attended by hundreds of thousands of mourners.

There was some disagreement about the exact cause of death. Bhutto's husband refused to permit an autopsy or post-mortem examination to be carried out. On 28 December 2007, the Interior Ministry of Pakistan stated that "Bhutto was killed when she tried to duck back into the vehicle, and the shock waves from the blast knocked her head into a lever attached to the sunroof, fracturing her skull". However, a hospital spokesman stated earlier that she had suffered shrapnel wounds to the head and that this was the cause of her death. Bhutto's aides have also disputed the Interior Ministry's account. On December 31, CNN posted the alleged emergency room admission report as a PDF file. The document appears to have been signed by all the admitting physicians and notes that no object was found inside the wound.

Muslim extremist organization affiliated with al-Qaeda that also attempted in 1999 to assassinate former Prime Minister Nawaz Sharif, is alleged to have been responsible for the killing of the 54-year-old Bhutto along with approximately 20 bystanders, however this is vigorously disputed by the Bhutto family, by the PPP that Bhutto had headed and by Baitullah Mehsud. On 3 January 2008, President Musharraf officially denied participating in the assassination of Benazir Bhutto as well as failing to provide her proper security.

On February 12, 2011, Anti-Terrorism Court in Rawalpindi issued an arrest warrant for Musharraf, claiming he was aware of an impending assassination attempt by the Taliban, but did not pass the information on to those responsible for protecting Bhutto.

Scotland Yard investigation: British detectives were asked by the Pakistani government to investigate the assassination. Although expressing reservations as to the difficulty in investigating due to the crime scene having been hosed down and Asif Zardari's was refusing permission for a post mortem, the Pakistani government announced on 8 February 2008 that Benazir Bhutto had been killed on impact by the knob of the sun roof following the bomb explosion.

UN inquiry: A formal investigation by the UN commenced on July 1, 2009. The report concluded that the security measures provided to Bhutto by the government were "fatally insufficient and ineffective".[Furthermore, the report states that the treatment of the crime scene after her death "goes beyond mere incompetence". The report states that "police actions and omissions, including the hosing down of the crime scene and failure to collect and preserve evidence, inflicted irreparable damage to the investigation."

In May 2007, Bhutto asked for additional protection from foreign contracting agencies Black Water and the British Firm Armor Group. The United Nation's investigation of the incident revealed that, "Ms. Bhutto's assassination could have been prevented if adequate security measures had been taken."

Legacy: The Pakistani government honoured Bhutto on her birth anniversary by renaming the Islambad International Airport as Benazir Bhutto International Airport after her. Prime Minister Yousaf Raza Gillani, a member of Bhutto's PPP also asked President Pervez Musharaf to pardon convicts on death row on her birthday in honour of Bhutto.

The city of Nawabshah in Sindh was renamed Benazirbad in her honor. A university in the Dir Upper district of NWFP is opened in her name.

Israel

Golda Meir - labor Zionist leader, diplomat and Israel's fourth Prime Minister - was born Golda Mabovitch in Kiev (Ukraine) in 1898. When she was eight years old, her family immigrated to the United States. Raised in Milwaukee, Wisconsin, she joined a Zionist youth movement, married Morris Myerson, and, in 1921, immigrated to Palestine, joining Kibbutz Merhavia.

Golda Meir
Ex- Prime Minister of Israel

In 1924 the Meyersons moved to Jerusalem, and Golda began a series of positions as an official of the Histadrut - General Federation of Labor, and became a member of its "inner circle." Over the next three decades, Golda Meir was active in the Histadrut, first in trade union and welfare programs, then in Zionist labor organization and fund-raising abroad, and later still in political roles. She was appointed chief of the Histadrut's political section - designed to use the Histadrut's growing power to advance Zionist aims such as unrestricted Jewish immigration. When, in 1946, most of the Jewish community's senior leaders were interned by the British authorities, Golda Meir replaced Moshe Sharett as acting head of the political department of the Jewish Agency until the establishment of the state in 1948. From then on she played a part both in internal labor Zionist politics and in diplomatic efforts - including her ultimately unsuccessful secret meeting with Jordan's King

Abdullah on the eve of the Arab invasion of Israel in 1948, in an attempt to reach agreement and avoid war.

In 1924 the Meyersons moved to Jerusalem, and Golda began a series of positions as an official of the Histadrut - General Federation of Labor, and became a member of its "inner circle." Over the next three decades, Golda Meir was active in the Histadrut, first in trade union and welfare programs, then in Zionist labor organization and fund-raising abroad, and later still in political roles. She was appointed chief of the Histadrut's political section - designed to use the Histadrut's growing power to advance Zionist aims such as unrestricted Jewish immigration. When, in 1946, most of the Jewish community's senior leaders were interned by the British authorities, Golda Meir replaced Moshe Sharett as acting head of the political department of the Jewish Agency until the establishment of the state in 1948.

From then on she played a part both in internal labor Zionist politics and in diplomatic efforts - including her ultimately unsuccessful secret meeting with Jordan's King Abdullah on the eve of the Arab invasion of Israel in 1948, in an attempt to reach agreement and avoid war.

In June 1948 Golda Meir was appointed Israel's first ambassador to the Soviet Union, a position she filled for less than a year. She was elected as a Member of Knesset in the 1949 elections, and served as Minister of Labor and National Insurance from 1949 to 1956 - years of social unrest and a high rate of unemployment, caused by mass immigration. She enacted enlightened social welfare policies, provided subsidized housing for immigrants and orchestrated their integration into the workforce.

During the following decade (1956-66), Golda Meir served as Minister of Foreign Affairs. She initiated

Israel's policy of cooperation with the newly independent nations of Africa, introducing a cooperation program based on Israel's development experience, which continues to this day. At the same time, she endeavored to cement relations with the United States and established extensive bilateral ties with Latin American countries. Between 1966 and 1968 she served as Secretary-General first of Mapai and then of the newly formed "Alignment" (made up of three Labor factions).

Upon the death of Prime Minister Levi Eshkol in 1969, Golda Meir - the "consensus candidate" - was chosen to succeed him. In the October 1969 elections, she led her party to victory.

Shortly after she took office, the War of Attrition - sporadic military actions along the Suez Canal, which escalated into full-scale war - ended in a cease-fire agreement with Egypt. Though the cease-fire was broken time and again by the advancement of Egyptian missiles on the Suez Canal front, it did bring a three-year period of tranquillity, shattered only in October 1973 by the Yom Kippur War.

As Prime Minister, Golda Meir concentrated much of her energies on the diplomatic front - artfully mixing personal diplomacy with skillful use of the mass media. Armed with an iron will, a warm personality and grandmotherly image, simple but highly effective rhetoric and a "shopping list," Golda Meir successfully solicited financial and military aid in unprecedented measure. [60]

Golda Meir showed strong leadership during the surprise attack of the Yom Kippur War, securing an American airlift of arms while standing firm on the terms of disengagement-of-forces negotiations and rapid return of POWs. Although the Agranat

[60] Israel Ministry of Foreign Affairs

Commission of Inquiry had exonerated her from direct responsibility for Israel's un-preparedness for the war, and she had led her party to victory in the December 1973 elections, Golda Meir bowed to what she felt was the "will of the people" and resigned in mid-1974. She withdrew from public life and began to write her memoirs, but was present in the Knesset to greet Egyptian President Anwar Sadat on his historic visit to Jerusalem in November 1977. Golda Meir died in December 1978, at the age of 80.

Myanmar

Ms. Aung San Suu Kyi is an opposition politician of Myanmar and a former general secretary of the national league for Democracy. She remained under house arrest in Myanmar for almost 15 of the 21 years from 1990 until her release on November 13, 2010. She was not allowed to receive the Nobel Peace Prize in 1991 by the military government.

Born: June 19, 1945: Rangoon, British Burma
Residence: Yangon
Nationality: Myanmar
Religion: Theravada Buddhism

Awards:
1990: Rafto Prize
1991: Nobel Peace Prize
1992: Jawaharlal Nehru Award
2005: Olof Pame Prize

Education
1964: Graduation from Lady Shri Ram College (Delhi) in politics
1969: BA degree in Philosophy, Politics, and Economics from St Hugh's College, Oxford

Service
Worked at the United Nations for 3 years

Name: Derives her name from relatives – **Aung San** from father, **Suu** from her grand mother and **Kyi** from her mother

1972: Marries Dr. Michael Aris
1973: Birth of first son
1977: Birth of second son
1988: Returns to Burma and leads the pro-Democracy movement
1998: Ph. D. at the school of Oriental and African Studies, University of London
1999: Husband dies

The government always urged her to join her family abroad during house arrest, but she knew that she would not be allowed to return. This separation she regarded as one of the sacrifices she had had to make in order to work for a free Burma. Aung San Suu Kyi was under **house arrest for nearly two decades** in her country Myanmar, yet she fights for justice for the people of her country and the world.

Nobel Award Ceremony Speech

Francis Sejersted, Chairman of the Norwegian Nobel Committee (1991) presented the award ceremony speech in honor of Aung San suu Kyi in her absence.

Your Majesties, You're Excellencies, Ladies and Gentlemen,

We are assembled here today to honour Aung San Suu Kyi for her outstanding work for democracy and human rights, and to present to her the Nobel Peace Prize for 1991. The occasion gives rise to many and partly conflicting emotions. The Peace Prize Laureate is unable to be here herself. The great work we are acknowledging has yet to be concluded. She is still fighting the good fight. Her courage and commitment find her a prisoner of conscience in her own country, Burma. Her absence fills us with fear and anxiety, which can nevertheless only be a faint shadow of the fear and anxiety felt by her family. We welcome this opportunity of expressing our deepest sympathy with them, with her husband, Michael Aris, and with her sons, Alexander and Kim. We feel with you, and we are very grateful to you for coming to Oslo to receive the Nobel Prize on behalf of your wife and mother.

Our fear and anxiety are mixed with a sense of confidence and hope. In the good fight for peace and reconciliation, we are dependent on persons who set examples, persons who can symbolize what we are seeking and mobilize the best in us. Aung San Suu Kyi is just such a person. She unites deep commitment and tenacity with a vision in which the end and the means form a single unit. It's most important elements are: democracy, respect for human rights, reconciliation between groups, non-violence, and personal and collective discipline.

Aung San Suu Kyi
Political Leader and Nobel Laureate in Peace

Our fear and anxiety are mixed with a sense of confidence and hope. In the good fight for peace and reconciliation, we are dependent on persons who set examples, persons who can symbolize what we are seeking and mobilize the best in us. Aung San Suu Kyi is just such a person. She unites deep commitment and tenacity with a vision in which the end and the means form a single unit. It's most important elements are: democracy, respect for human rights, reconciliation between groups, non-violence, and personal and collective discipline.

She has herself clearly indicated the sources of her inspiration: principally Mahatma Gandhi and her father, Aung San, the leader in Burma's struggle for liberation. The philosopher of non-violence and the General differ in many respects, but also show fundamental similarities. In both, one can see genuine independence, true modesty, and "a profound simplicity", to use Aung San Suu Kyi's own words about her father. To Aung San, leadership was a duty, and could only be carried out on the basis of humility in face of the task before him and the confidence and respect of the people to be led.

While no doubt deriving a great deal of inspiration from Gandhi and her father, Aung San Suu Kyi has also added her own independent reflections to what has become her political platform. The keynote is the same profound simplicity as she sees in her father. The central position given to human rights in her thinking appears to reflect a real sense of the need to protect human dignity. Man is not only entitled to live in a free society; he also has a right to respect. On this platform, she has built a policy marked by an extraordinary combination of sober realism and visionary idealism. And in her case this is more than just a theory: she has gone a long way towards showing how such a doctrine can be translated into practical politics.

Aung San Suu Kyi knows:

(a) For a doctrine of peace and reconciliation to be translated into practice, one absolute condition is fearlessness.
(b) It is not power that corrupts, but fear.

(c) Fear of loosing power corrupts those who wield it and fear of the scourge of power corrupts those who are subject to it.

The comment was aimed at the totalitarian regime in her own country. They have allowed themselves to be corrupted because they fear the people they are supposed to lead. This has led them into a vicious circle. In her thinking, however, the demand for fearlessness is first and foremost a general demand, a demand on all of us. She has herself shown fearlessness in practice. She opposed herself alone to the rifle barrels. Can anything withstand such courage? What was in that Major's mind when at the last moment he gave the order not to fire? Perhaps he was impressed by her bravery; perhaps he realized that nothing could be achieved by brute force.

Violence is its own worst enemy, and fearlessness is the sharpest weapon against it. It is not least Aung San Suu Kyi's impressive courage, which makes her such a potent symbol, like Gandhi and her father Aung San. Aung San was shot in the midst of his struggle. But if those who arranged the assassination thought it would remove him from Burmese politics, they were wrong. He became the unifying symbol of a free Burma and an inspiration to those who are now fighting for a free society. In addition to his example and inspiration, his position among his people, over forty years after his death, gave Aung San Suu Kyi the political point of departure she needed. She has indeed taken up her inheritance, and is now in her own right the symbol of the revolt against violence and the struggle for a free society, not only in Burma, but also in the rest of Asia and in many other parts of the world.

We ordinary people, I believe, feel that with her courage and her high ideals, Aung San Suu Kyi brings out something of the best in us. We feel we need precisely her sort of person in order to retain our faith in the future. That is what gives her such power as a symbol, and that is why any ill-treatment of her feels like a violation of what we have most at heart. The little woman under house arrest stands for a positive hope. Knowing she is there gives us confidence and faith in the power of good.

Aung San Suu Kyi was born in 1945. Her father was killed when she was two. She has no personal memories of him. Her mother was a diplomat, and Aung San Suu Kyi was to spend many of her early years and much of her later life abroad.

In 1967, she took a degree in Politics, Philosophy and Economics at St. Hugh's College, Oxford. From 1969 on, she worked for two years for the United Nations in New York.

In 1972 she married Michael Aris, a British specialist on Tibet. For a time the family lived in Bhutan, but in the mid-seventies they moved back to Oxford. In addition to being a housewife with two small children, Aung San Suu Kyi kept up her academic work, gradually concentrating on modern Burmese history and literature. She was a visiting scholar at Kyoto University in Japan and at the Indian Institute of Advanced Studies in New Delhi.

On her return to Burma in 1988, she broke off her studies at the London School of Oriental and African Studies. There is little in these outward events to suggest the role she was to embark on in 1988. But she was well prepared.

There is a great deal of evidence that the fate of her own people had constantly weighed on her mind. Her husband has told us how she often reminded him that one day she would have to return to Burma, and that she would count on his support Her studies, too, as we have seen, became increasingly concentrated on

Burma's modern history. The study of her father and the part he played in Burmese history no doubt increased her political commitment and sense that his mantle had fallen on her.

In moving to Japan, she was virtually following in her father's footsteps. During the Second World War, it was from a base in Japan that Aung San built up Burma's independent national army. When Japan invaded Burma, Aung San and his men went too. Before long, they switched from fighting the British colonial power to resisting the occupying Japanese and supporting the retaking of Burma by the Allies. After the war, he led the negotiations with the British, which were to lead to final independence. Aung San Suu Kyi appears to have felt an urgent need to study the process, which led to Burma's independent statehood, and to understand the ideals governing the politics. In a beautiful essay comparing the Indian and Burmese experience of colonization, she also brings out the special features of Burma's cultural heritage. History is important. You choose who you are by choosing which tradition you belong to. Aung San Suu Kyi seeks to call attention to what she sees as the best aspects of the national and cultural heritage and to identify herself with them. Such profound knowledge and such a deep sense of identity are an irresistible force in the political struggle.

The occasion of Aung San Suu Kyi's return to Burma in 1988 was, characteristically enough, not the political situation but her old mother's illness. The political turbulence had just begun, however. There had been demonstrations and confrontations with the police with some two hundred killed. The unrest continued while she was nursing her dying mother. That was the situation in which she resolved to take an active part in what she herself called "the second struggle for national independence".

The military regime had seized power in Burma in 1962. The disturbances, which broke out in 1988, were a reaction to growing repression. In the summer of that year, at a time when the situation was very uncertain, Aung San Suu Kyi intervened with a open letter to the government, proposing the appointment of a consultative committee of respected independent persons to lead the country into multi-party elections. In the letter, she emphasized the need for discipline and for refraining from the use of force on either side, and demanded the release of political prisoners.

A couple of days later, she addressed several hundred thousand people in front of the large Shwedagon Pagoda in Rangoon, presenting a political program based on human rights, democracy and non-violence. On the 18th of September, after hesitating for a few weeks, the armed forces reacted by tightening the restrictions. The so-called "State Law and Order Restoration Council" (SLORC) was established, and martial law was introduced under which meetings were banned and persons could be sentenced without trial.

Political parties were not prohibited (perhaps with meetings banned it was thought unnecessary). A week after the establishment of SLORC, Aung San Suu Kyi and a few other members of the opposition founded the National League for Democracy, the NLD. She went on to engage in vigorous political activity, defying the ban on meetings and military provocations, and holding heavily attended political meetings all over the country. One remarkable feature of her political campaign was the appeal she had for the country's various ethnic groups, traditionally at odds with each other.

It must have been her personal prestige, which caused the regime to hesitate so long, but in July 1989 she was placed under house arrest. In May 1990, elections were held, in which the NLD won an overwhelming victory and over 80 per cent of the seats in the national assembly. There is general agreement that this was principally a triumph for Aung San Suu Kyi.

Why did the SLORC allow free elections? Probably because they expected a very different result, a result, which would somehow have provided the legitimacy, they needed to retain power. The dilemma of such regimes was demonstrated - trapped in their own lies. At any rate, they refused to accept the election result. The election was in effect annulled. The SLORC continued, but with reduced legitimacy. Lack of legitimacy is often made up for by increased brutality. Amnesty International has reported continuing serious violations of human rights. Today, the Burmese regime appears to have developed into one of the most repressive in the world.

In recent decades, the Norwegian Nobel Committee has awarded a number of Prizes for Peace in recognition of work for human rights. It has done so in the conviction that a fundamental prerequisite for peace is the recognition of the right of all people to life and to respect. Another motivation lies in the knowledge that in its most basic form, the concept of human rights is not just a Western idea, but common to all major cultures. Permit me in this connection to quote a paragraph of Aung San Suu Kyi's essay *In Quest of Democracy*:

Where there is no justice there can be no security of peace.

Those just laws, which uphold human rights, are the necessary foundations of peace and security. These would be denied only by closed minds, which interpret peace as the silence of all opposition and security as the assurance of their own power. The Burmese associate peace and security with coolness and shade:

The shade of a tree is cool indeed.
The shade of parents is cooler.
The shade of teachers is cooler still.
The shade of the ruler is yet cooler.
But coolest of all is the shade of the Buddha's teachings.

Thus to provide the people with the protective coolness of peace and security, rulers must observe the teachings of the Buddha. Central to these teachings are the concepts of truth, righteousness and loving kindness. It is government based on these very qualities that the people of Burma are seeking in their struggle for democracy.

This is not the first time that political persecution at home has prevented a Peace Prize Laureate from receiving the prize in person. It happened to Carl von Ossietzky in 1936, ill in one of Hitler's concentration camps. It happened to Andrei Sakharov and to Lech Walesa. Ossietzky died before the regime fell, but Sakharov and Walesa saw their struggles succeed. It is our hope that Aung San Suu Kyi will see her struggle crowned with success.[61]

However, we must also face up to the likelihood that this will not be the last occasion on which a Peace Prize Laureate is unable to attend. Let that remind us that in a world such as ours, peace and reconciliation cannot be achieved once and for all. We will never be able to lower our standards. On the contrary, a better world demands even greater vigilance of us still greater fearlessness, and the ability to develop in us the "profound simplicity" of which this year's Laureate has spoken. This applies to all of us as individuals, but must apply especially to those in positions of power and authority. Show humility and show fearlessness - like Aung San Suu Kyi. The result may be a better world to live in.

---

[61] Nobelprize.org / Award Ceremony Speech

Conclusion:

Only brave women and men contest elections with new ideas, plans and programs to do justice to the people. If all of the elected candidates would try to award justice, peace and safety to all people of the world; we can make this earth a Heaven. And WORLD PEACE is possible.

Political parties need donations from industrialists. Political leaders want to remain in power for the life. So it is assumed that all political leaders amass personal wealth at the cost of the people and the state. But women Prime Ministers of different countries are not yet proved that they are prone to corruption. Hence, it is accepted that the countries are safe during their governance.

But women Prime Ministers of different countries are not yet proved that they are prone to corruption. Hence, it is accepted that the countries are safe during their governance.

However, it is not desirable to award reservations for women in elections for Parliament, Assembly or Senate. Let they prove their merit and efficiency as political leaders in Elections.

There should not be 'quota system' in service sector too. It is better that they should fight to achieve laurels in life. And it is possible.

All political posts such as President, Prime Minister, Governor, Chief Minister, Member of Parliament, and Member of Assebly or Senator should be elected or appointed for a term of 4-years in all countries. They could avail second term in their life through election or appointment as per constitution. But none should be permitted to enter to the Parliament or Senate for the third term.

Chapter VII

LOVE, MARRIAGE AND WAR

I, with a deeper instinct, choose a man who compels my strength, who makes enormous demands on me, who does not doubt my courage, or my toughness, who does not believe me naïve or innocent, who has the courage to treat me like a woman. --- Anaïs Nin

Love is blind and marriage is luck. Love is man-made and marriage is decided in heaven. So the lovers and beloveds should not mix both love and marriage as one institution. Failures in love-marriages cause disasters in the minds of young people, which can cause suicides and murders. This love-marriage is very slippery to climb to the heaven.

Love increases the potency to climb the tall tree, but it must be evaluated each time. Many persons have achieved laurels because they invest more time in constructive way, such as high academic performance or successful business career to please the love partner. But those who become mad after love and neglect their duties ultimately fail in marriage markets. Love should be an attachment of mind to soul and leave it to God to allow for a happy marriage. Those lovers, who take the full responsibility for success of love marriage, face more difficulties as friends and relatives oppose the marriage. And ultimately the love-episode faces the volcano or disaster. As a result, love relationship is marred; causes torture of mind and wrecks in the ocean of disaster, agony and misfortune.

The goons, rich and employed youth could achieve temporary success. Again they may fail in future leading to divorce. No body knows when it would succeed or fail.

It is better to go for marriage through negotiations by verifying the horoscope of both the young lover and beloved. But adjusting mind after the marriage could award long term marriage success. The love-letters written by youths make them poets, writers and singers. The love-letters are preserved by a true lover till his death, but these are destroyed by beloved partner before her marriage. Many lovers write manuscripts and keep it sealed to be published after 30 years of his death. True love is heaven and it cannot be compared with any other physical property.

The love of Mogul Emperor Shahjahan (1628 AD – 1658 AD) with beloved wife Mumtaz was so intense that it could create the Taj Mahal at Agra (India). This is a monument of beauty and love, stands out for its purity and serenity. This monument took 22 years for construction and 220 millions of Indian rupees were spent for the construction in the Seventeenth century. This is a clear reflection of his inexhaustible patience and love for beauty and love to his beloved queen. The Taj Mahal is considered as one of the SEVEN wonders of the world even today. He also constructed Mumtaz Mahal in Delhi in addition to other important constructions.

In this chapter, love, marriage and war is discussed to have a glimpse on the past events and for future guidance.

Interracil Marriages

Attitudes towards Interracial marriage have changed dramatically, in just the last generation. In the United States it was just 43 years ago when interracial marriage was made fully legal in all 50 states. Today, in many countries, interracial marriage is commonplace and most don't even give it a second thought. However, as we all know, it wasn't always this way in the past. This list includes individuals who didn't let the prejudice of society make their decisions in life, and also paved the way for interracial couples in the future.

1. Pearl Bailey and Louie Bellson (Married in 1952) Baileybelson

Pearl Mae Bailey was a famous actress and singer and Louie Bellson was a famous jazz drummer, composer and bandleader. Bellson was Duke Ellington's first white musician and met Bailey after being introduced by a trombone player. After a courtship lasting just four days they were married, in London. It was Bailey's third marriage and Bellson's first. Interracial couples were a rarity at the time, and even Bellson's presence in the Ellington band raised some eyebrows. During some dates in some Southern cities in the United States, Ellington would claim that Bellson was of Haitian background. After their wedding, Louie Bellson spent much of his time as Pearl Bailey's musical director, writing her arrangements and leading her accompanying bands. The Couple were married for 38 years, until Bailey's death in 1990, at age 72. Bellson died at age 84, in 2009. The couple adopted a boy, Tony, in the mid-1950s, and girl Dee Dee, in 1960.

Interesting Fact: Bailey served as a United Nations' Goodwill Ambassador under several Republican Presidential Administrations. Even after the majority of African-Americans moved from The Republican Party to The Democratic Party in 1964, Pearl Bailey remained with The Republican Party because The Republican Party was where she and Louis Bellson found the greatest acceptance for their interracial marriage.

2. Betty & Barney Hill (Married in 1960) Betty-And-Barney-Hill230

Betty and Barney Hill were from Portsmouth, New Hampshire. Barney worked for the post office and Betty was a social worker. The Hills were also members of the National Association for the Advancement of Colored People (NAACP) and community leaders. On the night of September19th, 1961, Betty and Barney Hill were heading back from a vacation in Southern Canada to their home in New England. They claimed to have observed a bright light in the sky that appeared to be following them. They arrived home at about 3 am and realized (later, when it was pointed out to them) that they had lost about 2 hours of time. Two weeks later Betty began having nightmares. In her nightmares, she described being taken aboard an alien spacecraft and then having medical experiments performed on her. Betty and Barney then decided to undergo hypnosis. In separate sessions, they described some similar experiences of being taken on board an alien spacecraft. Betty said she was shown a star map which she was able to memorize and reproduce later, which some believe is showing Zeta Reticuli as the aliens' home.

Under Barneys hypnotic session he said a cup-like device was placed over his genitals and thought that a sperm sample was taken. He also said he heard them speaking in a mumbling language that he did not understand. The UFO incident was distracting and embarrassing for Barney Hill. He feared that the tabloid publicity would tarnish his battle for equality and dignity. The Hills eventually went back to their regular lives but were always willing to discuss the UFO encounter with friends and UFO researchers. The release of the book "Interrupted Journey" in the mid-1960s, and a movie called The UFO Incident, starring James Earl Jones and Estelle Parsons turned Betty and Barney Hill into the world's most famous UFO "abductees."

Interesting Fact: Some psychiatrists suggested later that the supposed abduction was a hallucination brought on by the stress of being an interracial couple in early 60s. Betty discounted this suggestion, saying that her relationship with Barney was happy, and their interracial marriage caused no notable problems with their friends or family. Barney died of a cerebral hemorrhage in 1969, and Betty died of cancer in 2004. Many of Betty Hill's notes, tapes and other items have been placed in a permanent collection at the library of the University of New Hampshire, her alma mater.

3. Samuel Coleridge-Taylor and Jessie Walmisley (Married in 1899)

At the turn of the twentieth century, Samuel Coleridge-Taylor was one of Britain's most outstanding and celebrated composers. He was born to a white mother and black father and was raised in the London suburb of Croydon. At the age of just 23 he produced his most famous work; a musical called Hiawatha's Wedding Feast. Some describe it as one of the most remarkable events in English musical history. Coleridge-Taylor married Jessie Walmisley, in

1899. She was a pianist and a classmate of Samuel's in high school. Jessie's family had been vehemently opposed to the marriage and had done all in its power to prevent it. On the day before the wedding, Mrs. Walmisley invited Samuel to the family home where she and her husband shook his hand in a formal gesture of acceptance. Coleridge-Taylor and his family were targets of abuse from groups of local youths who would repeatedly shower him with insulting comments about the color of his skin. His daughter later recalled "when he saw them approaching along the street he held my hand more tightly, gripping it until it almost hurt."On September 1, 1912, Samuel Coleridge-Taylor died of pneumonia complicated by exhaustion from overwork. He was just 37 years old. Hundreds turned out for his funeral and a memorial concert which was held to raise money for his widow and his two children, Hiawatha and Gwendoline, who would both go on to have musical careers.

Interesting Fact: It emerged that the publishers of Hiawatha's Wedding Feast had paid Coleridge-Taylor just 15 guineas (£15.75) for the composition, which earned the company a fortune. Their refusal to grant the widow a fair royalty resulted in the formation of the Performing Rights Society, which has exacted fair dues for composers in Britain ever since.

4. Sammy Davis Jr. and May Britt (Married in 1960), Sammy-Davis-Jr-And-May-Br-009

When Sammy Davis Jr. married Swedish-born actress May Britt in 1960, interracial marriages were forbidden by law in 31 US states. Earlier that year the Democratic Convention took place in Los Angeles where John F. Kennedy would be elected as the Democrats' presidential nominee. When the introductions of Hollywood celebrities were being announced, Davis was booed by many of the white Southern delegates because he was engaged to a white woman. A headline over a New York Times story the next day read, "Delegates Boo Negro." JFK's father, Joseph Kennedy, was worried that Davis' marriage to a white woman on the eve of the November election might cost his son votes, so Davis reluctantly postponed the wedding until after the election. At the wedding Frank Sinatra was the best man along with many other stars, including Peter Lawford, Dean Martin, Janet Leigh, Shirley MacLaine, Milton Berle and Edward G. Robinson. During their marriage the couple received hate mail and was targets of nasty jokes and vicious slurs. Because Davis performed almost continuously he spent very little time with his wife. They divorced in 1968, after Davis admitted to having had an affair with singer Lola Falana. Davis and Britt had a daughter and also adopted two sons.

Interesting Fact: Before Davis met Britt, he had a relationship with actress Kim Novak. A contract by the mob was allegedly put out on Davis's life. Frank Sinatra intervened but Davis still feared for his life and married a black showgirl. The marriage only lasted a few months and was later annulled. Some consider Novak the love of Davis' life. Before he died of throat cancer, Davis's third wife, Altovise, allowed Novak to visit. She and Sammy spent hours talking and reminiscing just weeks before he died, in 1990.

5. George Schuyler & Josephine Cogdell (Married in 1928), Kaplan3

George S. Schuyler was a journalist, satirist, author and editor. During the mid 1920s, Schuyler was published in The Nation, and other left wing publications. Josephine Cogdell was an actress, model and dancer and came from a wealthy, former slave-owning family. She was intrigued by new ideas and radical politics and began corresponding with Schuyler, who was a brilliant and controversial journalist at the time. When she traveled to New York to meet him they would both write later that it was love at first sight. When they were married she proclaimed herself "colored." on the marriage certificate because of the dangers of crossing racial lines. The couple believed that intermarriage could "invigorate" both and help solve many of the United States' social problems. George and Josephine had one child named Philippa. Their daughter became a noted child prodigy. By the time she was four she was composing classical music for piano. When she reached adolescence, she was performing in the US and overseas. During the late 1940s, and the McCarthy Era, George Schuyler moved sharply to the political right. He believed that the American black could only succeed by working in cooperation with whites, within the democratic system, toward mutual economic gain. He started contributing to the American Opinion, the journal of the John Birch Society and, in 1947; he published The Communist Conspiracy against the Negroes. Schuyler continued his career as a journalist until 1966, when he published his autobiography, Black and Conservative. The couple remained married until George's death in 1977.

Interesting Fact: In 1967, their daughter, Philippa, had begun a career as a news journalist and traveled to Vietnam as a war correspondent. While attempting to rescue schoolchildren from a war zone, the helicopter crashed into the sea. She initially survived the crash but her inability to swim caused her to drown. She died at the age of 35. Film rights to her biography have been sold and it has been reported that she is to become the subject of a movie starring Alicia Keys. The above photo shows Phillipa, Josephine, and George Schuyler playing dominoes, around 1945.

6. Jack Johnson and Wives (Married in 1911, 1912 & 1925)

Jack Johnson was an American boxer and the first African American world heavyweight boxing champion, a title he held from 1908 to 1915. In addition to being a rich and famous athlete, Jack Johnson also performed for theatre companies between fights, singing, dancing and acting. He also led a very fascinating life, to say the least. Jack Johnson was married three times. All of his wives were white, which caused considerable controversy at the time. In January 1911, Johnson married Brooklyn socialite and divorcee Etta Terry Duryea, after meeting her at a car race. Their romantic relationship was often very turbulent. Sources also indicate that Johnson was physically abusive towards her and was often unfaithful. Etta suffered from severe depression, evidenced by her reportedly wild mood swings. In 1912, after just 8 months of marriage, Etta committed suicide by shooting herself in the head. Shortly afterwards he met his second wife, Lucille Cameron, who was an 18 year old prostitute. Less than three months after Duryea's suicide Johnson and Cameron were married, an act that outraged the public. In 1913, Johnson was convicted for transporting women across state lines for immoral purposes, which was part of the Mann Act. For the next seven years, the couple lived in exile in Europe, South America and Mexico. Johnson finally surrendered to the US authorities in 1920, and ended up serving eight months in federal prison. Four years later, Lucille filed for divorce on the uncontested charge of infidelity. In1925, Johnson married Irene Pineau after meeting her at a race track. Johnson would later call her his true love. She remained married to Johnson for the rest of his life. In 1946, Johnson was driving on Highway 1 near Raleigh, North Carolina, when he lost control of his car, which hit a light pole and overturned. He died three hours later.

Interesting Fact: At Johnson's funeral, Johnson's third wife Irene Pineau was asked by a reporter what she had loved about her husband. "I loved him because of his courage, he faced the world unafraid. There wasn't anybody or anything he feared." The photo above shows Johnson with his first wife, Etta Terry Duryea. Jack Johnson had no children.

7. Frederick Douglass and Helen Pitts (Married in 1884)

Frederick Douglass was an American writer, social reformer and statesman. He was born a slave in the early 1800s, the son of a female slave and her white owner. After he escaped from slavery in 1838, he married a free African American woman Anna Murray, and had 5 children. After Anna died in 1882, he met Helen Pitts, a white abolitionist and suffragist. Against the wishes of Douglas's children and her family, they married. The marriage was the subject of scorn by both white and black Americans, but the couple was firm in their convictions. Douglass's marriage was an affirmation of his personal belief in American unity, and his desire for a true melting pot of cultures within the United States. Douglas laughingly commented, "This proves I am impartial. My first wife was the color of my mother and the second, the color of my father." Helen Pitts said "Love came to me, and I was not afraid to marry the man I loved because of his color," The couple were married for eleven years, until his sudden death from a heart attack, in 1895. Douglass was also an advocate of equal rights for women. On the day he died he gave a speech on the topic of female equality and was a believer in granting women the right to vote. Helen is the one seated in the photo above. The woman standing is her sister Eva Pitts.

Interesting Fact: During Fredrick Douglass's first marriage he had a 26 year affair with German feminist Ottilie Assing. In 1884, when she read in the newspapers that Douglass was to marry Helen Pitts, who was 20 years-younger, she committed suicide in a public park in Paris. The letters Douglass wrote to her were burned, and she left all her money to Douglass.

8. Joseph Philippe Laroche and Juliette Lafargue (Married in 1908)

Joseph Philippe Lemercier Laroche was born in Cap Haitien, Haiti, in 1886. At the age of 15, he left Haiti and travelled to Beauvais, France, to study engineering in high school. While visiting nearby Villejuif, Joseph met his future wife, Juliette. After Joseph received his degree, they were married. Their daughter Simonne was born in1909, and a second daughter, Louise was born prematurely in 1910, and suffered medical problems. Because of racial discrimination it prevented Joseph from obtaining a high-paying job in France. The family needed more money to pay for their youngest daughters medical bills so Joseph planned to return to Haiti in 1913, to find a better-paying engineering job. However, in March of 1912 Juliette discovered that she was pregnant, so the family decided to leave for Haiti before her pregnancy became too far advanced. For a welcome present Joseph's mother in Haiti bought them steamship tickets on the La France, but the line's strict policy regarding children caused them to transfer their booking to the Titanic's second class. Racism towards the couple because of their interracial marriage was rampant aboard the ship, especially among the crew members.

After the Titanic struck an iceberg historians agree that Laroche was calm and heroic. As the ship sank, Joseph stuffed his coat packets with money and jewelry and took his pregnant wife and children up to the boat deck and managed to get them into the lifeboat. He wrapped the coat around his wife, and his last words were: "Here, take this, you are going to need it. I'll get another boat. God be with you. I'll see you in New York." Joseph Laroche died in the sinking and was the only passenger of black descent (besides his daughters) on the Titanic. His body was never found.

Interesting fact: When Juliette returned to Paris with her daughters she gave birth to a son, Joseph Lemercier Laroche. The White Star Line, the company that owned the Titanic, was later forced to issue a public apology for the derogatory statements made by the crew. When Louise Laroche died on January 28, 1998, at the age of 87 it left only seven remaining survivors of the Titanic.

9. Sir Seretse Khama and Ruth Williams (Married in 1948)

Seretse Khama was born in 1921, and is the son of the Chief of the Bangwato Tribe and ruler of the Bechuanaland (a protectorate by Great Britain) later known as Botswana. When his father died in 1925, Seretse's uncle, assumed the role as Seretse's guardian and Acting Chief. His uncle sent Seretse to England so he could continue his education. It was while he was in London, when studying for his bar examinations, that he met Ruth Williams. They shared their enthusiasm for jazz and eventually romance ensued and they were married a year later, in 1948. The interracial marriage sparked a furor among both the apartheid government of South Africa and the tribal elders. Seretse was at first banned from the chieftainship and the territory for breaking tribal custom, but was later re-affirmed and eventually became Chief. Because of the apartheid system in South Africa, the country could not afford to have an interracial couple ruling just across their border, so pressure was put on to have Seretse removed from his chieftainship. In 1951, the British government launched a parliamentary enquiry. They somehow proved that Seretse was unfit to be chief, and exiled Seretse and his wife Ruth from Bechuanaland. In 1956, Ruth and Seretse were allowed to return to Bechuanaland as private citizens, after he had renounced the tribal throne. In 1961, Khama founded the Nationalist Bechuanaland Democratic Party and became Prime Minister of Bechuanaland. In 1966, Botswana gained its independence and Seretse Khama became the country's first President. Ruth (Lady Khama) was a very influential and politically active first lady during her husband's tenure as president, from 1966 until his death in 1980. In 1966, Queen Elizabeth appointed Khama Knight Commander of the Most Excellent Order of the British Empire.

Interesting Fact: Botswana was among the world's poorest countries but during Seretse Khama's tenure as president, Botswana had the fastest growing economy in the world. Khama instituted strong measures against corruption and reinvested money into infrastructure, health and education. In 2009, Seretse and Ruth's fist son, Ian, won a landslide victory and became the fourth President of Botswana. Their younger son, Tshekedi, was elected as a parliamentarian.

10. Richard Loving and Mildred Jeter (Married in 1958)

This is at the number one spot because this couple's marriage overturned state laws in the United States that prohibited interracial marriages. Richard and Mildred were from VIrginia and met when he was 17 years old and she was 11. As they grew older, their friendship blossomed into romance. When Mildred was 18 she became pregnant so the couple decided to travel to Washington, D.C. to be married. Five weeks after their wedding, they were awakened at 2 a.m. by police and arrested for being married to one another. In 1959, they pleaded guilty to the charge against them and were sentenced to one year in jail. The sentence was suspended on the condition that the Lovings leave Virginia and not return for 25 years. The Lovings moved to Washington, D.C., and faced housing discrimination, compounded by deep unhappiness about not living close to their families. Mildred wrote a letter to Attorney General, Robert F. Kennedy. Kennedy then forwarded the letter to the American Civil Liberties Union. After many setbacks throughout a nine-year period, their case was heard before the U.S. Supreme Court. In 1967, The Supreme Court decided unanimously in their favor. Richard later said "For the first time, I could put my arm around Mildred and publicly call her my wife." In 1975, Richard Loving died at age 41, when a drunken driver struck the couple's car. Mildred Loving lost her right eye in the same accident. Mildred died of pneumonia in 2008, at the age of 68. The couple had three children, eight grandchildren and eleven great-grandchildren.

Interesting Fact: An annual celebration called Loving Day is held on June 12, the anniversary of the 1967 United States Supreme Court decision. Many organizations sponsor annual parties across the country, with Lovingday.org providing courtroom history of anti-miscegenation laws, as well as offering testimonials and resources for interracial couples.

11. Barack Obama, Sr. and Ann Dunham (Married in 1961)

Obama Parents

I wasn't going to include this couple in the list because their relationship was so short, but I know there would be many comments asking about them so I decided to include it as a bonus.

In 1960, after Ann Dunham graduated from high school in Mercer Island, Washington, her family moved to Honolulu. Dunham then enrolled at the University of Hawaii. Obama Sr. was 23 years old and had come to Hawaii to pursue his education, and was the university's first African foreign student, leaving behind a pregnant wife and infant son in Kenya. Dunham met Obama Sr. at the University while attending a Russian language class. When Dunham became pregnant they were married on the Hawaiian island of Maui. Obama Sr.'s wife in Kenya later said she had granted her consent for him to marry a second wife, in keeping with their countries customs. On August 4, 1961, at the age of 18, Dunham gave birth to her first child, Barack Obama II. Dunham took one month old Barack to Washington State where she took classes at the University of Washington from September 1961 to June 1962. Barack Sr. continued his studies in Hawaii until he graduated in 1962, and then left for Cambridge, Massachusetts, where he would begin graduate study at Harvard. Dunham returned to Honolulu to resume her education with her parents helping to raise Barack. Dunham then filed for a divorce in 1964, which was uncontested.

In 1971, Obama Sr. came to Hawaii to visit his 10 year old son, Barack. This would be the last time he would see him. Obama Sr.'s life fell into drinking and poverty back in Kenya. After a terrible car accident he lost both legs and subsequently lost his job. In 1982, at the age of 46, he was killed in another car accident in Nairobi. Obama Sr. had 7 children. In 1992, Ann, who was remarried to Lolo Soetoro, finally finished her doctoral dissertation and received her Ph.D. in anthropology. Two years later she complained of stomach pains. Months later, she was diagnosed with ovarian and uterine cancer. She died on November 7, 1995, at the age of 52. Ann Dunham had 2 children, Barack and a daughter, Maya, with Lolo Soetoro.

Interesting Fact: Following Ann Dunham's memorial service at the University of Hawaii, Obama and his half sister Maya spread their mother's ashes in the Pacific Ocean at Lanai Lookout on the south side of Oahu. Obama scattered the ashes of his grandmother

(Madelyn Dunham) who died November 2, 2008, in the same spot weeks after his election to the presidency.[62]

History's Most Famous Weddings

Romance, drama, passion, and notoriety are all highlighted in our list of history's most famous weddings. In fact, these star-studded unions often ignited lots of controversy. In some cases, these memorable ceremonies really captured the spirit of the times...If you love reading about Hollywood and the Royal Family, you'll enjoy this juicy list of famous weddings.

1. Liz and Dick (Elizabeth Taylor & Richard Burton)

Liz Taylor's legendary beauty led to fame, riches, and eight marriages...

The glamour and mystery of Elizabeth Taylor still endures today...from violet-eyed child star (National Velvet was her breakthrough role) to Hollywood temptress...this screen legend is known for her exquisite jewelry collection, her eight husbands, and her very real commitment too many worthwhile charities (such as AIDS research). A fascinating mixture of good girl/bad girl, Liz was at the height of her powers when she met charismatic, rugged Welsh actor Richard Burton. Of course, she was still married to Eddie Fisher then...and Richard was married to his long-suffering wife, Sybil...Liz and Dick were kindred spirits...they traveled the world together, acted

---

[62] Paul Holtum (2011), "10 Fascinating International Marriages in History", January 25, 2011, List verse Com / Note: Interracial marriage can convey a relationship between a Black and an Asian, a White and an Asian, a Hispanic and an Asian, a White and a Hispanic, etc. In this particular list I have included only black and white relationships.

together, and tried (more than once) to break off their illicit relationship – for the good of their families. However, this pair seemed destined for one another, and eventually, they dissolved the ties that kept them apart legally.

Then, they were wed...in Montreal, Canada, in 1967...Liz wore canary yellow and huge emeralds (bought by Richard)...her hair was a mass of tiny flowers. Dick smiled proudly in his suit, a bit dazed perhaps at marrying the world's most famous woman. His womanizing days were over as he committed 100 percent to his new bride...For years, they maintained their close bond, but, in time, cracks began to appear in their relationship. Richard wearied of Elizabeth's entourage and her possessiveness...she tired of his black moods and his heavy drinking...Their marriage ended in divorce in 1974. However, it's commonly believed, and very likely true, that they were more in love with one another than they ever were with anyone else...for this reason, the ceremony that joined Liz and Dick as man and wife has become one of the most famous weddings in history.

2. Wallis Simpson and Prince Edward (Duke of Windsor, formerly King Edward VIII)

Wallis and Edward were not destined to live out their married lives in this palace...

Born in June of 1896, the charms of Bessie Wallis Warfield were destined to threaten a Royal Empire. This American woman was twice-divorced, and considered wholly unsuitable as a legal wedded wife of the British King Edward VIII. When Edward proposed to Wallis after ascending to the Throne, it ignited a scandal and a constitutional crisis...In December of 1936, the King gave his shocking abdication speech, one that underlined his decision to marry the woman he loved – no matter the consequences. Restyled as the Duke of Windsor by the new King (his brother, George VI – the subject of the critically-acclaimed film, The King's Speech), he married Wallis Simpson half a year later...she became the Duchess of Windsor...

This couple continued to inspire heated public opinion throughout their time together...known as Nazi sympathizers; they earned the ire of the British government (and of many of its citizens). After the wedding ceremony on June 3rd, 1937, the couple went on to lead the lives of socialites, and often visited with wealthy friends in America and Europe. No members of the Royal Family attended their wedding.

3. Joe Di Maggio and Marilyn Monroe
Baseball legend Joe Dimaggio married Marilyn Monroe.

This romance seemed plucked straight from the pages of a glitzy contemporary romance novel...the famed New York Yankees baseball legend and the platinum-blond screen siren were married on January 14th, 1954. Instead of a glamorous white gown, Marilyn chose a modest, chocolate-brown suit with a fur collar as her wedding outfit. The couple was married in judge's chambers in San Francisco, with only 6 family members at their side...

DiMaggio, the son of Italian immigrants who were processed at New York's Ellis Island, was in the denouement of his baseball career when he married Marilyn. It was rumored that he missed the spotlight and found it hard to share his life with a woman who got more attention than he did. These two strong personalities were destined to clash...Marilyn could be a different woman every day, and she was known for her capriciousness.[63]

---

[63] Ciara O'Brien (2011), "History's most famous wedding", February 11, 2011

The couple divorced in October of 1954, but remained close friends after their breakup.

When Marriage Dream Fails

For a man and woman marriage is the second life to live. Both dream to experience the second stage of life "the marriage." Wish to become dominant members of the family comes true where they act their own ways. The own family and responsibilities give the opportunity to gain honor.

Woman's role in running a house is more important thus she gains significance. Therefore, for a woman marriage means more than anything in the world does.

For her, the marriage is an emotional attachment. For her marriage means, are freedom from parental restrictions and social pre-marriage compulsions.

Her first dream is the freedom of the sexual contact without the fear.

Her second dream to have her own identity as wife and mother. Own home is the place for her to exhibit her personality, being a wife is her dignity. For a wife husband/partner is not only the sexual partner rather he is her security, support, and strength, and the closest companion with whom she can share her feelings. For her husband is a partner she can share everything of her life, which she cannot share with, others even mother/father and kids.

Third dream is to have own children fathered by her husband/partner who is her closest companion.

Her husband is her asset; she likes to keep protected and would hate to share with others.

These dreams are the attractions, which contribute to emotions she possesses for the life after the marriage. She enters to second life to form her own house comprising husband and kids where she plays her dominant role. Therefore, for a woman marriage is emotional tie up to live together, share the feelings, and act independently for the house. For her the husband/partner is not the security alone he is rather a partner to play with the joy/sorrow, sweet/sour.

Her dreams of marriage and collected marriage values disintegrate when she finds her husband/partner is sharing with others what was meant for her. The partner is her/his own property and dignity that she does not want to loose. Her man for her is everything, whatever kind he is, she manages and sacrifices to get along as long as he is honest and dependable. Infidelity by her man is attack on her marital status and is suicidal for her:

She looses the trust and dependability; that would she trust when own man has cheated. She is devastated sensitively and mentally. She leads her tensed life with grieving emotions would be enough to develop mental and physical deceases.

Both partners believe sexual partner as a personal valuable asset that demonstrates dignity and pride. A sexual partner is most valued partner becomes own dignity thus loosing partner is loosing dignity. Unfaithfulness of the partner is an insult to the personal values. So the matter becomes unbearable and embarrassment if partner's sexual attraction goes into others hands is shameful and loosing self-respect. Her financial and other security is at risk. For a woman, her male partner is her security and safety. In addition, for a woman who is dependent, her man is the economic security. Her man shares her necessities, burdens, takes responsibilities of her, and kids. When he is there she is totally worry free. Loss of the best and emotional friend/partner she got. She, as she wished could share with partner her sentiments, anger, sorrow and everything of her was for her mental relief, what she cannot share with unknown. So is an emotional attack on her. For a woman it is pride when her man is around her. Absence of the partner results loneliness, which she would hate more than anything. Loneliness exists when is unable to share personal thoughts and sentiments with reliable person, is like killing self.

She/he is not worried of her/his relation out side marriage rather what worries him/her is loosing emotional attachment woven during the whole episode. So more than the security she looses the emotional values she possessed and shared. Security is for survival and emotional attachment is for the energy she needs for existence. That is why women feel totally distressed when her man deceives.

For a man his woman is his dignity and for a woman her man is her dignity and identity. Her man is her identity as father of her children. Her man is her identity as her security.

Living and sharing together is attachment of both souls they unknowingly build. Feeling of oneness contributes to energetic atmosphere. Feelings have meant for each other with who can fight, love, share, capitulate, expect, and involve sentimentally; all attachments are disintegrated when one cheats. Woman is more touching as uses heart more than the brain to visualize so is intolerable for her that her man shares his life with other woman too.

Infidelity is psychological syndrome created by attraction of the opposite, genetic and discontented behaviour, unrelenting sexual and emotional craving. Infidelity is an outcome of fading ambience, dislike, despair, humiliation, and loneliness. No adult person can escape the attraction of opposite sex, it influences our mind to admire and capitulate towards the quality. Some attractions are too strong to influence us to get involved emotionally despite married life; this involvement of extra marital is named by the society as infidelity.

Woman too is human, she too has feelings and her body chemicals too react by mental signals when comes in contact with attractive person. She too perceives the virtues of attraction and imagines relating with, but in many occasions her conscious prevents getting involved observing the danger of family and social consequences.

In developed countries she has rights to leave the partner for better. But when she keeps two philanders simultaneously becomes offence and is extra marital relation. Parents arrange most marriages in rural and urban developing countries. Both would be partners are unknown to each other.

Sufferings

In our religious fundamental world, woman is a second citizen so has to live with the person loaded on her.

Woman's role is to maintain home, taking care of children and at night to act as sexual toy, beyond these if she thinks is an offence which society can to tolerate. Woman has to accept all the terms and conditions of the male partner. If the partner is disgusting still she has to live under his cruelty, undependability and humiliation. She has no other choice as religious and social rights are curtailed; she suppresses her desires and dreams of married life and consoles, as this is her fate. For her life on earth is the penalty for sins she committed in her previous birth. Even Government laws cannot protect them as social and its religious laws are more effective. If she wants to live in the society she has to obey the social compulsions. She cannot leave the unmatched and seek partner of own choice because it is religious crime. If likes other man of own choice the only way-out for her is to make affair in her dreams. Fear of repentance is so dominant that she is scared even to dream the liking person. If by mistake the pre marital love affair is disclosed becomes humiliating for whole life. It is beyond imagination of her man to accept as her past relation hurts his dignity and pride for not having virgin woman as a wife. She has to succeed the test of virginity in the first night of marriage. If she fails is either sent back to the parents blaming her impurity or left to suffer for whole life.

Whether developed or undeveloped or religious fundamental country, woman is human she too possesses the sentiments and desire to look attractive to be liked by others. Woman by nature are very much conscious about their look is the nature's law and the sense behind this is to look attractive. The attraction is an enticement to men to act in order to lure women for physical contact. Some women escape keeping the social obligations in mind and some get lured to initiate relation. Attraction is such an enticement that some fall victim to it. Most women control emotions in fear of social consequences by suppressing their craving. Yet with some, emotions overpower so get involved unconsciously for emotional attachment. Impact of social obligations is too strong in religion-dominated countries that she is made to repent for her involvement. She is desecrated by the society for violating social norms and becomes hatred for family and society. She becomes evil and treatment is in accordance to her status:

(a) First she looses is the emotional attachment in the family with whom she felt comfortable. In case she despised, she may feel internally punishing the partner but externally she is still helpless and needs a home to live, as she cannot live alone in this unsecured world.

(b) She suffers when the truth comes out to deteriorate her married life, makes her life hell. She comes under threats, violence and humiliation from husband/partner.

(c) Her secret love affairs for craving is unbearable to the religion so she is punished and desecrated to set an example so others do not go for such conduct.

(d) Dependant woman looses her economic security and safety. Society and its religion quarantine her to discourage participation and involvement in social activities.

(e) Suspicion of husband/partner as father of her children becomes humiliation to her. She suffers identity crisis.

(f) Even though husband/partner forgives the infidelity yet the feelings and pain remains in the heart thus home is no longer sweet home to unfaithful wife.

(g) Break from the existing home is anxiety, which she has to carry whole life whenever her memory rebounds.

(h) A child questioning her for loss of father is embarrassment.

(i) She may be economically secured but not emotionally what she shared and stored.[64]

Division of property after separation

Divorce is a bad situation to be in! Life isn't always fair and sometimes, it may so happen that one needs to break away from a bond made for life. Overwhelmed by the emotional aspect of such a situation, one should not lose sight of the important question of financial security for the future, especially in a single income household.

---

[64] Www. Sadashivan.Com

Marriage is a partnership of equality but divorce may not be so anymore. The new provisions in the marriage and divorce laws tend to favour the wife over the husband when it comes to division of property.

The government in order to provide relief to women had introduced a Bill called the Marriage Laws (Amendment) Bill, 2010, which has been cleared by the Union Cabinet earlier this year bringing into effect many safeguards for women facing divorce. This bill aims to provide the wife with adequate financial means to sustain her life even after the annulment of the marriage.

No waiting period

As per the earlier provisions in the divorce laws in India, there was a stipulated cooling off period of six months for which the husband and wife had to stay together before the divorce was granted.

This sometimes worked against the woman involved as the husband might actually not provide for her needs during this period since technically the divorce was not in effect.

The new Bill provides for the "irretrievable breakdown of marriage" as a new ground for applying for divorce, in which this period of six months for a possible reconciliation is not necessary. Thus the wife can now apply for the division of property immediately after the decision to part ways has been taken by both the parties, who are free to approach the court straightaway.

Wife gets 50 percent of residential property

This was one of the most debated clauses in the new Bill, which aims to help out women after divorce through financial safeguards.

As per the new regulation, the wife will have 50 per cent rights over all residential properties that are in the name of the husband at the time of the divorce being granted.

The 50 per cent right to property of the wife extends to all properties acquired by the husband before or after the marriage. This is a new addition to the division of property after divorce regulations; earlier, the division was only applicable on the property acquired by husband after the marriage.

The new marriage Bill, however, stipulates that the division of property will be done only if the wife approaches the court for the same and not without any specific appeal from her.

Three-fourth share in joint property

Today many couples opt for joint registration of the residential property that they acquire after marriage. This is primarily done keeping in view the joint financial contribution, home loan and tax considerations.

However if the couple decides to seek divorce subsequent to buying a jointly registered property, the husband stands to lose a lot. The wife shall get the first 50 per cent of the property, which is in her name and also half of the husband's 50 per cent in the property which adds up to 75 per cent of the entire property leaving a meagre 25 per cent or one fourth for the husband. This particular clause has been viewed by many as purely pro-women and anti-men in its implications.

Rights of wife in other properties

Apart from the major share that the wife gets in the husband’s residential properties, she will also have a right to other properties owned by the husband.

However, the exact percentage of her share in such properties will have to be decided by the court as per each specific case.

The guiding factor in deciding the share of the wife in all other properties remains the "living standard of the wife", which is left to the courts to decide.

Wife's right to claim alimony

The statutes that cover the decision regarding payment of maintenance support to the financially weaker spouse (can be wife or the husband) in case of a divorce in India are the Hindu Marriage Act, the Special Marriage Act, the Parsi Marriage Act, and the Indian Divorce Act.

However in this case, the wife gets alimony only if she has no or lesser earning as compared to the husband. This is also applicable for the husband, who too can be awarded a maintenance amount in case his proven sources of income are minimal and less than that of the wife. Section 25 of the Indian Divorce Act categorically stipulates that such maintenance is provided to the wife irrespective of the ground of divorce as long as the financial need is proven in the court.

The amount of alimony that the wife is considered for is dependent on a number of factors:

(a)The duration of the marriage before the divorce is vital for alimony. If the duration has been more than 10 years, the court can award a lifelong alimony for the wife.

(b) The age of the wife at the time of divorce can be yet another important consideration in deciding the quantum of the alimony. The younger women will get alimony for a shorter duration.

(c) The difference between the earnings of the husband and the wife would also play a crucial role. The greater the difference higher will be the alimony awarded to the wife.

(d) The wife will get a higher alimony in case she is suffering from physical disability or prolonged disease.

The detailed calculation of the amount of alimony that a wife will receive depends on the different personal laws applicable for the couple. However in any case the wife now has a better chance of securing her financial future in case of a divorce.[65]

Salary of Wives

THE recent initiative of the UPA government, making it mandatory for husbands to pay a monthly 'salary' to their wives, has come in for severe criticism both from the rightists as well as feminists. One cartoon rightly depicted a husband saying to his wife, "here is your salary for the month of August 2012. However Rs. 3355 has been deducted as you were at your parents' home for a week." The Union ministry of woman and child development is drafting a Bill to make this proposal a reality. The ministry has termed this step as an initiative to empower women. If the Bill is passed, husbands will have to pay 10 to 20 per cent of their monthly salary to their wives.

Sometime back, the Supreme Court had questioned the government's census parameters which placed housewives and women engaged in domestic work in the same economic bracket as "prostitutes, beggars and prisoners". The court observed: "This bias is shockingly prevalent in the work of the census."

---

[65] Adhil Shetty (2012), "Division of property after separation", Deccan Herald, September 16, 2012

Domestic work is indeed more productive than working in an office because here one actually takes care of three people who go to work ~ two children who are the future of the nation and two elders who have given their best years towards serving the nation.

The apex court rightly observed: "Such categorization of about 360 million women in India by the authorities betrays a totally insensitive and callous approach towards the dignity of labour and is also indicative of a strong gender bias." The court noted that women make a "significant" contribution to national life, and referred to a report by the "Evangelical Social Action Forum and Health Brigade" which estimated the economic value of services by women in India at $612.8 billion annually. "One has to admit that in the long run, the services rendered by women in households sustain a supply of labour to the economy and keep human societies going by weaving the social fabric and keeping it in good repair. If we take these services for granted and do not attach any value to them, this may escalate the unforeseen cost in terms of deterioration of both human capabilities and the social fabric," observed Justice AK Ganguly.

The latest proposal has revived the debate about the recognition of domestic chores as productive work. The proposal has created a flutter among the people. There may be complications with the idea of husbands paying a "salary" to their wives. Many social rights activists are comparing it with the British policy of "divide and rule". Several questions arise. What is the history of recognition or non-recognition of wives' work as work in the western democracies? What are the justifications of treating domestic work as work? What has been the legislative activity in this regard?

We should seek to emancipate wives' labour in the household as well as in the market, and to do so, advocate "joint property" laws that would recognize wives' claims to marital assets to which husbands otherwise have title. Wives are entitled to joint rights in marital property by reason of the labour they contribute to the family economy. In seeking joint property in marriage ~ distribution of property commensurate with a wife's contribution to the household economy ~ we must insist that the work women perform for the family should be valued equally with men's work and reject the arguments that wives' labour should be emancipated in accordance with its market value because the market still devalues women's labour.

For centuries, the British common law of marital status was starkly hierarchical, imposing pervasive constraints on the lives of women. The common law charged a husband with the responsibility to represent and support his wife, giving him in return the use of her real property and absolute rights in her personality and "services" ~ all products of her labour. Unless her family was sufficiently rich to provide property in an equitable trust, a wife negotiated marriage as a dependent without property or the legal prerogative to earn it, and impaired in her capacity to contract, to convey or devise property, and to file a suit. If she survived her husband, she acquired a life estate in one-third of any real property he held during the marriage ("dower"), so long as the marriage produced an offspring. A husband who survived his wife was entitled to tenancy for life of any lands she held.

Till 1851, no country had recognized a wife's right in earnings of any sort. If a married woman worked for pay in or out of the home, it was the husband's prerogative to collect her wages. Wives frequently had no say in monetary decisions in the family. Even in the happiest of marriages, where husband and wife worked and shared together, the doctrine of marital service imposed itself because the law categorically defined wives as dependents. It effaced their contribution to the family and posed an affront to dignity in a culture that celebrated labour as the source of autonomy.

By the middle of the 19th century, some American states started reforming common law of marital status by enacting "Married Women's Property Acts". Some of these statutes exempted wives' real property from their husband's debts; others codified the equitable separate estate, allowing wives to hold, though frequently not to control or dispose of, property acquired before or during marriage. The reform legislations opened vistas beyond the ancient status doctrines of the common law, suggesting that the traditional consolidation of property interests in the husband might be supplanted by a regime of separate property ownership in marriage.

By 1850, the era of "earning statutes" had begun. It granted wives property rights in earnings from their "separate" or "personal" labour, and enabled wives to engage in many legal transactions in their own right. This was a significant development as it sought to alter the course of life of those women who had no property to hold in marriage other than the proceeds of their labour. A wife was granted the right to earnings acquired by "trade, business, labour or services carried on or performed on her sole and separate account". The earning statutes did not emancipate the common forms of wives' work, but instead left most forms of wives' labour subject to the doctrine of marital service. These statutes emancipated a wife's "separate" or "personal" labour: work performed by wife for family was often explicitly excluded, and, even when it did not, courts generally construed the statutes to give a wife rights only in income earned outside the family context that was not used for family support.

By the 19th century, growing numbers of men in the USA had begun to work outside the household, but wives continued to work in the family setting, and so their work increasingly appeared an indistinguishable part of "family life". Moreover, the development of a market economy left most wives dependent on their husbands for money. As it became more common for men to exchange their labour for money-wages, production for use came to be identified as a distinctly female activity, associated with the social, but not economic, maintenance of family life. Census measures of the economy that appeared in the aftermath of the Civil War characterized such labour as "unproductive", and, consistent with this gendered valuation of family labour. It excluded women engaged in income-producing work in the household from the count of those "gainfully employed". In so doing, they gave official expression to what were already deeply entrenched assumptions of popular discourse, which denied that wives' work was work. One should, therefore, not be surprised by the Indian census document which regards wives' work as unproductive and equates it with beggars and prostitutes.

THE so-called "cult of domesticity" depicted the economic developments of the era in an exaggerated, gender-conscious form. Family and market were treated as two distinct spheres, organized in accordance with fundamentally different norms. The market was a male sphere, by nature competitive and self-seeking; the home was regarded as a female turf, essentially a site for spiritual uplift that offered relief from the vicissitudes of the market forces. This gender construct was expressed in homilies that depicted the home as a place where men seek refuge, relaxation, sympathy and care.

Over time, marriage was redefined as a means of exchange of material for spiritual sustenance. Wives were, in turn, defined as economic dependents of their husbands. Nancy Folbre has rightly remarked: "The moral elevation of the home was accompanied by the economic devaluation of the work performed there." The tendency of "separate spheres" reinforced the legal ordering of family life and justified a husband's control of family assets.

It also reinforced both the social right and the power of husbands to claim the surplus value of woman's labour, both paid and unpaid. The economic aspect of the labour was invisible, and the very question of exploitation became pointless. One cannot confiscate what does not exist. The ideology of spheres made the non-economic character of domestic work a simple "fact of nature."

Thus the feminists used the marriage-as-slavery argument to expose contradictions between the ideology of domesticity and the institution of marriage, to pierce the veil of sentimentality shrouding the relation and to reveal its economic logic. More precisely, the argument demonstrated the role of law in perpetuating women's economically dependent status. Because the common law categorically defined wives as dependents and thereby obstructed their contribution to the family's economy, it demeaned women in a society that regarded labour as a source of dignity and autonomy.

But by simple inversion, the ideology of free labour provided the ground for contesting the legitimacy of marital status law. Labour (was) the foundation, of wealth; then the law's role in expropriating wives' labour amounted to "robbery of the rights and liberties that every 'free white male' takes to him as God given." By invoking simple precepts of free labour, feminists asserted that "the law which gives to the husband the power to use and control the earnings of the wife, makes robbery legal, and is as mean as it is unjust."

Women strongly demanded a right to "let us own ourselves, our earnings, and our genius". At the Worcester Convention in 1851, it was resolved "that since the economy of the household is generally as much the source of family wealth as the labour and enterprise of man, therefore the wife should, during life, have the same control over the joint earnings as per husband, and the right to dispose at her death of the same proportion of it as he."

The resolution was an improvement on the earlier demand of having a right to hold assets which wives brought or acquired during marriage as separate property in order to protect women from improvident, profligate or intemperate husbands. They argued that the title of family assets should be redistributed because the prevailing distribution of property in marriage was illegitimate, reflecting norms of gender status rather than individual desert. In making their case, joint property advocates attacked the premises of protectionism and illustrated how the state transformed economically productive wives into economic dependents. They eventually achieved success when the equal rights of wives in the matrimonial property were recognized.

In India, the debate on joint property rights of married women is not new. Mrs. Veena Verma did introduce a Bill in 1994 titled "The Married Women (Protection of Rights) Bill". In the statement of objects and reasons, she had said that the real cause of the exploitation of a woman by her husband is that she has no right in the house of her husband; she has no right on the property of the husband. Even our laws confer the right of property on a woman only after the death of her husband and not during her covertures. Her Bill provided that a married woman would be entitled to an equal share in the property of her husband from the date of her marriage and would also be entitled to dispose of her share in the property by way of sale, gift, mortgage, Will or in any other manner whatsoever.

The Marriage Laws (Amendment) Bill, 2010, redrafted on the basis of the recommendations of a parliamentary standing committee, was introduced in the Rajya Sabha in May 2012. It contains the provision to allow a woman a share in her husband's property, in it a progressive step in line with international trends; yet it does not go far enough. The share a woman is entitled to from her husband's property acquired during the period of the marriage is to be decided by the court on a case-by-case basis, taking into account the woman's financial position. There are too many caveats here, and leaving the question to judicial discretion and interpretation will only add to unnecessary legal battles over property.

In countries where irretrievable breakdown of marriage has been introduced as a ground for divorce, there exist laws relating to an equitable division of all marital assets. This is because the contribution of a woman in building up the household and in primarily taking care of children is recognized and considered to be as economically valuable as work outside the house.

In February 2012, the Planning Commission's working group on women's agency and empowerment had proposed a Right to Marital Property Act. That right aims to give separated or divorced women an equal share in property, with the onus of proving a husband's income resting on him rather than on the wife, as is the case in the current scheme of things. In Maharashtra, a Married Women (Property Co-ownership) Equality Bill is under discussion. It is meant to ensure equal rights for women in their husband's acquired property, especially in cases of divorce. Goa already has such a law, put in place by the erstwhile Portuguese rulers. In the event of a divorce, half of the husband's property goes to the wife. Indeed, large parts of the world have what is called the community property law, a regime that is based on the principle that property acquired after marriage and before actual separation (but for gifts or inheritance) is owned jointly by both spouses and is divided upon divorce, annulment or death. Such joint ownership recognizes the theoretically equal contributions of both spouses in the making and the functioning of a family entity.

Some scholars have drawn a comparison between marriage and slavery. Antoinette Brown Blackwell referred to the legal structure of marriage and slavery, using the comparison to great polemical effect: "The wife owes service and labour to her husband as much and as absolutely as the slave does to his master. This grates harshly upon the ears of Christendom; but it is made palpably and practically true all through our statute books, despite the poetic fancy which views woman as elevated in the social estate; but a little lower than the angels."

The glorification of women as devi in our country is not much different. Wives should certainly have the same rights in spending the earnings of the husband, but converting this right into an entitlement of monthly salary does not appear to be a sound proposition.

Will the UPA government consider amendments in various laws to ensure that a homemaker's contribution is scientifically assessed in the division of matrimonial property? Will it merely give them a status of an 'employee', entitled to some monthly wages or salary?[66]

---

[66] Faizan Mustafa (2012), " Salary of Wives", Statesman, September 25 and 26, 2012

Money and Marriage

Why the recent Marriage Laws (Amendment) Bill may not make much difference to a majority of rural women.

Should women cheer now that the Union Cabinet has approved the Marriage Laws (Amendment) Bill 2010? If it becomes law, women will have the right to an equal share of property acquired after marriage and divorce will become easier. The additional ground of "irretrievable breakdown of marriage" has been added and there is a shorter waiting period when both parties want to end a marriage.

Most television talk shows have focused only on the urban, educated, middle class women. There is an assumption that divorce and partition of marital property affects only them. There are also crazy scenarios being created about a "**divorce epidemic**".

Exercising rights

In fact, we have to ask whether such a change in law will make any difference to the majority of women, especially those living in villages. Most women do not know that under law they are granted many rights. Even if they do know — such as the right of daughters to inherit a share of their parents' property — they are forced or persuaded to sign away their right. A recent study by the Rural Development Institute (RDI) of women's land rights in Andhra Pradesh and Bihar noted that more than half the Hindu women surveyed had signed away their right to land they would have inherited.

Inheriting property or land is crucial for many women seeking some form of economic security. Yet, this is precisely where their lack of knowledge or ability to exercise the right forces them to continue living in abusive and violent marriages. To walk out of such a marriage means walking into destitution. But if they fight for their right and succeed in getting their share, they are ostracized by their own community. Nothing has changed the entrenched belief that a woman, once she leaves her natal home, has no right to anything there and that the dowry she carries with her is adequate compensation.

The other side of ignorance about rights is the absence of supportive structures to help women claim their right. According to the RDI study, 61 per cent of women said they had never gone to a revenue office and of these 99 per cent said this was because men handled such matters. Of course, it did not help that the majority of the lower level revenue officials were also men. A simple step like appointing more women to such posts might begin to make a difference.

Several studies have shown that women who have the ability to stand on their own feet are less likely to tolerate an abusive marriage. Of course, there are always exceptions to this rule, where she speaks about the abuse she suffered within the first four months of getting married. Economic independence did not protect Meena from domestic violence but it gave her the courage to walk out.

Double-edged

What about women living in villages, in highly patriarchal societies, where the majority of women accept that beatings and abuse are part of what marriage is all about. In such societies, inheriting property can become a double-edged sword.

A fascinating study on the link between economic independence and domestic violence is by feminist scholar Prem Chowdhry for UN Women. She could not have picked a more appropriate state for such a study. Haryana has one of the lowest female sex ratios in the country. It has become known for the horrendous incidence of so-called "honour" killings where young men and women are murdered merely for marrying a person of their own choice.

The National Family Health Survey-3 reports that 27 per cent of married women in Haryana have seen physical, emotional and sexual violence and 46 per cent of women and 33 per cent of men felt that a husband beating a wife was justified in certain circumstances. In such a State, where girls are not allowed to be born, can women escape such violence if they assert their right to a share of property?

As in the States surveyed by RDI, in Haryana too women tend to sign away their right to parental property. But now this has begun to change. With the spread of urbanization, property prices are hitting the roof. Girls are now demanding their share, often egged on by their in-laws. Of course, there is no guarantee that they will have control over the money if they manage to get it.

But the study cites many instances where the situation of women, and even of their daughters, has changed dramatically once they have money or property in their own name.

Studies like the one by Prem Chowdhry and many others firmly establish the link between women's economic independence — either by way of property or an assured income — and a reduction in domestic violence. Even as laws are changed in the name of empowering women, we have to take the first steps — of informing women of their rights and creating the supportive structures that will guarantee that they can exercise these rights.[67]

---

[67] Kalpana Sharma (2012), " Money and Marriage", The Hindu, April 1, 2012

Marriages in Different Religion

The cultural heritage in India is quite rich and diverse with a huge variety of marriages in different religions. All the different religions in India be it Hindu, Muslim, Christians or Sikhs have a different set of wedding customs. When one says Indian wedding the mind goes to the traditional Indian wedding. However, every religion has its unique way of celebration. The tradition and customs of marriages in different religions is different. The one common feature of weddings in India is the excitement and fun with a huge gathering of relatives and friends.

A Hindu marriage is different from marriages in other religions in the sense that the marriage ceremony goes on for several days. There are different rituals that are held in before, on and after the marriage days. Several customs like prayer to Lord Ganesha is held in the pre wedding day so that He can bless the couple. Other rituals like Mehendi, Barat, Sangeet, Tilak, Jai Mala, Vivah and Viladi. The ceremony is held in a big hall either in a rented marriage hall or in the lawn in the grooms' house.

The Muslim marriage is different from marriages of other religions and is also celebrated with pomp and show. There are various rituals before, during and after the wedding. In the pre wedding ceremony Mehendi is an important function. On the wedding day the rituals like welcoming the groom takes place. It is in the main wedding day that the main ceremony Nikah takes place in the home of the bride or in a commonly decided venue. The ceremony is performed in the presence of close relatives and friends. An elaborate dinner is arranged to celebrate the occasion.

The Christians too have their own tradition and celebrate their wedding with much pomp and show. The ceremonies are simple, charming and are conducted in the Church. On wedding day the best man greets the bride with a bouquet of flowers. In the presence of two witnesses from both sides the bride and groom declare themselves as husband and wife. There is an exchange of rings and blessing from the priest. Thus marriages in different religions have the same technical working despite diverse cultural background.[68]

Unsuccessful Marriages in India

Rather than falling into an unending legal hassle, couples now prefer to stay apart for a year before seeking a divorce. This trend has gained ground in urban families.

For many couples, making a marriage work is a Herculean task. But seeking a divorce poses more troubles. Living in a generation where everything is lacy, impatient couples want to get over the legal hassles of filing for a divorce as fast as possible. Thus, it is no surprise that couples increasingly prefer to live separately for a year before planning to file for a divorce. In the last five years, this trend has been on an upward spiral in the Capital. The process is simple since it saves time, money and, especially, agony.

Thirty-two-year-old advertising professional Deepti Agarwal, who recently underwent a divorce, says: "When my husband told me that he wanted a divorce, I was distressed and terrified. It was sad to know that my marriage had failed. But I was also scared that this signalled the start of a war between us. We were no longer a team — in fact, we were adversaries. Neither of us wanted to go through the tormenting process of seeking a divorce that would have lasted for years. Hence, we mutually decided to live separately for a year. I didn't have any intention to

---

[68] IndiaWeddingPlanner.com

slam him with my future expenses," says Agarwal. Today, she talks once in a while to her ex-husband and there are no bitter feelings.

However, marriage counselors are a disappointed lot. Dr Kamal Khurana, owner, Marriage Therapy, a marriage counseling centre, says: "It is sad that modern day couples are behaving like escapists. What they don't realise is that they are voluntarily entering into a vicious circle."

And there is no guarantee that one won't face similar issues with the next person. "One should not let go of a life-long commitment because of petty issues. There are no free lunches. Couples have to be patient, persistent and determined if they want to salvage their marriage. Sadly, these virtues are missing in them. If you love your partner, you have to accept their flaws," Khurana tells you.

Almost 9,000 divorce cases were filed in the Delhi family courts in last one year. 60 per cent couples opted for a divorce by mutual consent. With time at a premium, more couples in the 25-40 age groups prefer to separate this way. They don't make allegations against each other and the process is less traumatic.

Gaurav Bhattacharya, a lawyer in the family court, feels that people don't want to undergo the rigours of a long legal battle. "Seven of 13 divorce cases, I resolved last year, were settled through mutual consent," he says.

Another family court lawyer, Himanshu Mitra seconds Bhattacharya: "When a couple decides to part ways and files a divorce plea, the judge suggests mediation. If they don't agree to reconcile, the extensive court process begins.

To avoid this, most couples now-a-days opt for mutual consent. The couple ideally needs to live separately for about 18 months to get a decree of divorce. Rather than contest the divorce for years together in a court, couples want to end it with as little trauma as possible. This method allows them to do just that," says Mitra.

In another alarming trend, counselors say that over 50 per cent of mutual consent divorce petitions are from couples who have not even completed three years of Matrimony. Lawyers dealing with such cases say that couples with irrevocable differences prefer divorce by mutual consent as it goes a long way in saving time, money and effort.

"There is no mudslinging in this process. Allegations and counter-allegations are withheld, financial issues are easily sorted out and custody issues of children are amicably decided," says Karan Yadav, advocate, Delhi High Court.

But divorce itself is emotionally taxing for the partners. Dr Samir Parikh, chief psychiatrist, Department of Mental Health and Behavioral sciences, Max Healthcare, sights the case of a couple who separated by mutual consent, but still had to go through therapy and counselling. "It took them time to resettle.

Emotional trauma related to divorce is almost universal. It affects both partners. Even a divorce by mutual consent can lead to an upheaval," he adds.

Factsheet

(a) The divorce rate is India is amongst the lowest in the world
(b) Divorce rates in the metros have almost doubled in last five years

(c) Even the comparatively conservative Punjab has seen the number of divorces increase by an astounding 150 per cent
(d) Statistics show that only one out of 100 Indian marriages end up in a divorce which is quite low in comparison to America's 50 per cent of marriages ending in splitsville
(e) The divorce rate in India was lower in the previous decade, when only 7.40 marriages out of 1,000 marriages were annulled
(f) In 2006, 1,246 divorce cases were recorded in Bangalore. These pertained to the IT sector exclusively
(g) In 2006, 150 divorce cases on an average per month were recorded in Pune
(h) Kerala, known to be the most literate State, has experienced an increase of divorce rate by 350 per cent in last 10 years
(i) Around 20 years back India had a negligible divorce rate of around five per cent
(j) According to experts, there has been a 100 per cent increase in divorce rates in the past five years alone.[69]

The Shrinking Universe: **How convenient is your marriage?**

If a lot of the old marriages are stable, it is because they lack emotional investment, prioritizing convenience and mutual tolerance over companionship.

I am not any more surprised when young urban Indians tell me that they don't think of marriage as an absolute necessity in their lives and that they'd much rather stay single than be trapped in a loveless marriage. Marriage has moved from being a 'stage of life' phenomenon to a commitment that requires

---

[69] Shibani Roy Choudhury (2011), "So far so good", the Sunday Pioneer, October 2, 2011

more forethought, application and responsible mutuality. But I'm always pleasantly surprised when older people who've been through all the tribulations that marriage has laid at their doorsteps, also seem to increasingly express the same opinion. They hasten, of course, to clarify that they have no regrets about being married, but don't seem overly perturbed when their grandchildren of 'marriageable age' express this sentiment.

Admittedly they are still a small tribe, even if a growing one. Admittedly, the large majority of Indians are still obsessed, not just about mileage, but also about marriage and start planning for their children's weddings, about a week or so after they are born. Admittedly also, older Indians still believe that their younger counterparts place too much of premium on the mystical emotion of love rather than approaching their marriages with responsible stolidity as generations of their forefathers have done. After all, weren't marriages more stable in those days, is their argument clincher.

Reasons for stability

However, what I find promising is that over the last decade or so, more people are beginning to realise that an important reason for this apparent stability is that large numbers of couples settled into 'marriages of convenience', wherein, regardless of the lack of connectedness between each other, they didn't want to break away from each other. Equally, they were not prepared to make the effort to get their marriage to a more companionable platform. They led their own independent and parallel lives, neither questioning what the other did, neither making any demands of the other, and neither evincing any great interest in the life of the other. They were pretty much like roommates who have learned to give each other a wide berth (take it from me, this is not giving each other 'space').

Such marriages of convenience are not necessarily an 'olden days' phenomenon. Just look around you and you'll realise that they are in abundance today too. More often than not, there is very little bitterness, hostility or acrimony in such marriages. There may have been in the past, but not any more, since couples in marriages of convenience have chosen not to have any real emotional expectations of each other. They have worked out how to have their basic needs taken care of. Their conversations are limited to practical realities of day-to-day living. They come together around the children and do engage in some joint socialization. However, they have their own individual lives which the other is not privy to, and is in fact, not even interested in. If there are any peccadilloes, neither wants to know about this. Discretion is the primary requirement of each other.

I'm not for a moment suggesting that all stable marriages of yesteryears or today are based on convenience. I am perfectly aware that millions of couples have had, and continue to have, loving and companionable relationships after having worked through whatever issues bedevilled the early days of their married lives. But, it simply cannot be ignored that a significantly large number of marriages last the long haul because both partners prioritise convenience over companionship and may come together only to discharge the responsibilities of marriage, in an almost fiduciary manner.

Complex phenomenon

You might well ask me how convenient such marriages are and why people stay in them. The reasons are pretty complex. For starters, such people subscribe to a basic belief that whatever happens, one must hang in there, and divorce can never be a serious option and often use the 'known devil' explanation to rationalize their marriages. Sometimes, the reasons are economic. Put simply, neither partner can really 'afford a divorce', so they plod on together, doing the minimum required for each other to ensure that the marriage still chugs along. Oftentimes, couples feel that they have to live with each other for the sake of the children which, as I have argued ad nauseam in this column, are arguably the worst thing they can do for the kids. But the more important reason is the vague sense of security we feel with something or someone familiar that counterbalances the fear of the unknown.

You might also well ask, what's wrong with a marriage of convenience? After all, there is no hostility or resentment. Both partners seem to be sufficiently satisfied and everybody seems okay. If this is the question that springs to your mind, you obviously believe that marriage is just one of the many responsibilities that are placed in our paths as we struggle through our lives — just one more role we have to play in our lives. However, if you believe, like many younger, and some older Indians do, that marriage has a greater purpose than mere responsible procreation, then you'd probably like to get more out of your marriage by creating a platform of mutual companionship and harmony, rather than settling for mutual tolerance and lack of disharmony. If this is the case, you'd probably feel that close up; a marriage of convenience isn't really as convenient as it may appear from a distance.[70]

(B) WAR FOR WOMAN

A lady's imagination is very rapid; it jumps from admiration to love, from love to matrimony in a moment. — Jane Austen, Pride and Prejudice

---

[70] Vijay Nagaswami (2011), "The Shrinking Universe: How convenient is your marriage?" The Hindu, Sunday , October 30, 2011

Wars are caused for women, gold, land and prestige. It is practiced even in Twenty-first century.

The kings and monarchs were waging wars to occupy land of other kingdoms/ states/countries. They enjoyed in observing the blood baths of soldiers and cries of civilians. A winner king enjoys satisfaction and pleasure by torturing the defeated royal family members, and killing the king and soldiers in the battlefield. Why the United States of America and China are ready to face any military challenge? Why a country challenges the very survival of our human race and its civilization? Can the people tolerate nuclear war? War and threat of war is in the daily news.

The cause of war is not the people. It is caused by the government.

The history of war is long before we achieved civilization. Let us know how and why wars were caused in mythological era. Why we are not able cut down to military expenditure even today.

Ramayana

Ramayana is written by Rishi Valmiki and is written in Sanskrit comprising 24, 000 couplets in seven volumes.

It is the story of Rama, the eldest son of King Dasaratha of Ayodhya. The king had had three queens and four sons. The king wanted to install his eldest son as the crown prince. But his favourite queen Kaikeyi wanted the throne for her own son, Bharat. On the eve of the installation ceremony, she reminded the king of the two boons, she has promised long ego. She demanded that Rama should go to the forest for 14 years and Bharat should be placed on the throne.

Rama accepted his step mother's demands and left for forest life for 14 years along with faithful wife **Sita** and loving brother Lakshmana. Rama protected Aryan sages by fighting the marauding tribes of the forests in Dandaka forest near modern Nasik on the bank of the Godavari. Trouble came upon him. Ravan, the most notable non-Aryan king of Sri Lanka carried away Sita through a dramatic way of begging alms and snatched her, when both brothers were in the forest outside the hut.

Rama took the help of Sugriva, Hanuman and Bibhishan and fought against Ravan and got back Sita. It was a dangerous war in the pre-history period. Rama completed 14 years of forest life; returned to Ayodhya and became the king. Rama's subjects suspected the purity of Sita, on account of long stay in Ravan's kingdom. Rama knew that Sita's character was above suspicion, but he thought it to be his duty as a king to banish Sita as the public opinion was against her. He was very grieved at heart but he did his duty. Sita went to the hermitage of Valmiki and gave birth to two sons. Under the guidance of Valmiki, the sons became warriors. Rama knew that they are his sons and brought Sita, and two sons and declared them as his successors. And people accepted him as incarnation of God. **The war was caused to bring back Sita.**

Mahabharata

The story of Mahabharata is complex in character and its importance lies in the legends and long discourses on moral, religious, social and political topics. This epic was originally composed by the sage, Vyasa. The great epic Mahabharata is written in 18 volumes comprising 100, 000 couplets. The story is about the battle fought mainly between the Pandavs and the Kauravas. Pandu had five sons and Dhritarastra had 100 sons.

Pandu was the king of Hastinapur but he died young. So his elder brother Dhritarastra became the king of Hastinapur, although he was blind. His eldest son, Duryodhan conspired against the pandavs and got them exiled. Draupadi, the daughter of Panchal kingdom was facing Swayamavara (marriage by Choice among the invited sons of kings) with certain conditions. Arjun the third son of Pandu fulfilled the condition and won in the festival. This strengthened the relationship of the Pandavs with the Panchal king. The Kauravs misbehaved Draupadi in open durbar in front of Bhisma and all members of every body.

The Pandavs went on exile for 13 years and on return; the Kauravas did not return their kingdom. They approached Lord Krishna to get back their kingdom, but Dhritarastra denied because of Duryodhan.[71]

The Mahabharat war was the bloodiest war in pre-history period. Revenge and anger of Draupadi was the cause for death of 100 brothers of Kauravas and hundreds of thousands of brave soldiers.

The Sanjukta episode:

Prithvi Raj Chauhan, the king of Delhi wanted to marry Sanjukta, daughter of King Jayachandra; he took away his beloved on the back of a horse a long distance of 400 miles to his capital. Jayachandra took the help of Mohammed Ghori and fought two battles.

(a) First Battle of Tarain or Thaneswar (A.D. 1191): Prithvi Raj Chauhan defeated Mohammed Ghori.
(b) Second Battle of Tarain A.D. 1192—Mohammed Ghori defeated Prithvi Raj

[71] Glimpses of History part 1: by Xavier Pinto and E G Myall, Frank brothers.

> Chauhan. Ghori's victory paved the way for the establishment of Muslim rule in India.

The result was a Hindu ruler invited a Muslim ruler to fight against another Hindu ruler. The greater India now consists of India, Pakistan and Bangladesh because of Sanjukta, daughter of Jaychandra.

Women and War:

Acclimatized to violence

Women and children become a part of the `collateral damage' in war games. From nurturer to destroyer, women have come full circle.

FROM the small things of my life, from the seemingly safe, steady routines of cooking, cleaning, keeping house for my family, teaching, yoga classes, meeting friends, waiting for buses and trains, I receive subliminal messages from the millions of women not so fortunate. Everyday routine is not granted to everyone. To be safe and to know that tomorrow too will be safe is no longer a given. I have never been caught in a war-zone; in a world torn apart by war in this and the last century, a woman growing to middle or old age without being subjected to the savage compulsions of war or revolution is fortunate. And statistically one would be in a minority. Women, for no fault of their own, are never involved in the high-level negotiations that may precede a war, or even considered pawns in the games men play; they become either the spoils of war, or part of the "collateral damage". They are trapped in villages, towns and mountainous regions that one would have trouble identifying on a map, but which make headlines every day, because of civil war, armies going berserk, atrocities committed by terrorists or the military, invasion by a greedy superpower or neighbour and, of course, revolutions. And in these terrible situations, women pay the price.

Women and children usually strung together when spoken as if it were one word. Whole world's crash as violence erupts; homes are destroyed, children go missing, women are raped, mutilated and killed, fathers disappear for unfathomable reasons. Perhaps the most telling leitmotif of the last century is of a lost child crying or a woman sitting traumatized her face blank, as fires rage in the background. Or the long lines of the feeble and old, women carrying small children and whatever else they could salvage straggling up a hillside.... Eckhart Tolle, contemporary philosopher and teacher, says that a large part of our history has all the characteristics we would normally associate with a nightmare or an insane hallucination.

War! Single monosyllables like someone spitting, but it packs the impact of a jackboot descending. In German too, "der krieg" is like a harsh expletive, in French, "la guerre" is almost melodic, even romantic, but in whatever language, the word, the idea of being at war, does strange things to men; however much they may deplore the need to go to war, reasons are always found to justify, to excuse, to glorify war. There is the charge of adrenalin and hate, the demonisation of the enemy begins early in the game, war games start as part of training, great reserves of animal courage are called upon, young men flex their muscled bodies and mentally and physically prepare to kill the other, the enemy.

But the insanity does not end there. The human race has now become quite acclimatized to, almost blasé about, the sight of women in uniform whether they are guerrilla fighters or insurgents or as regular army personnel, whether in the U.S. army, or in some Central African republic, or in the Liberation Tigers of Tamil Eelam (LTTE), or in West Asia; we do not consider it unnatural anymore that women have become warriors, that they too, in the name of equal rights/opportunities, have become accustomed to the act of killing, maiming, hurling grenades at the enemy, setting landmines... .

Helene Cixous the famous French radical feminist writer and teacher, asks the simple question, "What is woman for man?" And, she quotes from a Chinese manual of strategy, a handbook for the warrior, written by the general Sun Tse. Asked to train the king's 180 wives, Sun Tse formed the women into two lines each headed by the king's two favourite wives, then asked them to listen to the language of the drumbeat. But the more he repeated the order, the more the women fell about laughing, chattering and laughing. Sun Tse decided that since they were so disobedient, he would condemn them to death. But the king objected to losing all his 180 wives; so Sun Tse, as an example, beheaded the two favourites at the head of the line. He had no more trouble with the women; they performed perfectly in silence, no more subversive laughter.

Women have also become workers

During the prolonged Vietnam war that later spilled over into Cambodia; I recall reading a report of the effects of what was happening on Cambodian society. The jungles were filled with young men and women insurgents trying to outwit the enemy. The report spoke with great seriousness of the value of women as soldiers, warriors. Their bodies are supple, they can melt into the background with greater ease; they can pass as peasants by carrying water, or a baby, or firewood, and carry messages with greater ease. A woman is her body, in a way that a man can never be. From the time she is a young girl entering puberty, her body adapts itself to lunar cycles, to the natural processes of preparing to give birth, to nurture and to protect. This same body, as a consequence of the politics and ideologies of the day, is trained to the unnatural processes of existence in the harshest of terrains, to develop the ferocity of men who attack and who are attacked, to become immunized to pain, to begin to think and act like men. Women who would, in normal times, be the storehouses of family history, cultural lore, religious traditions, teachers of songs, tellers of stories, keepers of social custom, become instead the destroyers of all that is human and decent about the human race.

In a recent article on women's cadres within the LTTE, it was estimated that at least half the members of the LTTE are women, often recruited as children. The LTTE is one of the few rebel groups that uses women not just as human bombs but as frontline troops fighting against a conventional army.

Radhika Coomaraswamy, the UN Special Rapporteur on Violence Against Women, questions the miniaturization of women, pointing out that it flies in the face of the humanism, non-violence, and the "celebration of life over death" that characterize the women's movement all over the world.

But, perhaps, this is the savage rejoinder of men to women seeking equality and empowerment, seeking a mutuality of understanding: You want to be equal? Come become us! [72]

Women fighting and dying in war,
Despite combat exclusion policy

By this Memorial Day, nearly 150 U.S. female troops have made the ultimate sacrifice in the Iraq and Afghanistan wars, with over 700 wounded. Although Department of Defense policy precludes women from being assigned to ground combat-infantry units, women have for years served in combat situations where they're just as vulnerable.

---

[72] Revathy Gopal (2003), "Women and War: Acclimatized to violence", Hindu, May 18, 2003

Marine Lance Corp. Angelica Jimenez, 26, was one of them.

On June 25, 2005, Jimenez was riding in the back of a truck carrying 14 female Marines near the Iraqi hotbed of Fallujah. The all-female unit was tasked with searching and questioning Iraqi women at security checkpoints, ensuring they were not armed with explosives. Since females were not allowed to sleep at the checkpoints as their male counterparts were, every day the women would be driven to and from an American base, making them a visible target each time they hit the road. It was only a matter of time before their luck would run out, and that night, it did.

A car approached their convoy, moments before it ran straight towards the women's truck. Packed with explosives, it detonated on impact, enveloping all 14 women in a deadly fireball. Most of the women were severely burned. Two women died immediately, one later that night, in what would become the deadliest attack on servicewomen since 1991.

Jimenez was knocked unconscious. She remembers waking up, directly in the line of insurgent fire, her flak jacket covered in blood, her M-16 gone. "Convoys are always dangerous, anything that involves going outside the base is dangerous, outside the base, those are all very much dangerous jobs," she said. Jimenez was part of a communications command, but was selected for the month of June to man security checkpoints into Fallujah, a role she served along with her fellow male Marines.

"We were doing the same thing," Jimenez said. "Women are just as capable. I don't like being called a 'female Marine' versus a 'Marine' -- we all graduated from the same boot camp."

Since 1994, the Department of Defense's combat exclusion policy prohibits the assignment of women to any unit below brigade level when the unit's primary mission is direct combat on the ground. However, according to DOD spokesperson Eileen Lainez, the policy does not "preclude women from being involved in ground combat." Blurring the lines further, the Army precludes women from being "assigned" to ground combat infantry units, but allows them to be "attached" to such units, where they often perform the same roles their male counterparts would.

"The nature of today's conflicts is evolving; there are no front lines in Iraq and Afghanistan," Lainez said. "While women are not assigned to units below brigade level whose primary mission is direct combat on the ground, this doesn't mean they are not assigned to positions in combat zones that could place them in danger."

The policy defines ground combat as "engaging the enemy on the ground with individual or crew served weapons, while being exposed to hostile fire and to a high probability of direct physical contact with the hostile force's personnel." Genevieve Chase, veteran of Operation Enduring Freedom and founder of American Women Veterans, found herself in that situation while serving in 2006 in the hotspots of Helmand and Bagram, where counter insurgency strategy emphasizes building relationships with locals including Afghan women who won't talk to a male stranger.

Chase told ABC News, "In both Iraq and Afghanistan, female troops have worked from day one outside the wire. In war, you do what you can. You can't withhold somebody because of his or her gender. If you are in charge of an aid station with three female medics, and this infantry unit needs another medic, you're sending them a medic. Rules in combat are very different."

But while Chase served alongside men and carried the same weapons, the policy precluded her from having the same combat training as the infantrymen. "When women are 'attached' to these ground infantry units, we are actually more vulnerable because we don't have the same level of training as the men that we support," she said. In addition, she said, teams train together as a unit, which allows them to create team cohesion, builds rapport, and understand everyone on the team's strengths and weaknesses so that in a combat situation, everyone knows what to do, and how each other will react. From the first day a soldier enters the Army, she said, the basic combat training that combat support units undergo differs greatly from the training that infantry units receive.

The policy also precludes female officers from leading ground combat units. Not only does the rule prevent women from gaining the experience they need to win promotions to the military's top ranks, Chase said, it does not always reflect reality on the battlefield.

Chase said, "Downrange, women have stepped up to serve in leadership roles when necessary, including acting as a commander of an all-male unit.

When asked about her colleagues experience Chase said, "She brought all her soldiers home, it doesn't matter who brings them home, as long as they all come home." "You want the best person leading your team. The ability to make decisions under pressure, keep your composure, remain calm and collected, all while maintaining your courage under fire -- those attributes are not gender specific."

Recently, the congressionally mandated Military Leadership Diversity Commission recommended that the DOD rescind the combat exclusion policy. Commission chair retired Air Force Gen. Lester L. Lyles said rescinding the policy is one way the military can get more qualified women into its senior leadership ranks.

Lyles said in March: Women serving in combat environments are being shot at, killed and maimed, but they're not getting the credit for being in combat arms.

Lainez said department officials "will thoroughly evaluate" the panels recommendations as part of their ongoing review of diversity policies. Meantime, she said, "Women will continue to be assigned to units and positions that may necessitate combat actions within the scope of their restricted positioning - situations for which they are fully trained and equipped to respond."

"The Department is committed to performing the comprehensive and expansive review of the laws, policies, and regulations restricting service of female service members, and will provide Congress with a report as required upon completion of the review," Lainez said.

Today, women make up about 15 percent of active-duty service members; 18 percent of National Guard and reserves; 10 percent of Iraq and Afghanistan combat veterans; and 10 percent of those who have served in the Iraq and Afghanistan theaters. The idea of women serving in ground combat infantry units has been controversial throughout U.S. history. Arguments against women serving in combat centers around the physiological and purported emotional differences between men and women, as well as the interaction between men and women that could distract from a mission. Specifically, opponents argue that women are physically weaker than men -- especially in upper body strength, and behave more emotionally than men. Also, sexual or romantic feelings that arise could affect unit cohesiveness or focus on a mission.

Chase said those arguments also do not reflect reality. "I served with men that were so macho and overprotective, then when it really actually got sticky, they weren't worried about me, the training kicked in, everybody did what they were supposed to do. We were professionals." Chase agrees there will have to be a thorough review on whether to rescind the policy, and that rescinding without a plan as to how to implement changes would be premature. But, she added, "It's long past time to revise the current policy so that it accurately reflects the capacity with which women have and will continue to serve in our armed forces. It gives combatant commanders the ability to truly build the most cohesive, well-trained and effective teams for their respective missions."

Jimenez, who still deals with the visible and invisible wounds inflicted from the attack, hopes that one-day, when people think Marine, it won't always be a man they picture. "No one will ever look at me like I was a Marine. When I tell people that I was a former Marine, they usually say, 'Are you serious?' As long as people acknowledge that we were there too.[73]

Poetry and the War - II

WOMEN were even encouraged to abstain from making a public display of grief, as it was widely believed that it could lower the morale of the soldiers on leave. Judith Lytton's poem: The Soldier articulates the mood of the hour:

Weaken him not with grief; with useless tears
Show not the bitter anguish of thy soul,
Lest he should lose the least of his control,
Lest he should hesitate with nameless fears

[73] Kristina Wong (2011), "Women fighting and dying in war, despite combat exclusion policy", ABC News, May 30, 2011

It was also generally assumed that as the soldiers had sacrificed themselves for a 'Holy War', so the expression of grief was inadmissible under such conditions.

As The Times reported in August 1914: "The stricken must determine for themselves how they may best meet their own longing to honour their cherished dead, but as the wishes entertained in the highest quarters rightly count for very much in matters of convention, we feel sure that a few words of timely approbation uttered from them would bring success to a movement that seems to us in many ways worthy and becoming the chastened grief of English hearts".

Thus women's right to express their legitimate grief came to be subjected to the whims and fancies of the patriarchal state. They were expected to be proud of the sacrifices of their lovers, husbands, brothers and sons for the nation and not mourn personal loss in public. In an untitled poem, Iris Tree voiced her anger against such interference of the state:

No more! And we, the mourners, dare not wear
The black that folds our heart in secrecy of pain,
But must don purple and bright standards bear,
Vermilion of our honour, a bloody train,
We dare not weep who must be brave in battle.

Regretting such restrictions on formal display of grief, the poem moves on to further lament:

Of all who died in darkness far away
Nothing is left of them but LOVE, who triumphs now,
His arms held crosswise to the budding day,
The passion-red roses clustering his brow

Denial of the display of grief invigorated the social trend to explore alternative private avenues for venting sorrow. On the other hand, it initiated a process of social repression of grief, which was to further culminate in the later decades. Denial of sorrow in public also contributed to the emergence of poetry as one of the alternative forms of expression of private grief for women. It served as a psychological anodyne for thousands of mourning women during the war. As psychologist Jeffrey Lerner observes in Changes in 'Attitudes toward Death':

The Widow in Great Britain in the Early Twentieth Century: The first public expressions about death and the war were poems. Poetry was the traditional medium for discussing death, so it is hardly unusual to find it employed....'

Hundreds of slim volumes of verse written and published by women poets during the war testify to the unprecedented nature of grief British women suffered. As this extract from Mary Boyle's sonnet sequence testifies, poetic space served the twin purpose of both displaying and commando rating private grief:

Since you loved words,
The words I bring to you
Woven in garlands to adorn your brow,
Wreathed sonnets are the gifts I bring you now,
Prismatic words, glowing in crimson blue

Besides commemoration of personal sorrow, most of these elegies belong to the sub-genre of family elegies which circuitously chronicles the social position of women as hapless victims of the war. The sudden demise of male members in the war forced female survivors to redefine their own images of life. These poems implicitly protest against the institutionalized male-centeredness' of the family, affirming the stereotypic gendered nature of women's citizenship during the war. Beyond their apparent simplicity in form and content, these elegies provide a fascinating insight into the psychology of women's grief of the war generation.

Unlike earlier elegists, women poets of the First World War often dealt with several successive personal losses at multiple levels, condensed within a brief span of time. Frequently the psychological distress was so important that the victim had no other alternative but to surrender to the extreme compulsion of seeking secret refuge in writing verse, often amidst difficult circumstances. Classical examples in this context are Vera Brittain's war elegies, which were mostly written during her period of active service in various military hospitals in London, Malta and France.

In her elegies, Brittain mourns the deaths of four men very close to her: her fiancé Roland Leighton, her friends Victor Richardson and Geoffrey Thurlow and her younger brother, Edward. In psychological terms, such a closely paced sequence of losses can have a paralytic effect on the mourning psyche.

As Vera Brittain observes in The Testament of Youth:

Pain beyond a certain point merely makes you lifeless and apathetic to everything but itself.

It is this sense of excruciating void that most women's elegists seek to redress in verse. Such a poetic redressal had to negotiate with grief in its myriad forms. It is well testified in various poems written by Vera Brittain, May Cannan, Mary Boyle, Eleanor Farjeon, Marian Allen, Isabel Clarke and several other poets who went on to lose family members or near ones in the war. Quite frequently temporary separation or farewell from loved ones eventually turned out to be a permanent one. Eleanor Farjeon's poetic record of an anxious moment of parting from Edward Thomas, in Now That You Too, represents the wider cultural anxiety of the period.

Eileen Newton's Last Leave echoes similar sentiments of resignation to fate.

It is through recurrent 'countless struggles' that the bereaved is finally reconciled with the loss. A close perusal of women's elegies written during and just after the war reveal this ongoing struggle for reconciliation. Mary Boyle's sequence of 30 sonnets commemorating her brother David or Alexandra Grantham's sequence of elegies for her dead son Hugo Frederick, testify to such 'countless struggles' being carried out in verse to be reconciled with the grief and loss.

This large body of elegiac verse represents a form of resistance to the 'dominant patriarchal logic of war'. Considered 'unpatriotic' during the time of the war and undesirable in the post-war period of renovation, the body of elegiac verse served as a 'leftover residue'. Being discordant with the dominant patriarchal ideology of the time, they also defied integration into the history of war. Inevitably they suffered from the predictable fate of being repressed. Beyond the surface reality of negotiating grief, they form a formidable force of protest and angst against the dominant patriarchal rhetoric of the war. These lyrics elegize and protest against the socio-political position of women of the time.[74]

Conclusion:

Love marriages would be successful when both husband and wife adjust mind and they live as friends. If both them would try finding mistakes of each other, it becomes a hell on earth.

Men cause woman harassment for sex. Rape has become a tragedy in India and in other countries.

---

[74] Argha Banerjee (2012), "Poetry and the War II", The Statesman", January 05, 2012

Love marriages need blessings of the Almighty for survival. Love marriages could be compared with rose flower with thorns.

Marriage with dowry is a social crime and it should be stopped. In many countries it has been denied by law of the land. But family torture still continues resulting in disaster. Use of liquor and addiction of drugs cause family disputes and it leads to disaster. KHAP[75] punishment leading to death must be stopped by law and practice.

Love marriages should be allowed by the family members instantly. **It is the best form of marriage.** Even inter-caste, inter-religion, inter-faith marriages might be allowed by the community.

If youths are satisfied with love marriages; they would live in peace. The society should not oppose this marriage. It would end violence against women.

Women are the root causes of family separation, family dissatisfaction, divorce, and family quarrels as some of them are selfish, lazy and insubordinate. They fight for justice without duties. They have the ability to manage the family with minimum expenditure. Women are also responsible for peace, harmony, progress, and can create a 'Heaven on Earth'. Without family life, the human kingdom might have been converted to hell.

Let the marriage of each couple result in peace and it would usher an era of peace; the WORLD PEACE is possible through successful marriages.

---

[75] It is a practice that none can marry in that gotra (kith and kin). If some one loves in his / her gotra and marry in courts or temples, both would be murdered by the local leaders.

Chapter VIII

RIGHTS OF A WOMAN

As a woman I have no country.
As a woman I want no country.
As a woman, my country is the whole world.
— Virginia Woolf

Women should try to protect them from physical and mental torture. Women must prove that they have the capacity to challenge men in education, intelligence, and competitive examinations. They must try to organize a political party and lead a stable government. They have the capacity to eradicate social evils and establish a value-based government. They can ensure justice to all and stop corruption, nepotism and bribery in the country. They can stop strikes; conflicts, revolutions and wars to stabilize peace everywhere. They would create an army of 'peace workers' to award peace to all.

The governments that are unable to offer good governance must be replaced by a government headed by a woman for better governance. Each government needs people oriented programs for peace and security.

In this chapter the famous speeches of Noeleen Heyzer, Hillary Rodham Clinton, Shirley Chisholm, Senator Margaret Chase Smith, Helen Keller, Susan B. Anthony, Senator Margaret Chase Smith and Lucretia Mott are presented for the welfare of women and the world.

Noeleen Heyzer

On topic 'Women's Role on Peace Consolidation' (2006)

Peace consolidation is an uncertain enterprise. It is one thing to agree to a ceasefire, and quite another to move from there to a point where societies can resolve conflicts through inclusive governance without reverting to armed combat. This year we have seen many examples – from Timor Leste to the Solomon Islands, Afghanistan to Iraq, the process of establishing a secure peace appears even more difficult than it did a year ago.[76]

With the setting up of the Peace Building Commission, the UN has strengthened its peace building architecture, increasing coherence in fulfilling its peace-building mandate. But today we must ask what else is urgently needed, and how **Security Council Resolution 1325** could be more effectively implemented to bring about just and sustainable peace.

From our work in over 20 conflict-affected countries, UNIFEM has learned what is needed to implement Resolution 1325 effectively in peace consolidation. Let me mention three points:

---

[76] Noeleen Heyzer (2006), " Women's Role on Peace Consolidation", Security Council, the United Nations, Washington D C, 2006

1. Peace-building efforts must ensure women's physical and economic security:

In peacemaking and peace building, the urgent often drives out the important. The urgent is the need to stop the fighting — which means placating former combatants and addressing the grievances of warring parties in peace talks and agreements. But parties to the conflict are not the same as parties to the peace. Peace building and consolidation require that all parties with an interest in peace are engaged in negotiating a new social contract, building institutions of a new society, and re-establishing livelihoods. Women are a crucial resource in this process. Peace agreements, early recovery and post-conflict governance do better when women are involved. Women make a difference in part because they adopt a more inclusive approach to peace and security and address key social and economic issues that provide the foundations of sustainable peace and that would otherwise be ignored.

The question is not only what women can bring to peace consolidation but also what peace building can do to promote women's human rights and gender equality—transforming social structures so they do not reproduce the exclusion and marginalisation that underlie conflict.

Women know the costs of war: what it means to be subject to sexual violence designed to destroy communities, what it means to be displaced, to flee their homes and property, to be excluded from public life and regarded as less than full citizens. Peace consolidation must include ending impunity for sexual violence and raising the political and economic costs to those who engage in it, making sure they are not rewarded with state power and high profile jobs as a result of negotiated peace agreements. Two of women's most urgent needs are for physical safety and economic security. Efforts to engage women in public decision-making will not succeed if women risk continued violence for taking on public roles, and they cannot be expected to be effective public actors if they have no source of livelihood.

What UNIFEM is seeing on the ground-- in Iraq, Afghanistan, and Somalia-- is that public space for women in these situations is shrinking. Women are becoming assassination targets when they dare defend women's rights in public decision-making. And everywhere there is evidence that sexual and gender-based violence is taken into homes and communities after conflicts have ended, as ex-combatants return with small arms, and social norms that protect women remain broken. In all of the conflict areas we have worked, we have witnessed women's willingness to take risks—reaching across borders, organizing to support dialogue and defying threats to their security. But we cannot rely on the bravery of women; we need systems to be in place. In peace consolidation, the international community must invest in reforming the security sector to ensure women's safety, particularly where armies or police have been a source of the violence they experience. In Rwanda, after police said they could not protect women as they lacked vehicles for rapid response, UNIFEM organized an inter-agency response to set up specialized gender desks in police stations and provide them with training, hotlines and motorcycles to reach women in remote districts.

2. Sustainable peace requires real justice for women:

To consolidate peace there must be justice for women in accordance with international human rights standards. This means removing all laws that discriminate against women, formulating new gender equality laws, strengthening rule of law institutions to implement them, and empowering women to access these institutions and demand their rights. To support these efforts, UNIFEM is working with the International Legal Assistance Consortium (ILAC) to support a global Partnership for Gender Justice, co-chaired by the Governments of Sweden and South Africa, to marshal Member States, UN system, and non-governmental resources to support these efforts.

Too often in conflict affected countries we see that laws on victim compensation do not include compensation for rape, which is regarded as a minor crime. I just returned from Kosovo with Goodwill Ambassador Nicole Kidman, where we met with women who had been brutally raped during the conflict. They feel doubly violated now as they seek justice, both locally and from international tribunals who promise to help them but never deliver. If we are serious about ensuring justice and consolidating peace, we must do more to provide legal training for judges and lawyers, witness protection, medical support services and compensation.

Family matters and personal status are typically left to traditional or customary legal systems—partly because they are an inexpensive system of dispute resolution, and partly to buy the cooperation of traditional or tribal leaders by giving them control over personal and family matters. The result is the perpetuation of honor crimes, exchange of women to resolve inter-clan disputes, denial of women's inheritance rights and other human rights violations. Justice for women cannot be done on the cheap, and women's rights cannot be bargained away for other political gains. Justice for women has to be featured as an integral and achievable part of any UN strategic plan of assistance.

3. Peace processes require institutional change and stronger accountability systems:

Women's engagement in peace consolidation requires consistent sustained investment in strategies to ensure that the institutions engaged in rebuilding governance, justice, security, economic, and social systems have the will and the capacity to respond to women's needs, and that women are taking leadership roles in influencing these processes.

UNIFEM's peace and security approach is based on five integrated elements:

(a) Bringing women to the peace table;
(b) Supporting women's engagement in building new constitutional and legal frameworks;
(c) Investing in women's leadership in the development of new institutions, including gender-sensitive judicial and law enforcement agencies;
(d) Building partnerships to generate and support national gender justice movements advocating to integrate women into national peace, security, development and rights agendas; and
(e) Support for women's participation in elections and political decision-making.

What we have learned is that the earlier women are recognized as peace agents and engaged in peace processes, from mediations to peace negotiations to constitutional reform, the more they are seen as legitimate actors. This is why in Uganda this week, UNIFEM is supporting the launch of a Peace Caravan with women from the Democratic Republic of Congo, Kenya and Uganda to demand that the international community respect Resolution 1325 and include women at the Juba peace talks. Some progress has been made in ensuring women's inclusion in post-conflict decision-making. A variety of quotas and reservation systems in Iraq, Burundi, Rwanda, Afghanistan and elsewhere have resulted in record numbers of women in national assemblies. But quotas alone will not ensure effective participation. A social group that has long been excluded from public decision-making must be supported to exercise the knowledge and skills needed to shape policy and legislation and enforce implementation.

This is not just a problem of women's capacities. It is about obstacles to gender equality in the institutions that shape the ways decisions are made, resources allocated, and policies implemented. Critical institutions – such as the military and ministries of finance and planning – do not automatically adopt gender equality goals even when peace agreements mandate them to do so.

Three changes are critical to enable public institutions to bring gender equality into their leadership, staff, and peace building work. These include:

(a) Top-level directives that make women's rights a key element of the institution's work;
(b) Incentive systems to reward efforts to address women's needs and
(c) Advance their rights measures to include gender equality in individual work plans and performance reviews.

Although more women have been brought into the military, the police and civilian staff of peacekeeping missions, they are still a token minority. Appointments of women to the top levels of mediation and facilitation teams, as well as peacekeeping missions, are still rare.

UNIFEM and other women's rights advocates must negotiate anew each time to bring women to peace talks or include women's priorities in post-conflict needs assessments, and even when they succeed, they find that resources are not allocated to meeting these priorities. In conclusion, if we want to consolidate peace we must stop rewarding those who are most socially destructive, and engage those with constructive, peaceful solutions.

Writing in the Sixteenth century, French philosopher Montaigne stated:

Women are not wrong when they decline to accept the rules laid down for them, since the men make these rules without consulting them.

One way of understanding peace consolidation is as a massive national effort to remake the rules of governance, justice, security and economic activity to eliminate the causes of conflict, distrust, and inequalities. For women of all social groups, this opportunity to participate in re-building the rules cannot be missed. Only then will we have peace under the laws of justice.

Hillary Rodham Clinton

On topic 'Women's Rights are Human Rights'
(1995)

Mrs. Mongella, distinguished delegates and guests:

I would like to thank the Secretary General of the United Nations for inviting me to be part of the United Nations Fourth World Conference on Women. This is truly a celebration — celebrations of the contributions women make in every aspect of life: in the home, on the job, in their communities, as mothers, wives, sisters, daughters, learners, workers, citizens and leaders.

It is also a coming together, much the way women come together every day in every country.

We come together in fields and in factories - In village markets and supermarkets - In living rooms and board rooms.

Whether it is while playing with our children in the par, or washing clothes in a river, or taking a break at the office water cooler, we come together and talk about our aspirations and concerns. And time and again, our talk turns to our children and our families.

However different we may be, there is far more that unites us than divides us. We share a common future. And we are here to find common ground so that we may help bring new dignity and respect to women and girls all over the world — and in so doing, bring new strength and stability to families as well.

By gathering in Beijing, we are focusing world attention on issues that matter most in the lives of women and their families: access to education, health care, jobs, and credit, the chance to enjoy basic legal and human rights and participate fully in the political life of their countries.

There are some who question the reason for this conference. Let them listen to the voices of women in their homes, neighborhoods, and workplaces.

There are some who wonder whether the lives of women and girls matter to economic and political progress around the globe. ...Let them look at the women gathered here and at Hairou...the homemakers, nurses, teachers, lawyers, policymakers, and women who run their own businesses.

It is conferences like this that compel governments and peoples everywhere to listen, look and face the world's most pressing problems.

Wasn't it after the women's conference in Nairobi ten years ago that the world focused for the first time on the crisis of domestic violence?

Earlier today, I participated in a World Health Organization forum, where government officials, NGOs, and individual citizens are working on ways to address the health problems of women and girls.

Tomorrow, I will attend a gathering of the United Nations Development Fund for Women. There, the discussion will focus on local — and highly successful — programs that give hard-working women access to credit so they can improve their own lives and the lives of their families.

What we are learning around the world is that, if women are healthy and educated, their families will flourish. If women are free from violence, their families will flourish. If women have a chance to work and earn as full and equal partners in society, their families will flourish. And when families flourish, communities and nations will flourish.

That is why every woman, every man, every child, every family, and every nation on our planet has a stake in the discussion that takes place here.

Over the past 25 years, I have worked persistently on issues relating to women, children and families. Over the past two-and-a-half years, I have had the opportunity to learn more about the challenges facing women in my own country and around the world.

I have met new mothers in Jojakarta, Indonesia, who come together regularly in their village to discuss nutrition, family planning, and baby care. I have met working parents in Denmark who talk about the comfort they feel in knowing that their children can be cared for in creative, safe, and nurturing after-school centers. I have met women in South Africa who helped lead the struggle to end apartheid and are now helping build a new democracy. I have met with the leading women of the Western Hemisphere who are working every day to promote literacy and better health care for the children of their countries.

I have met women in India and Bangladesh who are taking out small loans to buy milk cows, rickshaws, thread and other materials to create a livelihood for themselves and their families. I have met doctors and nurses in Belarus and Ukraine who are trying to keep children alive in the aftermath of Chernobyl.

The great challenge of this conference is to give voice to women everywhere whose experiences go unnoticed, whose words go unheard.

Women comprise more than half the world's population. Women are 70 percent of the world's poor, and two-thirds of those who are not taught to read and write.

Women are the primary caretakers for most of the world's children and elderly. Yet much of the work we do is not valued — not by economists, not by historians, not by popular culture, not by government leaders.

At this very moment, as we sit here, women around the world are giving birth, raising children, cooking meals, washing clothes, cleaning houses, planting crops, working on assembly lines, running companies, and running countries.

Women also are dying from diseases that should have been prevented or treated; they are watching their children succumb to malnutrition caused by poverty and economic deprivation; they are being denied the right to go to school by their own fathers and brothers; they are being forced into prostitution; and they are being barred from the ballot box and the bank lending office.

Those of us who have the opportunity to be here have the responsibility to speak for those who could not.

As an American, I want to speak up for women in my own country — women who are raising children on the minimum wage, women who can't afford health care or child care, women whose lives are threatened by violence, including violence in their own homes.

I want to speak up for mothers who are fighting for good schools, safe neighborhoods, clean air and clean airwaves... for older women, some of them widows, who have raised their families and now find that their skills and life experiences are not valued in the workplace... for women who are working all night as nurses, hotel clerks, and fast food chefs so that they can be at home during the day with their kids... and for women everywhere who simply don't have time to do everything they are called upon to do each day.

Speaking to you today, I speak for them, just as each of us speaks for women around the world who are denied the chance to go to school, or see a doctor, or own property, or have a say about the direction of their lives, simply because they are women.

The truth is that most women around the world work both inside and outside the home, usually by necessity.

We need to understand that there is no formula for how women should lead their lives. That is why we must respect the choices that each woman makes for herself and her family. Every woman deserves the chance to realize her God-given potential.

We also must recognize that women will never gain full dignity until their human rights are respected and protected.

Our goals for this conference, to strengthen families and societies by empowering women to take greater control over their own destinies, cannot be fully achieved unless all governments — here and around the world — accept their responsibility to protect and promote internationally recognized human rights.

The international community has long acknowledged — and recently affirmed at Vienna — that both women and men are entitled to a range of protections and personal freedoms, from the right to personal security to the right to determine freely the number and spacing of the children they bear.

No one should be forced to remain silent for fear of religious or political persecution, arrest, abuse or torture.

Tragically, women are most often the ones whose human rights are violated. Even in the late 20th century, the rape of women continues to be used as an instrument of armed conflict. Women and children make up a large majority of the world's refugees. And when women are excluded from the political process, they become even more vulnerable to abuse.

I believe that, on the eve of a new millennium, it is time to break our silence. It is time for us to say here in Beijing, and the world to hear, that it is no longer acceptable to discuss women's rights as separate from human rights.

These abuses have continued because, for too long, the history of women has been a history of silence. Even today, there are those who are trying to silence our words.

The voices of this conference and of the women at Hairou must be heard loud and clear.

It is a violation of human rights when babies are denied food, or drowned, or suffocated, or their spines broken, simply because they are born girls.

It is a violation of human rights when women and girls are sold into the slavery of prostitution.

It is a violation of human rights when women are doused with gasoline, set on fire and burned to death because their marriage dowries are deemed too small.

It is a violation of human rights when individual women are raped in their own communities and when thousands of women are subjected to rape as a tactic or prize of war.

It is a violation of human rights when a leading cause of death worldwide among women ages 14 to 44 is the violence they are subjected to in their own homes.

It is a violation of human rights when young girls are brutalized by the painful and degrading practice of genital mutilation.

It is a violation of human rights when women are denied the right to plan their own families, and that includes being forced to have abortions or being sterilized against their will.

If there is one message that echoes forth from this conference, it is that human rights are women's rights... And women's rights are human rights.

Let us not forget that among those rights are the rights to speak freely and the right to be heard.

Women must enjoy the right to participate fully in the social and political lives of their countries if we want freedom and democracy to thrive and endure.

It is indefensible that many women in non-governmental organizations who wished to participate in this conference have not been able to attend — or have been prohibited from fully taking part.

Let me be clear. Freedom means the right of people to assemble, organize, and debate openly. It means respecting the views of those who may disagree with the views of their governments. It means not taking citizens away from their loved ones and jailing them, mistreating them, or denying them their freedom or dignity because of the peaceful expression of their ideas and opinions.

In my country, we recently celebrated the 75th anniversary of women's suffrage. It took 150 years after the signing of our Declaration of Independence for women to win the right to vote. It took 72 years of organized struggle on the part of many courageous women and men.

It was one of America's most divisive philosophical wars. But it was also a bloodless war. Suffrage was achieved without a shot fired.

We have also been reminded, in V-J Day observances last weekend, of the good that comes when men and women join together to combat the forces of tyranny and build a better world.

We have seen peace prevail in most places for a half century. We have avoided another world war.

But we have not solved older, deeply rooted problems that continue to diminish the potential of half the world's population. Now it is time to act on behalf of women everywhere.

If wc take bold steps to better the lives of women, we will be taking bold steps to better the lives of children and families too. Families rely on mothers and wives for emotional support and care; families rely on women for labor in the home; and increasingly, families rely on women for income needed to raise healthy children and care for other relatives.

As long as discrimination and inequities remain so commonplace around the world — as long as girls and women are valued less, fed last, overworked, underpaid, not schooled and subjected to violence in and out of their homes — the potential of the human family to create a peaceful, prosperous world will not be realized.

Let this conference be our — and the world's — call to action.

And let us heed the call so that we can create a world in which every woman is treated with respect and dignity, every boy and girl is loved and cared for equally, and every family has the hope of a strong and stable future.[77]

Thank you very much. Let God's blessings on you, your work and all who will benefit from it.

Shirley Chisholm
On topic "Equal Rights for Women"
(1969)

Mr. Speaker, when a young woman graduates from college and starts looking for a job, she is likely to have a frustrating and even demeaning experience ahead of her. If she walks into an office for an interview, the first question she will be asked is, "Do you type?"

There is a calculated system of prejudice that lies unspoken behind that question. Why is it acceptable for women to be secretaries, librarians, and teachers, but totally unacceptable for them to be managers,

---

[77] Hillary Rodham Clinton (1995) "Women's Rights are Human Rights", Beijing China, September 5, 1995, The White House (in NARA) on the Remarks for the United Nations Fourth World Conference

administrators, doctors, lawyers, and Members of Congress?

The unspoken assumption is that women are different. They do not have executive ability, orderly minds, stability, leadership skills, and they are too emotional.

It has been observed before, that society for a long time discriminated against another minority, the blacks, on the same basis - that they were different and inferior.

The happy little homemaker and the contented "old darkey" on the plantation were both produced by prejudice.

As a black person, I am no stranger to race prejudice. But the truth is that in the political world I have been far oftener discriminated against because I am a woman than because I am black.

Prejudice against blacks is becoming unacceptable although it will take years to eliminate it. But it is doomed because, slowly, white America is beginning to admit that it exists. Prejudice against women is still acceptable. There is very little understanding yet of the immorality involved in double pay scales and the classification of most of the better jobs as "for men only." [78]

More than half of the population of the United States is female. But women occupy only 2 percent of the managerial positions. They have not even reached the level of tokenism yet No women sit on the AFL-CIO council or Supreme Court There have been only two women who have held Cabinet rank, and at

---

[78] Shirley Chisholm (1969), "Equal Rights for Women', Gifts of Speech – Equal Rights for Women, May 21, 1969, info please. com / history / equal rights for women

present there are none. Only two women now hold ambassadorial rank in the diplomatic corps. In Congress, we are down to one Senator and 10 Representatives.

Considering that there are about 3 1/2 million more women in the United States than men, this situation is outrageous. It is true that part of the problem has been that women have not been aggressive in demanding their rights. This was also true of the black population for many years. They submitted to oppression and even cooperated with it. Women have done the same thing. But now there is an awareness of this situation particularly among the younger segment of the population.

Senator Margaret Chase Smith

On topic 'Declaration of Conscience'

(1950)

Mr. President, I would like to speak briefly and simply about a serious national condition. It is a national feeling of fear and frustration that could result in national suicide and the end of everything that we Americans hold dear. It is a condition that comes from the lack of effective leadership in either the legislative branch or the executive branch of our Government. [79]

That leadership is so lacking that serious and responsible proposals are being made that national advisory commission is appointed to provide such critically needed leadership.

---

[79] Senator Margaret Chase Smith (1950), "Declaration of Conscience" U.S. Senate Washington, D.C., June 1, 1950, History Matters – National Suicides (from 'Declaration of Conscience' by Senator Margaret chase Smith and Statement of Seven Senators, June 1, 1950) Congressional Record, 82nd Congress and Congress Investigates: A Documentary History, New York, Chelsea House, 1963, pp. 84-88, info please, com

I speak as briefly as possible because too much harm has already been done with irresponsible words of bitterness and selfish political opportunism. I speak as simply as possible because the issue is too great to be obscured by eloquence. I speak simply and briefly in the hope that my words will be taken to heart.

I speak as a Republican. I speak as a woman. I speak as a United States Senator. I speak as an American.

The United States Senate has long enjoyed worldwide respect as the greatest deliberative body in the world. But recently that deliberative character has too often been debased to the level of a forum of hate and character assassination sheltered by the shield of congressional immunity.

It is ironical that we Senators can debate in the Senate directly or indirectly, by any form of words impute to any American, who is not a Senator, any conduct or motive unworthy or unbecoming an American—and without that non-Senator American having any legal redress against it—yet if we say the same thing in the Senate about our colleagues we can be stopped on the grounds of being out of order.

It is strange that we can verbally attack anyone else without restraint and with full protection and yet we hold ourselves above the same type of criticism here on the Senate floor. Surely the United States Senate is big enough to take self-criticism and self-appraisal. Surely we should be able to take the same kind of character attacks that we "dish out" to outsiders.

I think that it is high time for the United States Senate and its Members to do some soul searching—for us to weigh our consciences—on the manner in which we are performing our duty to the people of America; on the manner in which we are using or abusing our individual powers and privileges.

I think that it is high time that we remembered that we have sworn to uphold and defend the Constitution. I think that it is high time that we remembered that the Constitution, as amended, speaks not only of the freedom of speech, but also of trial by jury instead of trial by accusation.

Whether it is a criminal prosecution in court or a character prosecution in the Senate, there is little practical distinction when the life of a person has been ruined.

Those of us who shout the loudest about Americanism in making character assassinations are all too frequently those who, by our own words and acts, ignore some of the basic principles of Americanism—

(a) The right to criticize;
(b) The right to hold unpopular beliefs;
(c) The right to protest;
(d) The right of independent thought

The exercise of these rights should not cost one single American citizen his reputation or his right to a livelihood nor should he be in danger of losing his reputation or livelihood merely because he happens to know someone who holds unpopular beliefs. Who of us doesn't? Otherwise none of us could call our souls our own. Otherwise thought control would have set in.

Today our country is being psychologically divided by the confusion and the suspicions that are bred in the United States Senate to spread like cancerous tentacles of "know nothing, suspect everything" attitudes. Today we have a Democratic administration that has developed a mania for loose spending and loose programs. History is repeating itself—and the Republican Party again has the opportunity to emerge as the champion of unity and prudence.

The record of the present Democratic administration has provided us with sufficient campaign issues without the necessity of resorting to political smears. America is rapidly losing its position as leader of the world simply because the Democratic administration has pitifully failed to provide effective leadership.

The Democratic administration has completely confused the American people by its daily contradictory grave warnings and optimistic assurance — that show the people that our Democratic administration has no idea of where it is going.

The American people are sick and tired of being afraid to speak their minds lest they be politically smeared as "Communists" or "Fascists" by their opponents. Freedom of speech is not what it used to be in America. It has been so abused by some that others do not exercise it.

The American people are sick and tired of seeing innocent people smeared and guilty people whitewashed. But there have been enough proved cases, such as the *Amerasia* case, the Hiss case, the Coplon case, the Gold case, to cause Nation-wide distrust and strong suspicion that there may be something to the unproved, sensational accusations.

As a Republican, I say to my colleagues on this side of the aisle that the Republican Party faces a challenge today that is not unlike the challenge that it faced back in Lincoln's day. The Republican Party so successfully met that challenge that it emerged from the Civil War as the champion of a united nation—in addition to being a party that unrelentingly fought loose spending and loose programs.

The Democratic administration has greatly lost the confidence of the American people by its complacency to the threat of communism here at home and the leak of vital secrets to Russia through key officials of the Democratic administration. There are enough proved cases to make this point without diluting our criticism with unproved charges.

Surely these are sufficient reasons to make it clear to the American people that it is time for a change and that a Republican victory is necessary to the security of this country. Surely it is clear that this nation will continue to suffer as long as it is governed by the present ineffective Democratic administration.

Yet to displace it with a Republican regime embracing a philosophy that lacks political integrity or intellectual honesty would prove equally disastrous to this Nation. The Nation sorely needs a Republican victory. But I don't want to see the Republican Party ride to political victory on the four horsemen of calumny—fear, ignorance, bigotry and smear.

I doubt if the Republican Party could—simply because I don't believe the American people will uphold any political party that puts political exploitation above national interest. Surely we Republicans aren't that desperate for victory.

I don't want to see the Republican Party win that way. While it might be a fleeting victory for the Republican Party, it would be a more lasting defeat for the American people. Surely it would ultimately be suicide for the Republican Party and the two-party system that has protected our American liberties from the dictatorship of a one-party system.

As members of the minority party, we do not have the primary authority to formulate the policy of our Government. But we do have the responsibility of rendering constructive criticism, of clarifying issues, of allaying fears by acting as responsible citizens.

As a woman, I wonder how the mothers, wives, sisters, and daughters feel about the way in which members of their families have been politically mangled in Senate debate—and I use the word "debate" advisedly.

As a United States Senator, I am not proud of the way in which the Senate has been made a publicity platform for irresponsible sensationalism. I am not proud of the reckless abandon in which unproved charges have been hurled from this side of the aisle. I am not proud of the obviously staged, undignified countercharges that have been attempted in retaliation from the other side of the aisle.

I don't like the way the Senate has been made a rendezvous for vilification, for selfish political gain at the sacrifice of individual reputations and national unity. I am not proud of the way we smear outsiders from the floor of the Senate and hide behind the cloak of congressional immunity and still place us beyond criticism on the floor of the Senate.

As an American, I am shocked at the way Republicans and Democrats alike are playing directly into the Communist design of "confuse, divide and conquer." As an American, I don't want a Democratic administration "whitewash" or "cover-up" any more than I want a Republican smear or witch hunts.

As an American, I condemn a Republican "Fascist" just as much as I condemn a Democrat "Communist." I condemn a Democrat "Fascist" just as much as I condemn a Republican "Communist." They are equally dangerous to you and me and to our country. As an American, I want to see our Nation recapture the strength and unity it once had when we fought the enemy instead of ourselves.

It is with these thoughts I have drafted what I call a Declaration of Conscience. I am gratified that Senator

Tobey, Senator Aiken, Senator Morse, Senator Ives, Senator Thye and Senator Hendrickson, have concurred in that declaration and have authorized me to announce their concurrence.

The declaration reads as follows:

We are Republicans. But we are Americans first. It is as Americans that we express our concern with the growing confusion that threatens the security and stability of our country. Democrats and Republicans alike have contributed to that confusion.

The Democratic administration has initially created the confusion by its lack of effective leadership, by its contradictory grave warnings and optimistic assurances, by its complacency to the threat of communism here at home, by its over sensitiveness to rightful criticism, by its petty bitterness against its critics.

Certain elements of the Republican Party have materially added to this confusion in the hopes of riding the Republican party to victory through the selfish political exploitation of fear, bigotry, ignorance, and intolerance. There are enough mistakes of the Democrats for Republicans to criticize constructively without resorting to political smears.

To this extent, Democrats and Republicans alike have unwittingly, but undeniably, played directly into the Communist design of "confuse, divide and conquer."

It is high time that we stopped thinking politically as Republicans and Democrats about elections and started thinking patriotically as Americans about national security based on individual freedom. It is high time that we all stopped being tools and victims of totalitarian techniques—techniques that, if continued here unchecked, will surely end what we have come to cherish as the American way of life.

Helen Keller
On topic 'Strike against War'
(1916)

To begin with, I have a word to say to my good friends, the editors, and others who are moved to pity me. Some people are grieved because they imagine I am in the hands of unscrupulous persons who lead me astray and persuade me to espouse unpopular causes and make me the mouthpiece of their propaganda.

Now, let it be understood once and for all that I do not want their pity; I would not change places with one of them. I know what I am talking about. My sources of information are as good and reliable as anybody else's. I have papers and magazines from England, France, Germany and Austria that I can read myself. Not all the editors I have met can do that. Quite a number of them have to take their French and German second hand. No, I will not disparage the editors. They are an overworked, misunderstood class. Let them remember, though, that if I cannot see the fire at the end of their cigarettes, neither can they thread a needle in the dark. All I ask, gentlemen, is a fair field and no favor. I have entered the fight against preparedness and against the economic system under which we live. It is to be a fight to the finish, and I ask no quarter. [80]

The future of the world rests in the hands of America. The future of America rests on the backs of 80,000,000 working men and women and their children. We are facing a grave crisis in our national life. The few who profit from the labor of the masses want to organize the workers into an army, which will protect the interests of the capitalists. You are urged

---

[80] Helen Keller (1916), "Strike against War" New York NY, January 5, 1916, Her Socialist Years (International Publishers, 1967), Info pleases. Com

to add to the heavy burdens you already bear the burden of a larger army and many additional warships. It is in your power to refuse to carry the artillery and the dread - nougats and to shake off some of the burdens, too, such as limousines, steam yachts and country estates. You do not need to make a great noise about it. With the silence and dignity of creators you can end wars and the system of selfishness and exploitation that causes wars. All you need to do to bring about this stupendous revolution is to straighten up and fold your arms.

We are not preparing to defend our country. Even if we were as helpless as Congressman Gardner says we are, we have no enemies foolhardy enough to attempt to invade the United States. The talk about attack from Germany and Japan is absurd. Germany has its hands full and will be busy with its own affairs for some generations after the European war is over.

With full control of the Atlantic Ocean and the Mediterranean Sea, the allies failed to land enough men to defeat the Turks at Gallipoli; and then they failed again to land an army at Salonica in time to check the Bulgarian invasion of Serbia. The conquest of America by water is a nightmare confined exclusively to ignorant persons and members of the Navy League.

Yet, everywhere, we hear fear advanced as argument for armament. It reminds me of a fable I read. A certain man found a horseshoe. His neighbor began to weep and wail because, as he justly pointed out, the man who found the horseshoe might someday find a horse. Having found the shoe, he might shoe him. The neighbor's child might some day go so near the horse's hells as to be kicked, and die. Undoubtedly the two families would quarrel and fight, and several valuable lives would be lost through the finding of the horseshoe. You know the last war we had we quite accidentally picked up some islands in the Pacific Ocean which may some day be the cause of a quarrel between ourselves and Japan. I'd rather drop those islands right now and foret about them than go to war to keep them. Wouldn't you?

Congress is not preparing to defend the people of the United States. It is planning to protect the capital of American speculators and investors in Mexico, South America, China, and teh Philippine Islands. Incidentally this preparation will benefit the manufacturers of munitions and war machines.

Until recently there were uses in the United States for the money taken from the workers. But American labor is exploited almost to the limit now, and our national resources have all been appropriated. Still the profits keep piling up new capital. Our flourishing industry in implements of murder is filling the vaults of New York's banks with gold. And a dollar that is not being used to make a slave of some human being is not fulfilling its purpose in the capitalistic scheme. That dollar must be invested in South America, Mexico, China, or the Philippines.

It was no accident that the Navy League came into prominence at the same time that the National City Bank of New York established a branch in Buenos Aires. It is not a mere coincidence that six business associates of J.P. Morgan are officials of defense leagues. And chance did not dictate that Mayor Mitchel could appoint to his Committee of Safety a thousand men that represent a fifth of the wealth of the United States. These men want their foreign investments protected.

Every modern war has had its root in exploitation. The Civil War was fought to decide whether to slaveholders of the South or the capitalists of the North should exploit the West. The Spanish-American War decided that the United States should exploit Cuba and the Philippines. The South African War decided that the British should exploit the diamond mines. The Russo-Japanese War decided that Japan should exploit Korea. The present war is to decide who shall exploit the Balkans, Turkey, Persia, Egypt, India, China, and Africa. And we are whetting our sword to scare the victors into sharing the spoils with us. Now, the workers are not interested in the spoils; they will not get any of them anyway.

The preparedness propagandists have still another object, and a very important one. They want to give the people something to think about besides their won unhappy condition. They know the cost of living is high; wages are low, employment is uncertain and will be much more so when the European call for munitions stops. No matter how hard and incessantly the people work, they often cannot afford the comforts of life; many cannot obtain the necessities.

Every few days we are given a new war scare to lend realism to their propaganda. They have had us on the verge of war over the Lusitanian, the Gulf light, the Ancon, and now they want the workingmen to become excited over the sinking of the Persia. The workingman has no interest in any of these ships. The Germans might sink every vessel on the Atlantic Ocean and the Mediterranean Sea, and kill Americans with every one--the American workingman would still have no reason to go to war.

All the machinery of the system has been set in motion. Above the complaint and din of the protest from the workers is heard the voice of authority.

"Friends," it says, "fellow workmen, patriots; your country is in danger! There are foes on all sides of us. There is no difference between our enemies and us, except the Pacific Ocean and the Atlantic Ocean. Look at what has happened to Belgium. Consider the fate of Serbia. Will you murmur about low wages when your country, your very liberties, is in jeopardy? What are the miseries you endure compared to the humiliation of having a victorious German army sail up the East River? Quit your whining, get busy and prepare to defend your firesides and your flag. Get an army, get a navy; be ready to meet the invaders like the loyal-hearted freemen you are."

Will the workers walk into this trap? Will they be fooled again? I am afraid so. The people have always been amenable to oratory of this sort. The workers know they have no enemies except their masters. They know that their citizenship papers are no warrant for the safety of themselves or their wives and children. They know that honest sweat; persistent toil and years of struggle bring them nothing worth holding on to, worth fighting for. Yet, deep down in their foolish hearts they believe they have a country. Oh blind vanity of slaves!

The clever ones, up in the high places know how childish and silly the workers are. They know that if the government dresses them up in khaki and gives them a rifle and starts them off with a brass band and waving banners, they will go forth to fight valiantly for their own enemies. They are taught that brave men die for their country's honor. What a price to pay for an abstraction--the lives of millions of young men; other millions crippled and blinded for life; existence made hideous for still more millions of human being; the achievement and inheritance of generations swept away in a moment--and nobody better off for all the misery! This terrible sacrifice would be comprehensible if the thing you die for and call country fed, clothed, housed and warmed you, educated and cherished your children. I think the workers are the most unselfish of the children of men; they toil and live and die for other people's country, other people's sentiments, other people's liberties and other people's happiness! The workers have no liberties of their own; they are not free when they are compelled to work twelve or ten or eight hours a day. they are not free when they are ill paid for their exhausting toil. They are not free when their children must labor in mines, mills and factories or starve, and when their women may be driven by poverty to lives of shame. They are not free when they are clubbed and imprisoned because they go on strike for a raise of wages and for the elemental justice that is their right as human beings.

We are not free unless the men who frame and execute the laws represent the interests of the lives of the people and no other interest. The ballot does not make a free man out of a wage slave. There has never existed a truly free and democratic nation in the world. From time immemorial men have followed with blind loyalty the strong men who had the power of money and of armies. Even while battlefields were piled high with their own dead they have tilled the lands of the rulers and have been robbed of the fruits of their labor. They have built palaces and pyramids, temples and cathedrals that held no real shrine of liberty.

As civilization has grown more complex the workers have become more and more enslaved, until today they are little more than parts of the machines they operate. Daily they face the dangers of railroad, bridge, skyscraper, freight train, stokehold, stockyard, lumber raft and min. Panting and training at the docks, on the railroads and underground and on the seas, they move the traffic and pass from land to land the precious commodities that make it possible for us to live. And what is their reward? - A scanty wage, often poverty, rents, taxes, tributes and war indemnities. Statesmen or governments have never attempted the kind of preparedness the workers want is reorganization and reconstruction of their whole life.

The Germans found out years ago that they could not raise good soldiers in the slums so they abolished the slums. They saw to it that all the people had at least a few of the essentials of civilization--decent lodging, clean streets, wholesome if scanty food, proper medical care and proper safeguards for the workers in their occupations. That is only a small part of what should be done, but what wonders that one step toward the right sort of preparedness has wrought for Germany! For eighteen months it has kept itself free from invasion while carrying on an extended war of conquest, and its armies are still pressing on with unabated vigor. It is your business to force these reforms on the Administration. Let there be no more talk about what a government can or cannot do. All these things have been done by all the belligerent nations in the hurly-burly of war. Every fundamental industry has been managed better by the governments than by private corporations.

It is your duty to insist upon still more radical measure. It is your business to see that no child is employed in an industrial establishment or mine or store, and that no worker in needlessly exposed to accident or disease. It is your business to make them give you clean cities, free from smoke, dirt and congestion. It is your business to make them pay you a living wage. It is your business to see that this kind of preparedness is carried into every department on the nation, until everyone has a chance to be well born, well nourished, rightly educated, intelligent and serviceable to the country at all times.

Strike against all ordinances and laws and institutions continue the slaughter of peace and the butcheries of war. Strike against war, for without you no battles can be fought. You must strike against manufacturing scrape and gas bombs and all other tools of murder. You must strike against preparedness that means death and misery to millions of human being. Be not dumb, obedient slaves in an army of destruction. Be heroes in an army of construction.

Susan B. Anthony
On topic 'The Rights of Voting in an Election'
(1872)

Friends and fellow citizens: I stand before you tonight under indictment for the alleged crime of having voted at the last presidential election, without having a lawful right to vote. It shall be my work this evening to prove to you that in thus voting, I not only committed no crime, but, instead, simply exercised my citizen's rights, guaranteed to me and all United States citizens by the National Constitution, beyond the power of any state to deny.

The preamble of the Federal Constitution says:

We, the people of the United States, in order to form a more perfect union, establish justice, insure domestic tranquility, provide for the common defense, promote the general welfare, and secure the blessings of liberty to ourselves and our posterity, do ordain and establish this Constitution for the United States of America.[81]

It was we, the people; not we, the white male citizens; nor yet we, the male citizens; but we, the whole people, who formed the Union. And we formed it, not to give the blessings of liberty, but to secure them; not to the half of ourselves and the half of our posterity, but to the whole people - women as well as men. And it is a downright mockery to talk to women of their enjoyment of the blessings of liberty while they are denied the use of the only means of securing them provided by this democratic-republican government - the ballot.

---

[81] Susan B Anthony, 1872 Presidential Election Famous Speech, After Being Convicted Of Voting In The 1872 Presidential Election, Stump Speech in all 29 postal districts of Monroe County, New York, in 1873

For any state to make sex a qualification that must ever result in the disfranchisement of one entire half of the people, is to pass a bill of attainder, or, an ex post facto law, and is therefore a violation of the supreme law of the land. By it the blessings of liberty are forever withheld from women and their female posterity.

To them this government has no just powers derived from the consent of the governed. To them this government is not a democracy. It is not a republic. It is an odious aristocracy; a hateful oligarchy of sex; the most hateful aristocracy ever established on the face of the globe; an oligarchy of wealth, where the rich govern the poor.

An oligarchy of learning, where the educated govern the ignorant, or even an oligarchy of race, where the Saxon rules the African, might be endured; but this oligarchy of sex, which makes father, brothers, husband, sons, the oligarchs over the mother and sisters, the wife and daughters, of every household - which ordains all men sovereigns, all women subjects, carries dissension, discord, and rebellion into every home of the nation.

Webster, Worcester, and Bouvier all define a citizen to be a person in the United States, entitled to vote and hold office.

The only question left to be settled now is: Are women persons? And I hardly believe any of our opponents will have the hardihood to say they are not. Being persons, then, women are citizens; and no state has a right to make any law, or to enforce any old law, that shall abridge their privileges or immunities. Hence, all discrimination against women in the constitutions and laws of the several states is today null and void, precisely as is every one against Negroes.

Lucretia Mott

On topic "Discourse on Women"

(1849)

There is nothing of greater importance to the well being of society at large — of man as well as woman — than the true and proper position of woman. Much has been said, from time to time, upon this subject. It has been a theme for ridicule, for satire and sarcasm. We might look for this from the ignorant and vulgar; but from the intelligent and refined we have a right to expect that such weapons shall not be resorted to, — that gross comparisons and vulgar epithets shall not be applied, so as to place woman, in a point of view, ridiculous to say the least.[82]

This subject has claimed my earnest interest for many years. I have long wished to see woman occupying a more elevated position than that which custom for ages has allotted to her. It was with great regret, therefore, that I listened a few days ago to a lecture upon this subject, which, though replete with intellectual beauty, and containing much that was true and excellent, was yet fraught with sentiments calculated to retard the progress of woman to the high elevation destined by her Creator. I regretted the more that these sentiments should be presented with such intellectual vigor and beauty, because they would be likely to ensnare the young.

The minds of young people generally, are open to the reception of more exalted views upon this subject. The kind of homage that has been paid to woman, the flattering appeals which have too long satisfied her — appeals to her mere fancy and imagination, are giving place to a more extended recognition of her rights, her important duties and responsibilities in

---

[82] Lucretia Mott (1849), " Discourse On Woman", Library of Congress, Rare Book and Special Collection Division, National Women Suffrage Association Collection Philadelphia PA, December 17, 1849

life. Woman is claiming for herself stronger and more profitable food. Various are the indications leading to this conclusion. The increasing attention to female education, the improvement in the literature of the age, especially in what is called the "Ladies' Department," in the periodicals of the day, are among the proofs of a higher estimate of woman in society at large. Therefore we may hope that the intellectual and intelligent are being prepared for the discussion of this question, in a manner, which shall tend to ennoble woman and dignify man.

Free discussion upon this, as upon all other subjects, is never to be feared, nor will be, except by such as prefer darkness to light. "Those only who are in the wrong dread discussion. The light alarms those only who feel the need of darkness." It was sound philosophy, uttered by Jesus, "He that doeth truth cometh to the light that his deeds may be made manifest, that they are wrought in God."

I have not come here with a view of answering any particular parts of the lecture alluded to, in order to point out the fallacy of its reasoning. The speaker, however, did not profess to offer anything like argument on that occasion, but rather *a sentiment*. I have no prepared address to deliver to you, being unaccustomed to speak in that way; but I felt a wish to offer some views for your consideration, though in a desultory manner, which may lead to such reflection and discussion as will present the subject in a true light.

In the beginning, man and woman were created equal. "Male and female created them, and blessed them, and called their name Adam." He gave dominion to both over the lower animals, but not to one over the other.

The cause of the subjection of woman to man, was early ascribed to disobedience to the command of

God. This would seem to show that she was then regarded as not occupying her true and rightful position in society.

The laws given on Mount Sinai for the government of man and woman were equal; the precepts of Jesus make no distinction. Those who read the Scriptures, and judge for themselves, not resting satisfied with the perverted application of the text, do not find the distinction that theology and ecclesiastical authorities have made in the condition of the sexes. In the early ages, Miriam and Deborah, conjointly with Aaron and Barak, enlisted themselves on the side, which they regarded the right, united going up to their battles, and singing their songs of victory. We regard these with veneration. Deborah judged Israel many years — she went up with Barak against their enemies, with an army of 10,000, assuring him that the honor of the battle should not be to him, but to a woman.

Revolting as were the circumstances of their success, the acts of a semi-barbarous people, yet we read with reverence the song of Deborah: "Blessed above woman shall Jael, the wife of Heeber, the Kenite be; blessed shall she be above women in the tent. She put her hand to the nail, and her right hand to the workman's hammer; she smote Sisera through his temples. At her feet he bowed, he fell, he lay down dead."

This circumstance, revolting to Christianity, is recognized as an act-befitting woman in that day. Deborah, Huldah, and other honorable women, were looked up to and consulted in times of exigency, and their counsel was received. In that eastern country, with all the customs tending to degrade woman, some were called to fill great and important stations in society. There were also false prophetesses as well as true. The denunciations of Ezekiel were upon those women who would "prophesy out of their own heart, and sew pillows to all armholes,"

Coming down to later times, we find Anna, a prophetess of four-score years, in the temple day and night, speaking of Christ to all them who looked for redemption in Jerusalem. Numbers of women were the companions of Jesus, — one going to the men of the city, saying, "Come, see a man who told me all things that ever I did; is not this the Christ?" Another, "Whatsoever he saith unto you, do it." Philip had four daughters who did prophesy. Tryphena and Tryphosa were co-workers with the apostles in their mission, to whom they sent special messages of regard and acknowledgment of their labors in the gospel. Priscilla instructed a learned Jew, mighty in the Scriptures, in the way of the Lord more perfectly. Phebe is mentioned as a **servan***t* of Christ, and commended as such to the brethren. It is worthy of note, that the word **servant**, when applied to Tychicus, is rendered **minister.** Women professing godliness should be translated **preaching**.

The first announcement, on the day of Pentecost, was the fulfillment of ancient prophecy that God's spirit should be poured out upon **daughters** as well as sons, and they should prophesy. It is important that we be familiar with these facts, because woman has been so long circumscribed in her influence by the perverted application of the text, rendering it improper for her to speak in the assemblies of the people, "to edification, to exhortation, and to comfort."

If these scriptures were read intelligently, we should not so teach Christ, as to exclude any from a position, where they might exert an influence for good to their fellow-beings. The epistle to the Corinthian church, where the supposed apostolic prohibition of women's preaching is found, contains express directions how woman shall appear, when she prayed or prophesied. Judge then whether this admonition, relative to *speaking* and asking questions, in the excited state of that church, should be regarded as a standing injunction on woman's *preaching*, when that word was not used by the apostle. Where is the Scripture authority for the advice given to the early church, under peculiar circumstances, being binding on the church of the present day? Ecclesiastical history informs us, that for two or three hundred years, female ministers suffered martyrdom, in company with their brethren.

These things are too much lost sight of. They should be known, in order that we may be prepared to meet the assertion, so often made, that woman is stepping out of her appropriate sphere, when she shall attempt to instruct public assemblies. The present time particularly demands such investigation. It requires also, that "of yourselves ye should judge what is right," that you should know the ground whereon you stand. This age is notable for its works of mercy and benevolence — for the efforts that are made to reform the inebriate and the degraded, to relieve the oppressed and the suffering. Women as well as men are interested in these works of justice and mercy. They are efficient co-workers, their talents are called into profitable exercise, and their labors are effective in each department of reform. The blessing to the merciful, to the peacemaker is equal to man and to woman. It is greatly to be deplored, now that she is increasingly qualified for usefulness, that any view should be presented, calculated to retard her labors of love.

Why should not woman seek to be a reformer? If she is to shrink from being such an iconoclast as shall "break the image of man's lower worship," as so long held up to view; if she is to fear to exercise her reason, and her noblest powers, lest she should be thought to "attempt to act the man," and not "acknowledge his supremacy;" if she is to be satisfied with the narrow sphere assigned her by man, nor aspire to a higher, lest she should transcend the bounds of female delicacy; truly it is a mournful prospect for woman. We would admit all the difference, that our great and beneficent Creator has made, in the relation of man and woman, nor would we seek to disturb this relation; but we deny that the present position of woman, is her true sphere of usefulness: nor will she attain to this sphere, until the disabilities and disadvantages, religious, civil, and social, which impede her progress, are removed out of her way. These restrictions have enervated her mind and paralyzed her powers. While man assumes, that the present is the original state designed for woman, that the *existing* "differences are not arbitrary nor the result of accident," but grounded in nature; she will not make the necessary effort to obtain her just rights, lest it should subject her to the kind of scorn and contemptuous manner in which she has been spoken of.

So far from her "ambition leading her to attempt to act the man," she needs all the encouragement she can receive, by the removal of obstacles from her path, in order that she may become a "true woman." As it is desirable that man should act a manly and generous part, not "mannish," so let woman be urged to exercise a dignified and womanly bearing, not womanish. Let her cultivate all the graces and proper accomplishments of her sex, but let not these degenerate into a kind of effeminacy, in which she is satisfied to be the mere plaything or toy of society, content with her outward adorning, and with the tone of flattery and fulsome adulation too often addressed to her. True, nature has made a difference in her configuration, her physical strength, her voice, &c. — and we ask no change, we are satisfied with nature. But how has neglect and mismanagement increased this difference! It is our duty to develop these natural powers, by suitable exercise, so that they may be strengthened "by reason of use." In the ruder state of society, woman is made to bear heavy burdens, while her "lord and master" walks idly by her side. In the civilization to which we have attained, if cultivated and refined woman would bring all her powers into use, she might engage in pursuits, which she now shrinks from as beneath her proper vocation. The energies of men need not then be wholly devoted to the counting house and common business of life, in order that women in fashionable society may be supported in their daily promenades and nightly visits to the theatre and ball room.

The appeal of Catharine Beecher to woman some years ago, leading her to aim at higher pursuits, was greatly encouraging. It gave earnest of an improved condition of woman. She says, "The time is coming, when woman will be taught to understand the construction of the human frame, the philosophical results from restricted exercise, unhealthy modes of dress, improper diet, and other causes, which are continually operating to destroy the health and life of the young. Woman has been but little aware of the high incitements which should stimulate to the cultivation of her noblest powers. The world is no longer to be governed by physical force, but by the influence which mind exerts over mind. Woman has never wakened to her highest destinies and holiest hopes. The time is coming when educated females will not be satisfied with the present objects of their low ambition. When a woman now leaves the immediate business of her own education, how often, how generally do we find her, sinking down into almost useless inactivity? To enjoy the social circle, to accomplish a little sewing, a *little* reading, a little domestic duty, to while away her hours in self-indulgence, or to enjoy the pleasures of domestic life, — these are the highest objects at which many a woman of elevated mind, and accomplished education aims. And what does she find of sufficient interest to call forth her cultivated energies, and warm affections? But when the cultivation and development of the immortal mind shall be presented to woman, as her especial and delightful duty, and that too whatever be her relations in life; when by example and experience she shall have learned her power over the intellect and the affections, then we shall not find woman, returning from the precincts of learning and wisdom, to pass lightly away the bright hours of her maturing youth. We shall not so often see her, seeking the light device to embroider on muslin and lace, (and I would add, the fashionable crochet work of the present day ;) "But we shall see her, with the delighted glow of benevolence, seeking for immortal minds, whereon she may fasten durable and holy impressions, that shall never be effaced or wear away."

A new generation of women is now upon the stage, improving the increased opportunities furnished for the acquirement of knowledge. Public education is coming to be regarded the right of the children of a republic. The hill of science is not so difficult of ascent as formerly represented by poets and painters; but by fact and demonstration smoothed down, so as to be accessible to the assumed weak capacity of woman. She is rising in the scale of being through this, as well as other means, and finding heightened pleasure and profit on the right hand and on the left. The study of Physiology, now introduced into our common schools, is engaging her attention, impressing the necessity of the observance of the laws of health. The intellectual Lyceum and instructive lecture room are becoming, to many, more attractive than the theatre and the ballroom. The sickly and sentimental novel and pernicious romance are giving place to works, calculated to call forth the benevolent affections and higher nature. It is only by comparison that I would speak commendatory of these works of imagination. The frequent issue of them from the press is to be regretted. Their exciting contents, like stimulating drinks, when long indulged in, enervate the mind, unfitting it for the sober duties of life.

These duties are not to be limited by man. Nor will woman fulfill less her domestic relations, as the faithful companion of her chosen husband, and the fitting mother of her children, because she has a right estimate of her position and her responsibilities. Her self-respect will be increased; preserving the dignity of her being, she will not suffer herself to be degraded into a mere dependent. Nor will her feminine character be impaired. Instances are not few, of woman throwing off the encumbrances, which bind her, and going forth in a manner worthy of herself, her creation, and her dignified calling. Did Elizabeth Fry lose any of her feminine qualities by the public walk into which she was called? Having performed the duties of a mother to a large family, feeling that she owed a labor of love to the poor prisoner, she was empowered by Him who sent her forth, to go to kings and crowned heads of the earth, and ask audience of these; and it was granted her.

Did she lose the delicacy of woman by her acts? No. Her retiring modesty was characteristic of her to the latest period of her life. It was my privilege to enjoy her society some years ago, and I found all that belonged to the feminine in woman — to true nobility, in a refined and purified moral nature. Is Dorothea Dix throwing off her womanly nature and appearance in the course she is pursuing? In finding duties abroad, has any, "refined man felt that something of beauty has gone forth from her?" To use the contemptuous word applied in the lecture alluded to, is she becoming "mannish?" Is she compromising her womanly dignity in going forth to seek to better the condition of the insane and afflicted? Are not a beautiful mind and a retiring modesty still conspicuous in her?

Indeed, I would ask, if this modesty is not attractive also, when manifested in the other sex? It was strikingly marked in Horace Mann when presiding over the late National Educational Convention in this city. The retiring modesty of William Ellery Channing, was beautiful, as well as of many others, who have filled dignified stations in society. These virtues, differing as they may in degree in man and woman, are of the same nature and call forth our admiration wherever manifested.

The noble courage of Grace Darling is justly honored, leading her to present herself on the coast of England, during the raging storm, in order to rescue the poor, suffering, shipwrecked mariner. Woman was not wanting in courage, in the early ages. In war and bloodshed this trait was often displayed. Grecian and Roman history have lauded and honored her in this character. English history records her courageous women too, for unhappily we have little but the records of war handed down to us. The courage of Joan of Arc was made the subject of a popular lecture not long ago, by one of our intelligent citizens. But more-noble, moral daring is marking the female character at the present time, and better worthy of imitation. As these characteristics come to be appreciated in man too, his warlike acts, with all the miseries and horrors of the battleground, will sink into their merited oblivion, or be remembered only to be condemned. The heroism displayed in the tented field, must yield to the moral and Christian heroism, which is shadowed in the signs of our times.

The lecturer regarded the announcement of woman's achievements, and the offering of appropriate praise through the press, as a gross innovation upon the obscurity of female life — he complained that the exhibition of the attainments of girls, in schools' was now equal to that of boys, and the newspapers announce that "Miss Brown received the first prize for English grammar," & co. If he objected to so much excitement of emulation in schools, it would be well; for the most enlightened teachers discountenance these appeals to love of approbation and self-esteem.

But, while prizes continue to be awarded, can any good reason be given, why the name of the girl should not be published as well as that of the boy? He spoke with scorn that "we hear of Mrs. President so and so; and committees and secretaries of the same sex." But if women can conduct their own business, by means of Presidents and Secretaries of their own sex, can he tell us why they should not? They will never make much progress in any moral movement, while they depend upon men to act for them. Do we shrink from reading the announcement that Mrs. Somerville is made an honorary member of a scientific association? That Miss Herschel has made some discoveries, and is prepared to take her equal part in science? Or that Miss *Mitchell* of Nantucket has lately discovered a planet, long looked for? I cannot conceive why "honor to who honor is due" should not be rendered to woman as well as man; nor will it necessarily exalt her, or foster feminine pride. This propensity is found alike in male and female, and it should not be ministered to improperly, in either sex.

In treating upon the affections, the lecturer held out the idea, that as manifested in the sexes, they were opposite, if not somewhat antagonistic; and required a union, as in chemistry, to form a perfect whole. The simile appeared to me far from a correct illustration of the true union.

Minds that can assimilate, spirits that are congenial, attach themselves to each other. It is the union of similar, not opposite affections, which are necessary for the perfection of the marriage bond. There seemed a want of proper delicacy in his representing man as being bold in the demonstration of the pure affection of love. In persons of refinement, true love seeks concealment in man, as well as in woman. I will not enlarge upon the subject, although it formed so great a part of his lecture. The contrast drawn seemed a fallacy, as has much, very much that has been presented, in the sickly sentimental strains of the poet, from age to age.

The question is often asked, "What does woman want, more than she enjoys? What is she seeking to obtain? Of what rights is she deprived? What privileges are withheld from her? I answer, she asks nothing as favor, but as right, she wants to be acknowledged a moral, responsible being. She is seeking not to be governed by laws, in the making of which she has no voice. She is deprived of almost every right in civil society, and is a cipher in the nation, except in the right of presenting a petition. In religious society her disabilities, as already pointed out, have greatly retarded her progress. Her exclusion from the pulpit or ministry — her duties marked out for her by her equal brother man, subject to creeds, rules, and disciplines made for her by him — this is unworthy her true dignity. In marriage, there is assumed superiority, on the part of the husband, and admitted inferiority, with a promise of obedience, on the part of the wife. This subject calls loudly for examination, in order that the wrong may be redressed. Customs suited to darker ages in Eastern countries, are not binding upon enlightened society. The solemn covenant of marriage may be entered into without these lordly assumptions, and humiliating concessions and promises.

There are large Christian denominations that do not recognize such degrading relations of husband and wife. They ask no magisterial or ministerial aid to legalize or to sanctify this union. But acknowledging themselves in the presence of the Highest, and invoking his assistance, they come under reciprocal obligations of fidelity and affection, before suitable witnesses. Experience and observation go to prove, that there may be as much harmony, to say the least, in such a union, and as great purity and permanency of affection, as can exist where the more common custom or form is observed. The distinctive relations of husband and wife, of father and mother of a family are sacredly preserved, without the assumption of authority on the one part, or the promise of obedience on the other. There is nothing in such a marriage degrading to woman. She does not compromise her dignity or self-respect; but enters married life upon equal ground, by the side of her husband. By proper education, she understands her duties, physical, intellectual and moral; and fulfilling these, she is a helpmeet, in the true sense of the word.

I tread upon delicate ground in alluding to the institutions of religious associations; but the subject is of so much importance, that all, which relates to the position of woman, should be examined, apart from the undue veneration which ancient usage receives.

Such dupes are men to custom, and so prone,
To reverence what is ancient, and can plead a
course of long observance for its use,
That even servitude, the worst of ills,
Because delivered down from sire to son,
Is kept and guarded as a sacred thing.

So it was with woman. She has so long been subject to the disabilities and restrictions, with which her progress has been embarrassed, that she has become enervated, her mind to some extent paralyzed; and, like those still more degraded by personal bondage, she hugs her chains. Liberty is often presented in its true light, but it is liberty for man. Whose freedom is by sufferance and at will of a superior — he is never free. Who lives, and is not weary of a life Exposed to manacles, deserves them well.

I would not, however, go so far, either as regards the abject slave or woman; for in both cases they may be so degraded by the crushing influences around them, that they may not be sensible of the blessing of

Freedom. Liberty is not less a blessing, because oppression has so long darkened the mind that it cannot appreciate it. I would therefore urge, that woman be placed in such a situation in society, by the yielding of her rights, and have such opportunities for growth and development, as shall raise her from this low, enervated and paralyzed condition, to a full appreciation of the blessing of entire freedom of mind.

It is with reluctance that I make the demand for the political rights of woman, because this claim is so distasteful to the age. Woman shrinks, in the present state of society, from taking any interest in politics. The events of the French Revolution and the claim for woman's rights are held up to her as a warning. But let us not look at the excesses of women alone, at that period; but remember that the age was marked with extravagances and wickedness in men as well as women. Indeed, political life abounds with these excesses, and with shameful outrage. Who knows, but that if woman acted her part in governmental affairs, there might be an entire change in the turmoil of political life? It becomes man to speak modestly of his ability to act without her. If woman's judgment were exercised, why might she not aid in making the laws by which she is governed? Lord Brougham remarked that those of any political writer of the present time did not excel the works of Harriet Martineau upon Political Economy. The first few chapters of her 'Society in America,' her views of a Republic, and of Government generally, furnish evidence of woman's capacity to embrace subjects of universal interest.

Far be it from me to encourage woman to vote, or to take an active part in politics, in the present state of our government. Her right to the elective franchise however, is the same, and should be yielded to her, whether she exercise that right or not. Would that man too, would have no participation in a government based upon the life-taking principle — upon retaliation and the sword. It is unworthy a Christian nation. But when, in the diffusion of light and intelligence, a convention shall be called to make regulations for self-government on Christian, non-resistant principles, I can see no good reason, why woman should not participate in such an assemblage, taking part equally with man.

Walker, of Cincinnati, in his Introduction to American Law, says: "With regard to political rights, females form a positive exception to the general doctrine of equality. They have no part or lot in the formation or administration of government. They cannot vote or hold office. We require them to contribute their share in the way of taxes, to the support of government, but allow them no voice in its direction. We hold them amenable to the laws when made, but allow them no share in making them. This language, applied to males, would be the exact definition of political slavery; applied to females, custom does not teach us so to regard it." Woman, however, is beginning so to regard it.

"The law of husband and wife, as you gather it from the books, is a disgrace to any civilized nation. The theory of the law degrades the wife almost to the level of slaves. When a woman marries, we call her condition covertures, and speak of her as a *femme covert*. The old writers call the husband baron, and sometimes, in plain English, lord. The merging of her name in that of her husband is emblematic of the fate of all her legal rights. The torch of Hymen serves, but to light the pile on which these rights are offered up. The legal theory is that marriage makes the husband and wife one person, and that person is the *husband*.

On this subject, reform is loudly called for. There is no foundation in reason or expediency, for the absolute and slavish subjection of the wife to the husband, which forms the foundation of the present legal relations. Were woman, in point of fact, the abject thing which the law, in theory, considers her to be when married, she would not be worthy the companionship of man."

I would ask if such a code of laws does not require change. If such a condition of the wife in society does not claim redress? On no good ground can reform be delayed. Blackstone says, "The very being and legal existence of woman is suspended during marriage, — incorporated or consolidated into that of her husband, under whose protection and cover she performs every thing." Hurlbut, in his Essays upon Human Rights, says: "The laws touching the rights of woman are at variance with the laws of the Creator. Rights are human rights, and pertain to human beings, without distinction of sex. Laws should not be made for man or for woman, but for mankind. Man was not born to command, or woman to obey. The law of France, Spain, and Holland, and one of our own States, Louisiana, recognizes the wife's right to property, more than the common law of England. The laws depriving woman of the right of property is handed down to us from dark and feudal times, and not consistent with the wiser, better, purer spirit of the age. The wife is a mere pensioner on the bounty of her husband. Her lost rights are appropriated to himself. But justice and benevolence are abroad in our land, awakening the spirit of inquiry and innovation; and the Gothic fabric of the British law will fall before it, save where it is based upon the foundation of truth and justice."

May these statements lead you to reflect upon this subject, that you may know what woman's condition is in society — what her restrictions are, and seek to remove them. In how many cases in our country, the husband and wife begin life together, and by equal industry and united effort accumulate to them a comfortable home. In the event of the death of the wife, the household remains undisturbed, his farm or his workshop is not broken up, or in any way molested. But when the husband dies, he either gives his wife a *portion* of their joint accumulation, or the law apportions to her a *share;* the homestead is broken up, and she is dispossessed of that which she earned equally with him; for what she lacked in physical strength, she made up in constancy of labor and toil, day and evening. The sons then coming into possession of the property, as has been the custom until of latter time, speak of having to *keep* their mother, when she in reality is aiding to keep them. Where is the justice of this state of things? The change in the law of this State and of New York, in relation to the property of the wife, go to a limited extend, toward the redress of these wrongs; but they are far more extensive, and involve much more, than I have time this evening to point out.

On no good ground can the legal existence of the wife be suspended during marriage, and her property surrendered to her husband. In the intelligent ranks of society, the wife may not in point of fact, be as degraded as the law would degrade her; because public sentiment is above the law. Still, while the law stands, she is liable to the disabilities, which it imposes. Among the ignorant classes of society, woman is made to bear heavy burdens, and is degraded almost to the level of the slave. There are many instances now in our city, where the wife suffers much from the power of the husband to claim all that she can earn with her own hands. In my intercourse with the poorer class of people, I have known cases of extreme cruelty, from the hard earnings of the wife being thus robbed by the husband, and no redress at law.

An article in one of the daily papers lately, presented the condition of needlewomen in England. There might be a presentation of this class in our own country, which would make the heart bleed. Public attention should be turned to this subject, in order that avenues of more profitable employment may be opened to women. There are many kinds of business, which women, equally with men, may follow with respectability and success. Their talents and energies should be called forth, and their powers brought into the highest exercise. The efforts of women in France are sometimes pointed to in ridicule and sarcasm, but depend upon it, the opening of profitable employment to women in that country is doing much for the enfranchisement of the sex. In England also, it is not an uncommon thing for a wife to take up the business of her deceased husband and carry it on with success.

Our respected British Consul stated to me a circumstance, which occurred some years ago, of an editor of a political paper having died in England; it was proposed to his wife, an able writer, to take the editorial chair. She accepted. The patronage of the paper was greatly increased, and she a short time since retired from her labors with a handsome fortune. In that country however, the opportunities are by no means general for Woman's elevation.

In visiting the public school in London, a few years since, I noticed that the boys were employed in linear drawing, and instructed upon the black board, in the higher branches of arithmetic and mathematics; while the girls, after a short exercise in the mere elements of arithmetic, were seated, during the bright hours of the morning, *stitching wristbands*. I asked, why there should be this difference made; why they too should not have the black board? The answer was that they would not probably fill any station in society requiring such knowledge.

But the demand for a more extended education will not cease, until girls and boys have equal instruction, in all the departments of useful knowledge. We have as yet no high school for girls in this state. The normal school may be a preparation for such an establishment. In the late convention for general education, it was cheering to hear the testimony borne to woman's capabilities for head teachers of the public schools. A resolution there offered for equal salaries to male and female teachers, when equally qualified, as practiced in Louisiana, I regret to say was checked in its passage, by Bishop Potter; by him who has done so much for the encouragement of education, and who gave his countenance and influence to that convention. Still the fact of such a resolution being offered augurs a time coming for woman, which she may well hail. At the last examination of the public schools in this city, one of the alumni delivered an address on Woman, not as is too common, in eulogistic strains, but directing the attention to the injustice done to woman in her position in society, in a variety of ways. The unequal wages she receives for her constant toil, &c., presenting facts calculated to arouse attention to the subject.

Women's property has been taxed, equally with that of men's, to sustain colleges endowed by the states; but they have not been permitted to enter those high seminaries of learning. Within a few years, however, some colleges have been instituted, where young women are admitted, nearly upon equal terms with young men; and numbers are availing themselves of their long denied rights. This is among the signs of the times, indicative of an advance for women. The book of knowledge is not opened to her in vain. Already is she aiming to occupy important posts of honor and profit in our country? We have three female editors in our state — some in other states of the Union. Numbers are entering the medical profession — one received a diploma last year; others are preparing for a like result.

Let woman then go on — not asking as favor, but claiming as right, the removal of all the hindrances to her elevation in the scale of being — let her receive encouragement for the proper cultivation of all her powers, so that she may enter profitably into the active business of life; employing her own hands, in ministering to her necessities, strengthening her physical being by proper exercise, and observance of the laws of health. Let her not be ambitious to display a fair hand, and to promenade the fashionable streets of our city, but rather, coveting earnestly the best gifts, let her strive to occupy such walks in society, as will befit her true dignity in all the relations of life. No fear that she will then transcend the proper limits of female delicacy. True modesty will be as fully preserved, in acting out those important vocations to which she may be called, as in the nursery or at the fireside, ministering to man's self-indulgence. Then in the marriage union, the independence of the husband and wife will be equal, their dependence mutual, and their obligations reciprocal.

In conclusion, let me say, "Credit not the old fashioned absurdity, that woman's is a secondary lot, ministering to the necessities of her lord and master! It is a higher destiny I would award you. If your immortality is as complete, and your gift of mind as capable as ours, of increase and elevation, I would put no wisdom of mine against God's evident allotment. I would charge you to water the undying bud, and give it healthy culture, and open its beauty to the sun — and then you may hope that when your life is bound up with another, you will go on equally, and in a fellowship that shall pervade every earthly interest."

Conclusion:

Women are not able to get justice in all countries. The UN Security Council resolution 1325 could be more effectively implemented to bring sustainable peace.

Peace-building efforts must ensure women's physical security and economic security. Sustainable peace requires real justice for women. Peace processes require institutional change and stronger accountability systems.

Women must be involved in peace making and peace building processes. Women know the cost of war. Women must be saved from violation of human rights. In USA, women constitute more than 50 percent of population, but they occupy only 2 percent of managerial posts and they are discriminated more than colour discrimination.

Women are not wrong when they decline to accept the rules laid down for them, since the men make these rules without consulting them. Women comprise more than 50 percent of world's population; women are 70 percent of the world's poor, and 67 percent of those who are not taught to read and write.

We also must recognize that women will never gain full dignity until their human rights are respected and protected. The cause of death of women from age 14 to 44 is the violence of human rights in their own homes. Moreover, young girls are brutalized by the painful and degrading practice of genital mutilation. It is a violation of human rights when women are denied the right to plan their own families, and that includes being forced to have abortions or being sterilized against their will.

+++++

Chapter IX

WORLD PEACE IS POSSIBLE

The world is very different now. For man holds in his mortal hands the power to abolish all forms of human poverty and all forms of human life. And yet the same revolutionary beliefs for which our forebears fought are still at issue around the globe—the belief that the rights of man come not from the generosity of the state, but from the hand of God.

John Fitzgerald Kennedy (January 20, 1960)

The world has advanced in theory and practice; science and technology; satisfaction and comfort, trade and commerce, knowledge and achievements and looks to a horizon of peace. It is possible, if there would prevail equality between man and woman, opportunity of food security to all and justice to all. So, the United Nations and the member countries should take a decision in the Security Council to achieve human rights, food security and justice to all within a time frame.

It is time to end violence against women. It is time to complete the judicial procedure within three months or in a record time on women atrocities. It is time to punish female child abortion; torture of women by family members and torture by husband, which promised to take care of his wife life-long. It is time; all people should change their mindsets for a new horizon of peace and progress.

The Marriage formula

Beyond functional stability, a marriage needs intimacy to survive the years meaningfully.

Pretty much everyone I meet, whether they express it not, wants from me a magic formula that would guarantee them marital happiness. When I got married, I too was looking for one such. And now, almost 25 years later, a young man whom I know well, asked me on the eve of his wedding, whether I could distil my personal and professional knowledge and give him a formula for a happy marriage. He loved his fiancée very much, he told me, but with wisdom beyond his years, he felt that this alone was not enough. He was absolutely right. While love is very important in a relationship, it can't make for a successful marriage on its own. Also, he didn't want a marriage like that of his parents which he felt was not particularly bad in that they didn't fight very much, but not particularly good either since they were not really close to each other.

Key to happiness: So, after some thought, I gave him my formula for a happy marriage: I = C3. [83]
Intimacy = Commitment + Connectedness + Companionship

[83] NB: Sustained marital happiness is experienced primarily on account of Intimacy (I). In turn, Intimacy is a function of three Cs — Commitment, Connectedness and Companionship.

Of course, there are many couples who believe their marriages are doing fine because they have successfully negotiated marital minefields and have achieved a degree of solidity. And I have no quarrel with them on this, for; their marriages are obviously functionally stable. However, if we are looking for marital happiness, then the absence of unhappiness can at best be seen as a beginning and not the end point.

As a nation, we are not too hot on the idea of intimacy, since we shoot more for marital comfort rather than for marital happiness. If the couple doesn't fight too much, everybody thinks of them as being 'the ideal couple'. But marriage can actually be configured to offer us much more than this. Often when I ask couples how good the intimacy is in their marriage, the response I usually get has to do with their sex lives. However, intimacy is not just about sex. It is basically about emotional closeness which can only enter the marriage when both partners mutually experience feelings of commitment, connectedness and companionship.

Merely hanging on in a marriage is not, as is commonly believed, a sign of commitment. As is well known, thousands of couples in our country live together even if they're not particularly happy with each other simply because they don't know what else to do, or because social norms dictate that they must, or they cannot find good enough reasons to part ways. As I see it, the term commitment refers to both partners determinedly seeking and finding solutions to issues that bedevil them and their marriages. As any couple therapist will tell you, solutions to marital problems are based more on common sense than any scientific principles, and that, closely connected couples will usually find very creative ways out of their bottlenecks. Not because they have to, but because they want to. As a result, most couple therapists work not towards finding solutions for couples' problems but towards helping increase their commitment to and connectedness with each other. When two people are committed to each other, they build a bond of connectedness and may actually have fun finding ways and means around their problems, particularly when they realise that two heads and two hearts work better than one. And when they do this often enough, they experience a feeling of companionship that ensures they enjoy the time they spend with each other, even if they have widely varying interests.

Necessary conditions

However, for this formula to work, two preliminary conditions need to be fulfilled. The first of these is the recognition that bonding is not, as many people fear, bondage. The bond of connectedness is based purely on a voluntary desire to connect, and not because the partner demands it. The second condition is that it takes two to bond. Of course, both partners may express their need for connectedness differently, since men and women are quite different when it comes to expressing and responding to intimacy needs. However, once both partners start the process, believe me, they will find the wherewithal to not only deal with their issues, but to forge a resilient bond that holds them together even during storms, and is flexible enough to accommodate their respective requirement for personal space.

The consequences of low-intimacy marriages, even those where the partners love each other, may or may not be disastrous. Some couples may just hang in there, but others may feel unstipulated or unsupported and lead parallel lives. Some others may find their marriages visited by what American relationship researcher John Gottman refers to as "the four horsemen of the Marital Apocalypse" — criticism, defensiveness, contempt and stonewalling — which can together make for an extremely distressing marital experience. However, if couples conceive of marriage as a space they can jointly configure in any way they choose and put the I = C3 equation to work, then words like 'apocalypse' can remain where they belong — in dictionaries. [84]

What Women Really Want for Valentine's Day

Valentine's Day has long celebrated love with caring notes, decadent chocolates and romantic arrangements of flowers. But this Valentine's Day, perhaps it's time to celebrate with a gift many of the world's women desperately want and need: reproductive health.

According to the United Nations Population Fund (UNFPA), 1,000 women die every day due to pregnancy or childbirth, or one woman every 90 seconds. Ninety-nine percent of these deaths occur in the developing world, 90 percent in Africa and Asia. A handful of complications account for 80 percent of these maternal deaths -- severe bleeding, infections, high blood pressure, obstructed labor, and unsafe abortion -- and the bulk of these deaths are preventable.

Reproductive health, including access to the information and means to plan a family, is a human right the world's nations have recognized in various forms since 1968. Access to family planning and other reproductive health services safeguard the lives of women and their children and promote families that are emotionally and economically healthy.

In my book, More: Population, Nature, and What Women Want, I explore centuries of reproductive history and conclude that, if given the chance to do what they really want, women on average have

---

[84] Vijay Nagaswami (2011), "The Marriage Formula", The Shrinking Universe, The Hindu, August 7, 2011

smaller families, with childbirths later in their lives. This pattern is safer for women and children, and promotes environmental sustainability through the slower population growth that lower fertility rates and later births bring about.

The Health of Women and Children

The UNFPA report Women and Girls in a World of 7 Billion notes that poverty, marginalization, and gender inequalities based on culture are key challenges to reproductive health. The report relays that women own less than 15 percent of the land worldwide; their wages, on average, are 17 percent lower than men's; and they make up two-thirds of the world's 776 million illiterate adults.

This means that women, particularly in the developing world, must often rely on men for financial support -- creating situations in which women are subject to their partners' views on contraception, feel trapped in physically or emotionally abusive relationships, and marry and have children young instead of pursuing further education or employment outside the home. In the developing world, one in seven girls will be married before she turns 15, and worldwide, complications from pregnancy and childbirth are the leading causes of death for girls 15-19.

Many women are not empowered to make their own decisions regarding if or when to have children, how many to have, and how long to wait in between them. Some 40 percent or more of pregnancies are unplanned, with more than 21 percent of all births resulting from such pregnancies worldwide, according to estimates of the Guttmacher Institute. If given access to family planning, and permission by their families and societies to use it, fewer women and children would die from unsafe abortions and high-risk pregnancies.

The Health of the Planet

The United Nations Foundation sponsors Girl Up, an organization that encourages a world where young girls can avoid the pitfalls of too-early marriage and childbearing and can instead go to school, enjoy health and safety, and grow into the next generation of leaders. In the Amhara region of Ethiopia, where half of adolescent girls are married, Girl Up is helping to promote education for young girls. The project offers basic literacy classes, family planning information, and agricultural training.

When women and girls are empowered with education and the capacity to make choices about sex, marriage and childbearing, they have opportunities to realize futures as farmers, businesswomen, politicians, or whatever dream drives them. These benefits ripple out from the lives of individual women and girls to their families, their communities, their nations -- and ultimately to the entire world.

In the World Watch report Population, Climate Change, and Women's Lives, I suggest that if women are given access to increased reproductive health, they are better able to more naturally control the size of their families and counterbalance the resource depletion and pollution that are exacerbated by unabated population increases.

The importance of women and the autonomy they exercise may be far greater to the climate's future than most experts and negotiators on climate change have realized.

What Women Really Want

Reproductive health is not about state-mandated family sizes; it is about freeing women to make their own choices about when and how often to give birth.

In all countries where affordable access is offered to family planning resources and women have the option of safe and legal abortions, women's fertility rates drop to two or less children per woman? Such rates are normal for nearly half the world and are less than the "replacement fertility" rate of slightly more than two children per woman, that fuels present and future population growth.

When women are free to make their own choices, they improve their own health and that of their families. A study by the UNFPA and the Guttmacher Institute suggests that it would take USD $24 billion to fulfill unmet reproductive health needs in developing countries, several times what countries spend today. According to the report, such an investment would "provide every woman with the recommended standard of maternal and newborn care" and would "[r]educe unintended pregnancies by more than 66 percent, prevent 70 percent of maternal deaths, avert 44 percent of newborn deaths, and reduce unsafe abortion by 73 percent."[85]

Wise women offer wonderful words

Eleanor Roosevelt wasn't commander in chief or the executive leader of our powerful country. She didn't single-handedly make powerful decisions that would affect numerous generations after and certainly, no one put a check beside her name on the ballot that fateful November; but, like so many other first ladies America has experienced and from which we have profited, she knew a thing or two about our world today. She only presented this wise information when necessary and in a poised manner. A person had no choice but to stop and pay attention.

---

[85] Robert Engelman (2012), "What Women Really Want for Valentine's Day", February 10, 2012

A brilliant illustration of this knowledge Mrs. Roosevelt passed on to Americans was a response she once gave when asked about world peace and what she thought needed to be done in order to achieve a thing that seemed unreachable.

She stated, "It isn't enough to talk about peace. One must believe in it. And it isn't enough to believe in it. One must work at it." Said at a time when no one was quite sure what peace truly represented, this statement was put quite beautifully and tastefully and to the point. People today might believe in true peace to a certain extent but few are willing to commit and do what is necessary to obtain a realistic sense of peace, not just throughout the country, but, more importantly, around the globe.

Let's face it. Peace isn't exactly at the top of anyone's priority list. What people fail to realize is that if we all took the time to allow ourselves the privilege of peace everything would subsequently fall into place. We have allowed ourselves to focus all our attention on all the wrong things. Machines have printed and will continue to print our paper-based economy, whether this works or not. The very people who allow this to happen are the same people who wear their paychecks like an invaluable piece of jewelry for everyone to admire. Is this what we as a human race should base our very existence on? Does the number of zeros on your bank statement define who you are? Perhaps if the inhabitants of the whole world, not just the United States, put all their materialistic thoughts aside — perhaps, if we did more than simply talk about how provident the concept of peace truly sounded while sitting behind our business desks, and instead took the first step towards achieving this goal. Maybe then, we could allow ourselves to believe. But remember, believing is not enough.

The question for many still remains, "How do you 'work' at peace?" The answer to this often-asked question comes in numerous forms, many of which may surprise you. Working at peace doesn't always have to involve winning a Noble Prize, feeding thousands of starving children in Third World countries, or attending rallies that support the idea of peace. All these things are huge in the progress of peace, but simpler things that people do not find themselves doing enough of can have more of an effect sometimes than painting your face and waving a flag. What is this simple solution to a problem we have always faced you ask? Simple - The little things in life that, more often than not, can only be found in picture books and young children's imaginations.

There are several examples of these things. Smiling at a stranger in line at a grocery store when they look like they've been worn down by the constant demand of life is working at peace. Holding the hand of a lonely older lady as she stumbles to make the light across the street is working at peace. Treating people, strangers and friends alike, with utmost respect is working at peace. Sounds easy I'm aware but the fruit harvested by actually taking the time to pay forward the feeling of wholeness that peace provides is what the world needs today. As a final thought, I end with three basic concepts, provided by Eleanor Roosevelt herself. Talk, believe, and most importantly, act. This process can be a gradual one but also has to be given effort by everyone. Everyone has to realize what's possibly at stake if we don't change something. What problem couldn't peace fix easily? What value would you rather have internally? With peace comes all else, and according to another fabulous lady that fills the pages of our history books today, Mother Teresa, "Peace begins with a smile." It's as simple as that.[86]

---

[86] Paige Barnes (2009), "Wise women offer wonderful words" Peabody Gazette Bulletin, November 4, 2009

Battle over Women Bishops

Twenty years after women were first allowed to become priests, the Church of England is bracing itself for a week of bitter rows over the consecration of female bishops as traditionalists gear up for a last-ditch attempt to stop full equality.

The thorny issue of whether women can hold the most senior positions in the church has dominated Anglican debates for much of the past 10 years. But next week things will come to a head as the church's General Synod ~ its parliament ~ votes on a crucial debate that is seen by many within the pro-women lobby as a last-minute attempt to scupper their progress.

The issue of women bishops still threatens to tear the church in two. Previous Synods have consistently voted in favour of allowing women to become bishops, in what has been a tortuous and lengthy legislative process for a church that prides itself on welcoming a multitude of opinions. But a minority coalition of traditionalists, conservatives and Anglo-Catholics has always opposed them, believing that Jesus intended men to lead the church.

The dissidents have demanded that the church create a separate category of male bishops who are ordained by men only, and therefore able to cater to parishioners who cannot countenance a female bishop. The pro-women lobby and argue that such a move would create a two-tier system where women bishops are effectively second-class citizens within their own church. In an attempt to find a compromise and stop mass defections at a time of dwindling church attendance, the Archbishops of Canterbury and York, both of whom support women bishops, have risked the wrath of liberals by throwing their support behind a controversial suggestion that would allow traditionalists to reject female leadership. Under their plans, those parishes that feel unable to be led by a woman could request oversight from a male bishop who does not serve under a female.

The same amendment was narrowly defeated in 2010 but has since been resurrected by the Bishop of Manchester, who has argued that Synod should vote on it again. In the opposite corner is the Bishop of Southward, who has tabled a separate amendment calling on Synod to pass the legislation as it stands.

The row will come to a head on Wednesday, with observers expecting bitter recriminations. If Southward wins the argument, the likelihood is that women could become bishops by 2014, once the legislation passes on to Synod for final approval in July and then to Parliament. Those opposed to them would either have to leave the church or grudgingly accept their authority.

If Manchester wins, the House of Bishops would be under pressure to rework the legislation and provide some sort of opt-out for dissenters.

Guessing which way Synod will vote is difficult. The Church of England prides itself on being a "big tent" that welcomes multiple opinions, and there is a strong feeling that compromises should be made to try to keep the anti-equality faction within the church. But after two decades of female priests, many believe it is absurd to keep women away from the church's most senior positions. [87]

The women Bishop should be permitted to continue, if they are knowledgable and capable.

---

[87]Jerome Taylor (2012), "Churchmen Close Ranks (Again) In Battle Over Women Bishops", the Statesman, February 6, 22012 / the Independent (News).

Don't be a Brute

Many a time husband's cruelty-physical and verbal is cited as a reason for seeking a divorce.

While some may be using this accusation to get a divorce easily other men, high on male ego, are still harbouring the myth that to control the wife the man must be brutal. Domestic violence is a brutal reality, rampant even in our times. Women continue to be tortured for reasons ranging from dowry to infertility.

Mostly, it is a result of the deviant personality of the husband. His inability to manage his anger, his need to control and feeling of a sense of power over his wife manifest themselves in the form of domestic violence. This behavior not only causes her grievous injury but also preys on the psyche, paralyzing her strength and slowly killing her spirit. Many men are under this warped illusion that to keep a woman on a tight leash, he needs to exercise his brute force and that doing so is a sign of masculinity. Nothing could be farther from truth. Men don't need to use force in order to rule over wives. They can rule them by love and affection.

One may ask why a woman should put up with domestic violence, but only the woman in question would be able to answer that. The Domestic Violence Act of 2006 is a liberating step for many caged souls.[88]

How can a woman help herself? Never ever tolerate violence, in any form. Once any one is a victim; he is always a victim. If the husband shows signs of violent behavior, immediately bring it to the notice of your parents. Enlist the support of a woman's organisation. If the husband is willing, get him psychiatric help.

---

[88] Narayan Reddy (2012), "Don't be a Brute", Deccan Chronicle, February 9, 2012

Women and their world

What better way to celebrate International Women's Day than to announce the all-women long list for the Orange Prize, the £30,000 bonanza that awaits women authors, much to the chagrin of their male counterparts?

This year it has rained historical novels — starting from the Homeric period to World War II, there's a list of 20 glittering authors, which includes five debut novels and four "seconds". Joanna Trollope, as the chair of the jury, has already ploughed through all 143 submissions. An author herself, she remarked, obviously impressed with the quality, "Fiction is a way into life's great dilemmas" and found that women were "extraordinarily unafraid" to enter that emotional space.

The Orange Prize has been known to create a great buzz around the winning book — and the presence this time of established authors such as Emma Donoghue and Ali Smith will make the competition much tougher. The authors include those from the UK, America, Sweden and Canada, and one of them, Madeline Miller, has taken 10 years to complete her book, The Song of Achilles.

No doubt this long list will lead to another round of betting on the likely outcome. I would thus like to lay a wager on Ann Patchett for her book, State of Wonder. Not because I know that she will win (though I certainly hope she does), but because I have shared a stage with her at the Hay literary festival, and I was astonished to find how much the two of us, our books and their female protagonists had in common! (With one huge difference — I haven't had the good fortune of making it to the Orange long list!). Even though our writing styles and plots were completely different, I got a real spooky sense of déja vu when I met her. How did we, coming from such different backgrounds, have such similar thoughts?

To add to the coincidences, Hay was also where I met Joanna Trollope as we were all staying at the same hotel, and she had mentioned in a newspaper interview that at that time she was reading my book. So, having accidentally bumped into some of the Orange Prize participants and judges, I shall take renewed interest in the longlist, and the prize!

However, for the past few years, it is the Americans who have walked off with the honours. Téa Obreht, Barbara Kingsolver and Marilynne Robinson...

Meanwhile, Prime Ministers, former and present, have all jumped onto the gender bandwagon on International Women's Day — each being more politically correct than the other. British Prime Minister David Cameron is trying for a stricter law to safeguard women from "unwanted verbal, non-verbal or physical conduct of a sexual nature with the purpose or effect of violating the dignity of a person, in particular when creating an intimidating, hostile, degrading, humiliating, offensive environment". And, according to campaigners who have been fighting for the law, punishable offences could even include wolf whistles and sexist comments.

The legislation would also allow the easy annulment of forced marriages and has already been enacted in over 18 countries in the European Union. But will the new law strike terror in the hearts of Britain's roadside Romeos? Once upon a time the "whistle" was seen as a compliment, but no more, as there could be other unpleasant connotations. The British Crime Survey has an estimate of 120,000 incidents of stalking, of which less than half have been actually registered with the police in recent years. A negligible number of offenders received a custodial sentence, and only 10 per cent were imposed a fine or given a probation order. Campaigners hope that things will change and the new legislation will have a positive impact on the life and security of women.

Not far behind, trying to establish his own "equality" credentials, former British Prime Minister Gordon Brown has announced his intention to work towards the abolition of child brides, through a newly launched global education fund. According to his estimates, 10 million girls under the age of 18 are married every year and 1.5 million of them are under the age of 15. In Niger, 36 per cent of girls are married by the age of 15, but the highest number of child brides is in India, with 45 per cent of under-18s already married, according to Mr Brown. One wonders if he will be soon tramping through the villages of Rajasthan, snatching away child brides and putting them back in school.

And no column would be complete without at least mentioning Siobhan Benita — one of the more interesting new candidates for the upcoming mayor's election. Ms Benita may not be exactly setting the Thames on fire, but at least she is creating a ripple of interest in the Asian community as her mother had come to the UK in 1959 from India. Standing as an independent, the former civil servant hopes that the stranglehold of the two main parties over the mayor's post will be diminished if she wins. Displaying a canny knack in identifying the freebies that might propel her to victory, Ms Benita has already declared that she will freeze fares for public transport at current levels, introduce a monthly "free London" day in which Londoners would travel free and get loads of discounts on the high street... and will also make London the best Wi-Fi enabled city in the world.

She claims that the early positive influences in her life were her parents from whom she learnt "unconditional" kindness, and so, perhaps, if elected, she will improve the marginalised areas of London.

Interestingly, she has experience of both the government and the private sector, working with former Cabinet secretary Sir Gus O'Donnell and businessman Peter Jones on a joint initiative on innovation. The only problem with Ms Benita might be that she sounds too "normal": both the main contenders — present mayor, wild-haired Boris Johnson, and ex-mayor, tough-talking Ken Livingstone — have carefully nurtured attention-grabbing eccentricity. But we wish Ms Benita luck as it would be fabulous if London got a mayor of Indian origin.

As regards the health of Queen Elizabeth II, and how she manages to travel around the world without falling sick, as a royal rule apparently, is to avoid shellfish, salad and watermelon... so, on your next trip, check it out.[89]

Changing times for women

The Judiciary in India has been the guiding force behind a number of legislations that have helped in bettering the lives of women. Thanks to landmark judgments, women are now eligible for a share in ancestral property, able to work in offices in dignity, exercise their reproductive rights, continue using their maiden names after marriage, and secure equal rights in the armed forces. The judiciary has also been instrumental in fine-tuning laws related to marriage and divorce, inheritance, guardianship of minor children, child prostitution and protection of sex workers from exploitation.

Right from Shah Bano to Visakha and Geeta Hariharan, the Supreme Court of India has been in the forefront, not only protecting the rights of women, but also ensuring that they get their due.

---

[89] Kishwar Desai (2012), "Women and their world", Deccan Chronicle, March 10, 2012

Courts in India have touched on practically every aspect concerning women, redefining the term 'homemaker' in so far as compensation under the Motor Vehicles Act is concerned, giving a new meaning to the increasing 'live-in' relationship, or interpreting the Shariat in the light of the Quran with regard to divorce of Muslim women.

However enlightened the courts' judgments; what works against litigants is the long time it takes to get justice. This works against everyone but particularly against women who have fewer resources.

Lawyer T. Vasantha Lakshmi emphasises the need to reduce procedural delays once a case related to women reaches the court. "Procedural delays often help the accused to find ways to escape from the clutches of the law," she says.

Though the Supreme Court has delivered several judgments that are considered 'landmark' judgments, women in India continue to suffer because of the different laws governing them and the lack of a court with a common jurisdiction to deal with issues related to women.

Women are forced to approach different foray to seek each relief separately. Women have to grapple with numerous legislations for the same or related issues, for example, Hindu women are governed by the Hindu Marriage Act (for divorce), Hindu Adoption and Maintenance Act (for maintenance), Guardians and Wards Act (for custody of children), and the Hindu Succession Act (for inheritance). Muslim women are governed by the Shariat Act and the Muslim Women Protection of Rights Act, while the Indian Divorce Act and the Indian Succession Act are primarily meant for Christian women.

Referring to multiplicity of Acts governing women, the department of women and child development,

Government of India, in its document on court cases agrees that each of these acts vests jurisdiction in a different court.

"This multiplicity of litigation increases the physical and financial burden of litigation manifold." Some laws still need strengthening. Says senior advocate Ch Nirmalatha, "In many divorce cases, women do not get maintenance as the divorced husbands disobey the decree. There should be stringent laws to ensure that maintenance is paid. Courts should work out a mechanism to oversee the payment."

Judicial activism notwithstanding, political pressure often creates hurdles in the delivery of justice to victims. "Political pressures have been on the rise and this impact the fair functioning of the police department.

It is not good for democracy if the police fail to act in cases of violence against women. In Andhra Pradesh the Sri Lakshmi case was a landmark judgment as the culprit was severely punished," says legal expert J. Jnanamba.

The top court created a history of sorts in the Visakha case, which is now cited in almost every legal argument related to women. It protected women from sexual harassment at the work place, and framed detailed guidelines for both prevention and redressed. There have been a number of orders, which state that the character of a rape victim should not form part of the proceedings during trial.

Women's rights groups have been largely satisfied by the Supreme Court guidelines in the Visakha case that they feel no new legislation is needed to protect the rights of women. P. Durga Bhavani, vice-president of the AP Mahila Samakhya (Women's organization) observes that existing laws are sufficient to protect women. "What we need is proper implementation of the legislations and judgments.

It is often the implementation of orders that causes more trouble. The Domestic Violence Act is a case in point. It is observed more in the breach. -- Social activist T. Shakuntala

Advocate S.K. Nagoor says loopholes in the Constitution are the cause of the trouble. "The Constitution is prowomen only on paper," she argues. "Loopholes in acts should be plugged. An amendment should be made to Section 498-A to make women-related cases non-bailable offences."

Taking the approach of an activist, the Supreme Court drew up guidelines for dealing with the exploitation of sex workers.

Counselling, cajoling and correction should be adopted to eradicate child prostitution and rescue girls from red light areas. – Supreme Court, India

In the Gita Hariharan case the court held that the mother too could be treated as a natural guardian under the Hindu Adoption and Maintenance Act, which hitherto has treated the father as the sole natural guardian.[90]

A woman and the world

Events at Westminster Hall are always done with an exquisite grandeur, and that was how it was when Aung San Suu Kyi arrived in London, for the first time since she left the United Kingdom in 1988.

---

[90] Syed Akbar and S A Ishaqui (2012), "Changing times for women", Deccan Chronicle, March 11, 2012

The orchestra arranged just below the enormous stained glass windows at one end played on while the crowds of ministers and MPs and all of us, including British Prime Minister David Cameron, gathered below, at various levels. The setting was serious yet celebratory.

The only awkward moment in the gathering was when Cherie Blair got a seat in the front row just next to Gordon Brown, the former Prime Minister of Britain, whom she had once (allegedly) accused of being a liar. If body language said anything, here it spoke volumes as she deliberately turned and faced the other way. The Browns, Sarah and Gordon sat stoically through it all except at the end.

Despite the fact we had all been informed that cameras were not allowed inside the hall, Ms Sarah Brown suddenly leapt to her feet when Ms Suu Kyi came around to shake everyone's hand and started taking photographs on her phone, possibly for her Twitter account. We all know how addictive social media can be. Looking at her, all of us took out our personal mobile phones and began clicking pictures.

And my memorable moment came when Ms Suu Kyi walked down the aisle towards us, and I shook her hand. She gave me a big grin when I told her that I, too, was from Lady Shri Ram College - A moment of bonding. If only everyone from LSR had her courage and equanimity.

The speech Ms Suu Kyi gave was unforgettable, a master class in forgiveness. It was almost like the 24 intervening years of incarceration had disappeared and the soft-spoken Ms Suu Kyi had always been with us.

.

She did not mention her own suffering but instead spoke of having visited 10 Downing Street to meet Mr. Cameron, earlier in the day. She had been reminded of when her own father had last visited there. Apparently, Jawaharlal Nehru had given him his own heavy overcoat to protect him from the British cold. And indeed, her father, Aung San, had worn that coat to Downing Street.

Her speech was highly personal but immensely moving as each time she reminded us how precious democracy is and how we must hold fast to it.

But listening to her I wondered whether we Indians have let her down in the recent past? Had we been more proactive, Ms Suu Kyi should have made her first official visit, post-incarceration, to India where she had attended her school and college and where her family has such close associations? It may be because of our connections with the dubious military regime of Burma that we missed a historic chance.

And thus Ms Suu Kyi chose to go to Europe and collect the Nobel Prize she won long ago. She also visited Oxford, which must have brought back poignant memories of when she had lived there with her husband and two children.

The amazing thing is that despite having sacrificed everything, her husband, her children and her whole life, she continues to believe in the ideal of democracy for Burma. Her faith is so unshakeable that she chose to remain powerless, trapped by a cruel regime. But today she has become a worldwide icon of grace under pressure, of peaceful resistance. And yet she does not appear to have an ounce of bitterness in her. She wears those beautiful flowers in her hair like a symbol of peace and inner tranquility, and her gentle smile and much understated sense of humour says it all.

The British MPs had a good laugh when Ms Suu Kyi said that she one day hoped there would be Prime Minister's Questions (which take place every

Wednesday, rather acrimoniously, in Westminster) even in the Burmese Parliament. And she got a long-standing ovation both when she entered and when she left. For most of us after Nelson Mandela, Ms Suu Kyi is probably one of the most heroic figures of recent times.

But there are plenty of people in this world who despite having got "everything" and having become the perfect "material girls" would still want more to be happy. Yes, you guessed it, this is about our anti-hero, Madonna, who wanted to play up her bad girl image when recently in the middle of her stage performance in Istanbul, she pulled out a breast, almost as though to demonstrate that she is still a sex symbol.

The British papers, especially the tabloids, gleefully printed the picture, while pretending to be outraged over why a 50-year-old woman (and the mother of three — or is it four? — children) would want to parade in fishnet stockings and thongs, yanking off her underwear on stage.

One answer could be that this is all marketing technique and that in a democratic country; fortunately, you can still do anything you like. But possibly the most accurate answer is that Madonna knew that a provocative photograph like that would swiftly go viral, grabbing headlines everywhere. It's called staying abreast of things.[91]

On International Women's Day:

12 innovations that are lifting women out of poverty

International Women's Day (March 8) celebrates women's achievements. Innovative ideas and

---

[91] Kishwar Desai (2012), "A Woman and the World", Deccan Chronicle, June 30, 2012

programs, such as the 12 below, are helping women better care for themselves and their families.

Women have proven to be a powerful force in the fight against global hunger and poverty, especially in agriculture. Worldwide roughly 1.6 billion women rely on farming for their livelihoods, and female farmers produce more than half of the world's food. In sub-Saharan Africa alone, women account for 75 percent of all the agricultural producers.

Today we observe International Women's Day, a global celebration and recognition of women's achievements. Women farmers face a variety of obstacles, including a lack of access to information technology, agricultural training, financial services, and support networks like co-operatives or trade unions. Without these services, women cannot develop resilience to political, economic, social, or environmental upheaval, and they remain dependent on their male family members.

The good news is that women worldwide are developing and utilizing agricultural innovations to sustainably nourish their families and communities. Today we celebrate 12 innovations that are helping women get access to credit, improve their incomes, feed their families, introduce sustainable crops to markets, and reduce rural poverty:

Co-operatives: Cooperatives are a type of business characterized by democratic ownership and governance. In the war-torn country of Côte d'Ivoire, Marium Gnire partnered with Slow Foods International to organize a women's farming cooperative that would provide quality local food for school meals in her village of N'Ganon, increasing both the women's income and the health of the community.

Creating Links Between Women Producers and Markets: In Africa's Western Sahel, the production of shea butter is boosting women's entry into global markets. Women-run cooperatives across the region are tapping into the global demand for fair trade and organic beauty products by selling the skin-care cream they produce from the shea nut crop to cosmetics firms such as Origins and L'Oréal. These companies in turn pay a fair price for the products and invest in the women's communities.

Educating Girls on Family Planning: The United Nations Foundation sponsors Girl Up, an organization that encourages a world where young girls can avoid the pitfalls of too-early marriage and childbearing and can instead go to school, enjoy health and safety, and grow into the next generation of leaders. In the Amhara region of Ethiopia, where half of adolescent girls are married, Girl Up is helping to promote education for young girls. The project offers basic literacy classes, family-planning information, and agricultural training. In delaying motherhood, even for a few years, girls can gain critical years of education, where they often gain knowledge about successful agricultural practices.

Empowering Young Girls through Agriculture: When young girls learn valuable agricultural skills, they gain the power to avoid dependence on men for food and financial security. In Rwanda, the 'Farmers of the Future Initiative' helps to empower young girls and other students by integrating school gardens and agricultural training into primary school curriculums. Over 60 percent of students in Rwanda will return to rural areas to farm for a living after graduating instead of going on to secondary school or university. As young girls learn these skills, they become self-sufficient and empowered.

Extension Services: Extension services are an important way of disseminating agricultural knowledge to farmers, but unfortunately, women have been excluded from many extension programs, whether as service providers or recipients. When women are included in extension programs, they receive an education, raise their agricultural yields, increase their incomes, raise the nutritional status of their household, and contribute to the improvement of their communities. To improve female inclusion in extension programs, the International Institute of Tropical Agriculture's Sustainable Tree Crops Program created videos that women could watch in their homes or in groups, without disrupting their childcare or fuel-gathering obligations. Since 2006, nearly 1,600 farmers in Côte d'Ivoire and Ghana have received cocoa-production training directly through Video Viewing Clubs.

Female Trade Unions: In developing countries, women are commonly disenfranchised and not offered the same opportunities and rights as men, such as access to credit and land ownership. The Self Employed Women's Association (SEWA), a female trade union in India that began in 1992, works with poor, and self-employed women by helping them achieve full employment and self reliance. SEWA is a network of cooperatives, self-help groups, and programs that empower women. Small-scale women farmers in India have particularly benefited from this network that links farmers to inputs and markets.

Increasing Access to Water: In sub-Saharan Africa, improved access to water means the difference between barely scraping by and eating balanced meals, affording education, and owning a home. In Zambia, Veronica Sianchenga, a farmer living in Kabuyu Village, saw improvements in her family's quality of life when she began irrigating her farm with the "Mosi-o-Tunya" (Pump that Thunders), a pressure pump that she purchased from International Development Enterprises. In many parts of sub-Saharan Africa, the task of gathering water can take up to eight hours of labor per day and usually falls to women. Because of the pump, her children are eating healthier and she is enjoying increased independence.

Microfinance Credit: Globally, women fall well short of receiving the same financial benefits and opportunities as men. Only 10 percent of the credit services available in sub-Saharan Africa, including small "microfinance" loans, are extended to women. The New York-based nonprofit Women's World Banking is the only microfinance network focused explicitly on women, providing loans of as little as $100 to help women start businesses. Microfinance institutions from 27 countries provide the loans to women who in many cases have no other way to access credit.

Vertical Farming: Over 800 million people globally depend on food grown in cities for their main food source. Considering that women in Africa own only 1 percent of the land, a practice called vertical farming gives these women the opportunity to raise vegetables without having to own land. Female farmers in Kibera, Nairobi's largest slum, have been practicing vertical farming using seeds provided by the French NGO Solidarities'. This innovative technique involves growing crops in dirt sacks, allowing women farmers to grow vegetables in otherwise unproductive urban spaces. More than 1,000 women are growing food in this way, effectively allowing them to be self-sufficient in food production and to increase their household income. Following the launch of this initiative, each household has increased its weekly income by 380 shillings (equivalent to $4.33).

Urban Farming: In Kenya, about 20 urban farmers grow fruits and vegetables on a small strip of land in Kibera, an urban slum in Nairobi with nearly 1 million people. These farmers do not formally own this land

and farm through an informal arrangement. More than once, they have been forced to stop farming, and they often see their water supply cut. However, the farmers are continuing to come up with innovative ways of raising food – and incomes – on the farm. With the help of the farmers' advocacy group Urban Harvest, the farmers are not only growing food to eat and sell, but, perhaps surprisingly, becoming a source of seed for rural farmers.

Women's Collectives: In many countries, women's subordinate position in society makes them easy targets for domestic and sexual violence when working in the agricultural sector, which greatly inhibits their ability to work to their full potential. In India, the Tamil Nadu Women's Collective focuses on advocating for women's rights and improving food and water security. The collective reaches over 1,500 villages spread across 18 districts in India's Tamil Nadu state and has helped many women see an increase in crop yields. The collective provides counseling and support for female victims of domestic violence, promotes women's participation in local government, and helps women strengthen local food systems through education on natural farming techniques.

Women-Run Community Seed Banks: Studies have shown that women farmers typically have lower crop yields than their male counterparts. Rural women farmers' lower productivity compared to male farmers may be due to women lacking access to high-quality seeds and agricultural inputs. The GREEN Foundation has partnered with NGOs including Seed Savers Network and The Development Fund to create community seed banks in India's Karnataka state. Women run these seed banks, gaining leadership skills and acquiring quality organic seeds that yield profitable crops and their food security and incomes.[92]

Although these innovations inevitably help men as well as women, it is important that policymakers, scientists, farmers' groups, and the funding and donor communities focus on ensuring that these women harness the power of these innovations so we can create a more equitable and nourished planet.

Conclusion:

Women can strengthen the peace movement in the world through the following programs. These are:

1. Women should form '**Women's Rights Organizations**' in all the countries with grass root societies to mobilize and concectrate their might to award justice to the vulnerable societies.

2. **Education:** Women organizations should assist the vulnerable groups in education, training and career building programs.

3. **Decoding Mind:** Human mind is a seat of perception where information from all the senses is gathered and processed. They must adjust their mind for peace. They should think thoroughly the effects of their work. Once they decide to undertake some work for a meaningful achievement, they should go ahead to achieve it through their organization. There are many problems, which cannot be solved alone. It is better to fight united for a region or state. A call to women world is also possible now-a-days because of internet facility, news, facebook etc. If women of the world make their homes 'sweet homes', world peace would be possible quicker.

---

[92] Reuters, Nourishing the Planet, The Christian Science Monitor, March 8, 2012

4. **Physical Fitness:** Do not take hasty decisions. You must remember that the problem for which you desire to take strong action needs yours physical fitness, soundness of mind and some expenditure. So you should practice YOGA or meditation regularly. There are eight steps of yoga. Yoga controls blood pressure, develops immunity, improves respiration, lowers stress, improves nervous system and body becomes fit to undertake hard work.

5. **Avoid inferior complexity:** Never think that women are inferior to others in power, position, education or intelligence. Women are more blessed by God and their parents. They should fight for a cause for the welfare of the 'women world'. They can fight for justice in a mass movement.

6. **Devotion to God:** Women must pray God for His blessings for the benefits of all people. Unless His creations are not saved, the human kingdom would be destroyed with deseases, accidents, natural calamities and war. Women can do the prayer for the survival of others and this beautiful World. The prayers should be performed at right time each day. If women of the world chant the God's name 108 times at a stretch and pray to save the world from disaster. World Peace would be possible if 7 billion people pray God and desire to live in peace.

7. **Humanity**: HUMANITY can reduce or eliminate tensions among the religions because it is a product of all religions. If the Chiefs or Heads of religious institutions come forward for negotiations in the religious conflicts, and cooperate with the administration, tensions at the borders could be reduced. Once a peace process starts, the result would maximize in the following years.

HUMANITY aims at discipline in all sectors. HUMANITY can decrease the disparities of income of the people. HUMANITY can debar the sale of sons or daughters by hungry mothers, stop starvation deaths, reduce court cases and check inhumane activities being practiced towards innocent, poor, diseased or peace-loving and sober people. HUMANITY can grow in a society through participation of religious organizations and can be enriched through state laws. Disparity in legal systems for different religions results in chaos. (Refer: World Peace – Volume Seven)

8. **Decisions:** Each person, institution or the country should take decisions for playing a long term game. Good decisions must be taken up in cool mind.

You should help:

(a) A needy individual;
(b) Take a patient to hospital;
(c) Attend a religious meet;

Women should accept membership in organizations like:

(a) Peace Movement
(b) End of Violence against Women
(c) Food Security Campaign and
(d) Justice for All

The Women organizations should think for and take decisions as these are noble duties of a human being. If there are no such organizations in your locality, you should try to organize these organizations for people and peace. Revengeful attitude, false propaganda, corrupt friends and harm to enemies must be avoided as these are the negative factors of progress and development.

9. **Skewed Sex Ratio:** For example, let us study sex ration in India. The average count of girl child (upto 6 years) has dropped to 914 per 1000 boys as per the Census 2011 from a relatively high level of 927 in the 2001 Census. The ratio is particularly dismal in Punjab, Haryana, Rajasthan, Uttar Pradesh, Bihar,

Maharastra and Delhi. More over, states like Jammu and Kashmir, Uttarakhand, and M.P. fared badly.

This explains the number of boys exceed girls in India. So there are marital problems on the country. Women are torchured even by relations. The crime is of a more incestuous nature. So female infanticide and dowry torture must be stopped and the parents must be punished by law of the land. Illegal and painful activities against women must be stopped by law and action. There is 'no law' for marital rape; hence Domestic Violence Act should be initiated against the husband.

10. **Justice System:** The First Track Court should deliver judgement on atrocities against child, girl and women within three months in closed chambers with or without advocates.

Quicker judgement would reduce the criminal activities.

There is no need to change Law and punishment. Only quicker judgement would solve the problem. In case of rape and murder, if the First Track Court awards death penality to the accused, terming his heinous crime as the 'rarest of rare case', the accused should be permitted to challenge the verdict in the Supreme Court directly by-passing the High Court. But the Apex Court must decide the case within 3 months. It should not be forwarded to the Hon'ble President of the country for pardon.

The court should award fines in cash to the friends of victim, police officer, parents, hostel superindent and principal, if they have neglected in their duties on the day it happened.

The media should report the judgement of court in one para only. All bad events should be reported in abdriged form.

The media cannot describe the detailed history and photographs to create panic in society. It should not explain the episode in pages and pages each day to train the young mind to go wrong. The media cannot explain the wrong doings in visual form and make cinema shows on actual or virtual cinematography. Media should not be a forum to disseminate facts in cimema or TV.

Let us hear that people are practicing peace and avoiding controversy, destruction and war.

Man is a social animal, so animal instinct is prevalent in many cases.

So controlling mind is the only solution to avoid unnecessary botheration and punishment. The people can get rid of animal cruelty by reading religious books and attending prayers daily as a rutine task. Let us pray that God would show the way to these cruel people. And it is possible.

THE END

AUTHOR INDEX

+++++

SUBJECT INDEX

A MOVEMENT FOR A PEACEFUL WORLD

AUTHORS

Professor Suresh Chandra Mallick (b 1944) was a faculty member of the OUAT, Bhubaneswar (India) during 1968 - 2004. He is a researcher, writer, thinker and social worker. He is an Agricultural Economist with specialization in Agriculture, Poverty, Marketing, Policy and World Peace to motivate people's involvement in peace process. He held the post of Vice President, Indian Society of Agricultural Marketing during 2003 - 05. At present, he is the Chairperson of the Institute of Development Studies & Policy Research, Bhubaneswar.

Pritam Mallick (1975–2006) was extremely noble, friendly and knowledgeable and possessed extraordinary memory. He received B.A. (Honors) from Utkal University, M.A. from Central University, Hyderabad and M. Phil. Degree from Jawaharlal Nehru University and completed Ph. D. courses in JNU. He was a specialist in Monetary Economics and Econometrics. He remembered the Oxford Dictionary and Roget's Thesaurus to master English literature. He acquired deep knowledge in Astrology, Palmistry, Mathematics and Statistics. He contributed enormously for WORLD PEACE manuscripts as co-author. But his heavenly demise occurred on August 4, 2006.